Praise for
When We Were the Boys

"Stevie Salas has been my rock 'n' roll buddy for the past twenty-five years. He's achieved the greatest thing in our game: he lived a life worth living, and then was able to remember it all long enough to write it down!"

—Slim Jim Phantom, The Stray Cats

"It's funny but when I met Stevie Salas it was like meeting myself in my younger career.
Having two Scorpios working together meant Fire without the Fear.

He stepped in loud, dreaming, with his volume turned up.
Speaking through his guitar and givin' up the funk.
You see, music speaks the truth, it never lies,
it's like one big soul with nothin' to hide.

I named him Stevie-No-Wonder just because you never knew what he was gonna say.
I will always be his big brother living a simple life of Plug & Play.

Thanks, little brother, for always staying true to the passion that you possess.
Music & love is that thang that we 'Self-Express.'
Stay funky, my friend!"

—Bootsy Collins

"Stevie Salas is the ultimate insider, and *When We Were the Boys* is your backstage pass. This book is a vibrant, unfiltered collection of stories from a rookie guitarist earning his stripes with rock legends—from hazing to Hooters girls and everything in between."

—Spike Feresten, Emmy Award–winning writer, producer, and comedian whose work includes *Seinfeld*

"Rock 'n' roll pirate Stevie Salas spins a captivating yarn about his days aboard the great ship Rock Star. A fast and fun read, full of brass, balls, and bollocks, much like the man himself."

—Sass Jordan, multi-platinum recording artist

"We met Stevie shortly after he left the Rod Stewart Band. Jeff Healey was a funny cat when it came to guitar players. He would interact with very few during our live shows, but he really dug Stevie's playing from day one and would have him sit in whenever possible. This led to a great friendship and writing partnership—as well as some killer good times."

—Tom Stephen, manager/drummer, The Jeff Healey Band

"Stevie's expertise and diverse musical abilities were invaluable when we worked with contestants from *American Idol*. Now, after reading *When We Were the Boys*, I think that most of his 'diverse musical abilities' came on the fly!"

—Stirling McIlwaine, music business manager

"Stevie's one of the busiest people in the biz, but at the end of each day, he's just a kid who's a massive fan of music. It's great to be able to have this book by one of the most sought-after guys in music—and read about ALL of the things he was up to."

—Mike Halloran, legendary alt-rock radio DJ

"I loved *When We Were the Boys*. . . . The craziness of being on a major rock 'n' roll tour is all here: the private jets, the trashed hotel rooms, the limousines that Stewart occasionally stole, the booze, the drugs, and the women—lots and lots of women. This book is well-written and contains great photos. You won't want to put it down!"

—Jim McInnes, legendary San Diego radio DJ

"This book isn't a front row seat—it's an unlimited access backstage pass to the world of rock 'n' roll. Two masters of their crafts, Stevie Salas and Bob Yehling, pool their talents to put you onstage with Stevie in what could be described as one of the most amazing true 'rock 'n' roll fantasies' ever. A great, great read."

—Ken Kebow, Emmy Award–winning producer/director

WHEN WE WERE THE BOYS

WHEN WE WERE THE BOYS

Coming of Age on Rod Stewart's Out of Order Tour

Stevie Salas

With Robert Yehling

TAYLOR TRADE PUBLISHING
Lanham • Boulder • New York • London

Published by Taylor Trade Publishing
An imprint of The Rowman & Littlefield Publishing Group, Inc.
4501 Forbes Boulevard, Suite 200, Lanham, Maryland 20706
www.rowman.com

16 Carlisle Street, London W1D 3BT, United Kingdom

Distributed by NATIONAL BOOK NETWORK

British Library Cataloguing in Publication Information Available

Library of Congress Cataloging-in-Publication Data

Salas, Stevie, author.
When we were the boys : coming of age on Rod Stewart's Out of order tour / Stevie Salas with Robert Yehling.
pages cm
ISBN 978-1-58979-988-2 (pbk. : alk. paper) — ISBN 978-1-58979-989-9 (electronic)
1. Salas, Stevie. 2. Guitarists—United States—Biography 3. Rock musicians—United States—Biography. 4. Stewart, Rod. 5. Rock musicians—England—Biography. I. Yehling, Robert, author. II. Title.
ML419.S1923A3 2014
782.42166092—dc23
[B]
2014007915

∞™ The paper used in this publication meets the minimum requirements of American National Standard for Information Sciences Permanence of Paper for Printed Library Materials, ANSI/NISO Z39.48-1992.

Printed in the United States of America

This book is dedicated to my amazing Father,
Hilario Salas,
because without him nothing would have been possible,

and to my dear, sweet Tonjua Twist,
who knew me like no other.

Also, to all the dreamers in the world . . . never give up,
because the day you give up might be the day before
your dream comes true.

It was late 1984 when I looked up at the marquee: ROD STEWART. I wanted to see Rod on his Camouflage tour so badly, but I couldn't afford a ticket.

As I drove on the I-5 freeway past the San Diego Sports Arena, I said to myself, "I'm going to play guitar for Rod Stewart, Mick Jagger, and David Bowie." For some reason, I believed this with all my heart.

A few short years later, I ran onto a stadium stage, playing the opening chords to "Hot Legs" as Rod Stewart belted out the lyrics.

Later, I would play with Mick Jagger. As for Bowie, I am still working on that dream.

This is the story of how it all started, how a young kid got a lucky break that changed his life, and molded him into a musician and a man.

This is about the year when we were the boys . . .

CONTENTS

ABOUT THE PHOTOGRAPHS

1. A Revolution Is Almost Born. Jerry Jones, one of my best friends in tenth grade, and I started a band with dreams of playing backyard parties for our friends. We named our band Revolution, but since we could only play three songs, we never made it out of the garage . . . but we sure had some fun. (L to R: Me, Eddie Binder, Tom Kerr, Jerry Jones; photo: Steve Jones)

2. This Kids. In 1980, I didn't realize that I had a gift for spotting talent that I would later put to use as a record producer and music director for some of the biggest names in music and television. I was the youngest in the band and still in high school, but when I saw Pat Pinamonti sing at a jam session, I thought, *that guy's a star lead singer.* No one believed me at first, but three months after we put This Kids together, we were the biggest thing going. (L to R: Paul Martinez, Pat Pinamonti, Greg Hammond, Me; photo: Allen Carrasco)

3. Rock Star in Training. It was so weird. All of a sudden, it was like This Kids was the mini Duran Duran or Beatles, with girls screaming and crying at our shows. I was also really into the Beatles then (note the hollow guitar played up high like George Harrison). I would do a long tour with Duran Duran in 1993, but by that time, their screaming wild girl fans had grown into calm cougars. (Photo: Allen Carrasco)

4. Broke and Homeless at Baby O. I quit This Kids and moved to Hollywood in 1985, where I soon found myself homeless. I must have had an angel on my shoulder, because Baby O Recording studio owner Rick Perratta and David Pahoa from The Plimsouls offered to let me sleep on the studio lounge couch in exchange for looking after their rehearsal room. This photo was shot in Studio A, where I would soon meet and record with George Clinton. (Courtesy of Stevie Salas Archives)

5. Stand by This Man. In San Diego, my then-girlfriend, Deirdre, was the stepdaughter of legendary country singer Tammy Wynette. During my struggles to make it in Hollywood, Tammy and her husband George Richey would always encourage me to keep going. People never talk about Tammy's great sense of humor, but the way she signed this photo for me says it all: *Stevie, who says it's over after 40?? Babe it's what's up front that counts!!* (Courtesy of Stevie Salas Archives)

6. We Want the Funk. Everything happens for a reason. At Baby O Studios during my homeless period, George Clinton was working on his R & B album, *Skeletons in the Closet*, for Capitol Records. He needed a guitar player for a 3:00 a.m. session—and I was in the right place at the right time when he woke me up from the studio couch and asked me to play. After I recorded with George, people in the music business began to take me seriously. (L to R: Gary Shider, Me, George Clinton; courtesy of Stevie Salas Archives)

7. "We're Hooters Girls!" My first U.S. concert with Rod Stewart at the Big Sombrero, the Tampa Bay Buccaneers' football stadium, was a big learning experience. When I saw these funny-dressed gals walking around backstage, I didn't know what to think; after all, they didn't have Hooters girls in California in 1988. I found a golf cart, put a keg of beer on it, and spent the afternoon making friends and learning about the perks of being in a big rock band. (Courtesy of Stevie Salas Archives)

8. The Wind Cries "Maggie!" While performing "Maggie May" at Miami's Joe Robbie Stadium, Rod had the stadium in the palm of his hand. (Photo: Dale Lawrence)

9. Madre Mia Maria! I was having some fun with actress Maria Conchita Alonso, who sat on my side of the stage during our Miami concert. The next night, she invited me to her yacht to watch a private screening of *Vampire's Kiss*, a new movie in which she was starring with Nick Cage. (Photo: Dale Lawrence)

10. Saké Party on Sting's Private Plane. Our plane wasn't ready when the tour started, so we borrowed Sting's plane for the South Florida gigs. One night, Rod ordered us a massive spread of sushi and saké. After several sakes, he decided to leave a little note for Sting on the plane's beautiful wood table—and used a sharp knife to carve it. Word was, Sting wasn't too happy about it. (L to R: Kelly Emberg, Don Archell, Rod, and Tony Brock; courtesy of Stevie Salas Archives)

11. Our Home Away from Home. Our Rod Stewart tour plane arrived in Atlanta, and we practically lived on the plane from this point on. We flew twice per day, four to five times per week. If you were a musician with a fear of flying, this wouldn't be the gig for you. (L to R: Tour Manager Henry Newman, me, Carmine Rojas; courtesy of Stevie Salas Archives)

12. Every Picture Tells a Story. Jeff Golub and I shared lead guitar duties, and what a music lesson that was. I stole a lot of tricks from Jeff, and I am not ashamed to admit it. In 1990, guitar fans in France, Germany, Japan, and the U.S. voted me into several guitar magazine readers' polls for best new guitarist. I owe a lot of that to Jeff. (Photo: Bruce Kessler)

13. Nice Selfie. There is nothing quite like the blend of energy and exhaustion you feel after a great two-hour show with twenty thousand screaming fans. To balance this out, we would often go straight to the bar on the plane and start hitting the drink. Rod and the boys taught me how to be a professional musician, which was great. They also taught me how to be a professional drinker, which wasn't so great . . . but it was fun. (Courtesy of Stevie Salas Archives)

14. Once More for Me Ol' Mucker. Rod and his valet, Don Archell, who was an old-school English singer who knew the classics; we lovingly called him "Dad." We would often tell the girls that he was Rod's father, and would the girls eat Dad up! They didn't call Don the Silver Fox for nothing! (Courtesy of Stevie Salas Archives)

15. Spongy and Me. Singing into the mic with my big brother Carmine was always a mind blower. Only three years before that a poster of Carmine hung on my wall at my dad's house in Oceanside. Now we were in a band together! He had many nicknames, but the most popular was "Spongy." I never asked him why, but I figured it was due to the fact that his Afro looked like a sponge. (Photo: Bruce Kessler)

16. A Rock 'n' Roll Rite of Passage. I had heard many rock 'n' roll stories about bands like The Faces, The Who, and Led Zeppelin destroying hotel rooms. I got back to my room late one night in Kansas City and had a funny feeling something was not right. Rod and some of the boys had given me my rock 'n' roll initiation (yes, it was very expensive). (Courtesy of Stevie Salas Archives)

17. Too Rolling Stoned. One night, legendary *Rolling Stone* writer Robert Palmer hitched a ride on the RS band plane bound for New Orleans. I had never been to New Orleans, so Robert took me on a 3:00 a.m. custom tour to some seriously funky spots. He also joined our band ritual: after every show, once we were on the plane, we would do a dance and sing a song while Rick or Nick mixed Mudslides. (Courtesy of Stevie Salas Archives)

18. The Singer. Words cannot describe the feeling one gets from playing a classic song like "Mandolin Wind" with Rod Stewart singing it. (Photo: Bruce Kessler)

19. King Size Children. This is a rare shot of Jeff Golub on the plane *without* his Four Seasons robe. When it was too hot, he would just rock the hospital pants. Our drummer, the legendary Tony Brock, had an issue with Jeff's style, but Rod's co-manager, Randy Phillips, didn't seem to mind. (L to R: Jeff Golub, Tony Brock, Randy Phillips; courtesy of Stevie Salas Archives)

20. Arnold, Get to the Chopper! In Las Vegas, we jumped out of our private plane into jet helicopters and then raced down the Strip to our concert. Rod's manager, Arnold Stiefel, was the unlucky one stuck with me in my helicopter and was frazzled after the flight. I lost my mind on the chopper, bouncing back and forth like a wild man shaking it to and fro while screaming like a commando on a raid. When Arnold screamed, "Stop it!" I knew I was in trouble. (Courtesy of the Stevie Salas Archives)

21. The Boys Bringin' It. Once this band came together as brothers, we were the baddest band in the land. We could make rock feel huge and funky, and we could make soft folk music fill an arena. (L to R: Tony Brock, Jeff Golub, Carmine Rojas, Me, Rod; photo: Allen Carrasco)

22. Soul Mate. I met Tonjua Twist, an incredible *Vogue* magazine stylist, when I was with Rod and Carmine in New York City—and something changed in me. If she said it was okay to wear something, I felt safe doing it . . . otherwise, I never would have worn these crazy gold pants for my video shoot! Since her death, I have never been the same. She was indeed the love of my life. (Courtesy of the Stevie Salas Archives)

23. You're Kidding, Right? After leaving Rod, I made records, toured the world many times, and also was lucky to have my pick of projects as a producer, music director, writer, and guitar player. When Bill Laswell called in 1991 with a band idea, I couldn't believe it: Buddy Miles from The Jimi Hendrix Band of Gypsies, Bootsy Collins . . . and little ol' me? I was afraid to do it, but Bootsy convinced me that it would put me in a new light as a musician. (Courtesy of the Stevie Salas Archives)

24. You Gotta Love Your Friends. In 1993, I wasn't finished with my second Colorcode record, so I decided to make *The Electric Pow Wow*, a record that featured a lot of my rock star friends jamming with me. I am truly blessed to have so many talented friends. When I saw Cheap Trick open for KISS when I was a kid, I could have never imagined they would some day be playing on my record. (L to R: Matt Sorum, Tom Peterson, me, Sass Jordan, Brian Tichy, Rick Nielsen; courtesy of the Stevie Salas Archives)

25. It's a Big World. After the mid-1990s, I no longer toured the U.S., but I would spend months in Europe, the UK, and Asia. Music has given me a chance to see the world like a VIP. This concert photo was shot at a gig in Inchon, Korea a few years back. (Photo: Invisible Hands Music UK)

26. Anything Is Possible! When I was learning how to play guitar, I drove my Mom, Dad, and sisters crazy while trying to play Led Zeppelin songs. Here I am in Tokyo with the great Jimmy Page telling me a joke while fans take our picture. My bro Zakk Wylde and I both thought this was pretty cool. (L to R: Jimmy Page, Me, Zakk Wylde; courtesy of the Stevie Salas Archives)

27. Papa-San. My dad always encouraged me to follow my dreams. He wasn't sure if I would ever really succeed, but he never had a negative thing to say, so when I did make it, I felt like we'd *both* made it. He loved to see my Rod Stewart concerts, and when I went solo, I wrote and recorded a song for him, "Indian Chief." I was doing a big in-store press event in Tokyo and the fans loved it when Dad got onstage, chanting, "Hey Chief!" (Courtesy of the Stevie Salas Archives)

28. A Little Less Shattered. In 2001, I was doing all I could just to get out of bed. I was suffering from depression after the death of Tonjua Twist but trying to keep it hidden from my then-girlfriend, Nikita Ager. I couldn't play guitar, I couldn't write a song, and my life felt over. Out of nowhere, I got a gift from God. The phone rang, and the voice on the other end said, "Can I speak to Stevie Salas? This is Mick Jagger calling." Mick inspired me to get it together, starting my healing process. This is a cool photo of me and my long time rock 'n' roll partner Bernard Fowler with Mick and Hugh Jackman after playing on *Saturday Night Live* in New York. (Courtesy of the Stevie Salas Archives)

29. 25 Years Later, and It Still Feels Like a Dream. (Photo: Greg Hackett)

30. How Did a Native American Guitar Player with a High School Education Get a Job at the Smithsonian? I have always been proud of my heritage, but have never thought of myself as a Native American guitar player. During a speech I gave at the 6 Nations Indian Reservation in Canada for the opening of a great studio, Jukasa, Tim Johnson, Associate Director at The Smithsonian's National Museum of the American Indian, liked what I had to say. Before I knew it, Tim and I were working in Washington, D.C., on an exhibit about Native American musicians and their role in pop music history. (L to R: Me, Robbie Robertson [formerly of The Band], Tim Johnson. Photo: Jefferson Miller)

31. There Is No Place Like Home. After all these years, I still am the same guy with my same best friends from Oceanside, California. It's a great balance to play a big concert in Germany, then come home and surf with one of my best friends, Allen Carrasco. Allen liked to sit in my room after school and watch me jam. No matter how bad I sounded, Allen never let on. (Courtesy of the Stevie Salas Archives)

32. I Am Too Young for This! Over the years, I have received some great music awards, including gold and platinum discs, but the Native American Lifetime Achievement award feels best. I spent the first twenty years of my career focused on me, but in 2008, I decided to focus on helping people in Indian country. The things I learned from working with Rod Stewart, *American Idol*, Justin Timberlake, George Clinton, Mick Jagger, The Smithsonian, and all the others can't be learned in a school. (Photo: Kimberlie Acosta)

FOREWORD

When Stevie Salas called me in spring 2013, we began a writing adventure like no other I've experienced in my career as an author and journalist.

Six months prior, I'd seen Stevie play in his hometown of Oceanside. I wrote a blog about the benefit concert for his late cousin's family. After the blog went viral, he thought enough of it to ask me about collaborating with him on a very special memoir. He wanted to commemorate the twenty-five-year anniversary of his first professional tour, when he played lead guitar on Rod Stewart's Out of Order Tour.

I was intrigued, for two reasons. First, the Out of Order Tour was one of the last wild, uncut tours of a dying era, when musicians carried a larger-than-life aura, mystique, and mystery . . . and treated themselves to an endless succession of outrageous days and nights. Legend-building nights. You rarely see that anymore. Second, who the hell rises from playing backyard parties to center stage with a rock 'n' roll legend in three years? What was the story behind that? Behind Stevie?

Stevie and I share history, though amazingly, we'd never worked together before. We grew up five miles from each other in North San Diego County. In the late 1970s, while he was emerging as the teenage guitar sensation for This Kids, I managed one of the area's other red-hot bands, Seraphim. Stevie spent his teenage years playing guitar; I spent mine writing concert reviews and interviewing musicians. Let's just say that when I saw the movie *Almost Famous* in 2000, it took my breath away, because I was the second teenaged journalist to regularly interview big acts at the San Diego Sports Arena. Cameron Crowe, the one-time *Rolling Stone wunderkind* and eventual writer of *Almost Famous* and *Jerry Maguire*, was the first.

Fast forward to 2006. Once again, Stevie and I were in the same place without crossing paths, working at opposite ends of the *American Idol* universe. He was the music director and consultant for several of the show's most successful contestants, including Daughtry, Jordin Sparks, and Adam Lambert, while I was the editorial director of *American Idol Magazine*. I spent time with the idols as they rose up the ranks, giving many their first serious print media coverage. Once there, Stevie molded them into legitimate professional acts.

Now, nearly thirty-five years after our parallel journeys began, we finally join forces to bring you Stevie's memoir, *When We Were the Boys*.

Stevie grew up amidst great hardship and personal tragedy in North San Diego County, whetted his taste buds to the promise (and allure) of rock 'n' roll with This Kids, and then did what every young person with a burning dream should muscle up and do—whatever it takes to make your dream come true. In his case, it meant two-plus years of starving, and sleeping on studio couches, closets, and guesthouses in L.A. The experience chiseled his ability and toughened him mentally, just in time for funk-rock legend George Clinton to discover the young, homeless guitar player sleeping on the couch and invite him to play in a wee-hours recording session.

You can read what happens next in *When We Were the Boys*, a memoir that is equal parts touching, hilarious, self-reflective, and . . . well, rock 'n' roll. In a nutshell, Stevie found his way into amazing (and risky) film and music projects, including the number-one box-office smash *Bill & Ted's Excellent Adventure* and Was (Not Was), which had a number-one hit in "Walk the Dinosaur" in 1987. He then pulled off one of the bigger coups in pop music, landing the gig as Rod Stewart's lead guitarist for the Out of Order Tour in 1988. Many were skeptical about Rod's ability to still command audiences (not to mention his hiring an untested twenty-four-year-old guitarist). However, when his three-month tour turned into a two-year extravaganza, the skeptics were silenced. Much of it was thanks to the youthful, hard-working ball of fire to Rod's left.

Stevie minces no words about his time on the Out of Order Tour. He delivers the goods hot and raw, combining blunt honesty with a large helping of wonderful tales, told by a natural storyteller and filled with juicy backstage and bedroom moments that long-time rock 'n' roll fans love to see. He not only shares stories, but also makes us feel part of them. Then he runs deeper. He pokes at his own follies, peels away the layers of invincibility with which we anointed our rock stars in the 1970s and 1980s, and shows us many painful lessons he learned on the road to stardom. He writes of how those lessons molded him into a better man, a better musician, and more versatile recording artist (selling more than two million solo albums), songwriter, music director, and producer on three fronts—music, television, and film.

What impresses me most about Stevie is his commitment to other musicians, his service-oriented nature, and his status as a lifelong fan. The title of this book, *When We Were the Boys*, spells out that quality: he speaks of his brothers in The Rod Stewart Band almost as much as himself. Also, Stevie is a walking Rolodex; he knows everyone. All you have to do is visit his Facebook fan page and hop onto the story train to realize that. He's played with seemingly everyone, too, from Rod Stewart, Mick Jagger, and P. Funk's George Clinton and Bootsy Collins to Sananda Maitreya (the artist formerly known as Terence Trent D'Arby) and The Jeff Healey Band. (Healey was the legendary blind guitarist in the Patrick Swayze film, *Road House*.) He recently cut the song "Dead and Gone" with Justin Timberlake and hip-hop star T.I. He's the executive producer and star of *Arbor Live*, the Canadian comedy-music TV series, and recently completed a two-year consultancy as the Advisor to Contemporary Music at the Smithsonian Institution.

I love talking with Stevie about music, because unlike so many of today's packaged stars, who can't see their way out of their own illusory boxes, he holds a lifelong love and admiration for the works of many. Plus, he's a veritable encyclopedia of pop and rock music knowledge, much of which he experienced directly. He has worked with the biggest rock star in history, Mick Jagger; *American Idol*, one of the highest-rated television series in U.S. history; and with the biggest museum in the world, the Smithsonian Institution. When he paints his memoir with refreshing brushstrokes of incisive musical perspective, you know it is borne of his vast experience.

How does a kid rise from backyard parties to center stage in seventy-thousand-seat stadiums in three years—and use that experience to launch such a diverse and successful career on four continents, for which he continues to log 150,000 air miles per year?

By getting to the show on time, and playing his heart out, night after day after night.

Enjoy.

—Robert Yehling, coauthor

I

CALL TO AUDITION

I took a deep breath and walked into Audible. This huge Burbank, California, rehearsal studio was a very intimidating place for any young musician. Only the biggest acts could afford to rehearse at Audible, but I knew where to go, because I had jammed and auditioned there for alt keyboard legend Thomas Dolby several months before.

Now, on March 29, 1988, I found myself in Audible for a gig that seemed beyond my wildest dreams. Actually, it *was* my wildest dream, laid down in San Diego a few years before: to play with Rod Stewart.

When I arrived, a person working for Rod told me to hang out for a minute and they would call me when it came my turn to audition. I was really confident, because it felt like everything was going my way. I was twenty-four years old and enjoying great success on many fronts, in large part because of my management: the Bill Graham Management Group. Bill was the greatest rock 'n' roll promoter who ever lived, and the man who single-handedly turned the San Francisco psychedelic music scene into a global phenomenon in the late 1960s. That happened partially through his twin venues—the Fillmore West in San Francisco and Fillmore East in New York. He also was a tough-as-nails manager who, along with his staff, worked his ass off to succeed. Plus, Bill and his company really believed in me.

So yes, as I stood in Audible, I had the buzz. The music gods were working in my favor. What other reason could explain the audition with

Rod? I was at least ten years younger than any of the other musicians, and I had zero touring experience—unless you want to count my van tours with This Kids, my band from San Diego. We cut two EPs and played in Southern California, Arizona, and the Southwest. I really was underqualified for a gig like this, but none of it mattered, because when you get a buzz in Hollywood, you can ride it to the bank, if you're lucky.

While waiting for my audition, I walked into the kitchen looking for a bottle of water. As I turned the corner to enter the kitchen—*boom*—right there, leaning against the refrigerator, was Rod Stewart!

I stopped dead in my tracks. Rod was one of my favorites, an idol to me, whose concert I had badly wanted to see in San Diego but couldn't afford. He was one of the three British legends with whom I wanted to play someday, an artist whose *Gasoline Alley* and *Atlantic Crossing* albums helped to light a fire inside this kid from Oceanside. But right now, I couldn't let him see the wide-eyed fan jumping up and down inside me. I had to play it cool.

I quickly scanned the room for water, as if running into him wasn't a big deal. I glanced side to side near the cupboards, but I could feel him staring at me, his eyes burning a hole in the side of my face.

When I finally met him eye to eye, he looked me up and down. "Hey," he said, nodding his head.

"Hey," I said, trying my best to be cool. You know how hard it is to keep cool while freaking out?

Rod walked back into the music room and auditioned another guitar player while I grabbed my water and waited in the hall.

After a short bit, the auditioning guitarist walked out of the studio, instrument in hand. I thought to myself, *Man, that guy does not look like a rock star.* He was dressed like a plumber. Then I thought, *Hmm, did I overdress? I don't want them to think I'm a showboat. I am looking cool . . . aren't I?*

That made me nervous. I was wearing black Let It Rock jeans with Mexican conchas down the legs tied with black leather, along with custom-made short black suede and python cowboy boots with chains around them and some kind of cool T-shirt. I know it sounds lame now, but that shit was hella cool in trashy L.A. in the late 1980s. That was the music scene, and you both played and dressed the part. Especially when auditioning for a stadium rocker like Rod Stewart. *Oh man, hopefully Rod doesn't think I'm a joke for dressing like a rock star when I'm not quite there yet!*

I took a breath and calmed down, and then said to myself, "This is who I am and *this is my gig.*"

A man called me over and walked me into the room. "Hey, I am Tony Thompson," he said. "I'm music director for the tour."

Tony Thompson? As in, my favorite drummer in the world? I grew up listening to his records with Chic, not to mention his studio work with Madonna, The Power Station, David Bowie, and countless others. Tony then introduced me to bass guitarist Carmine Rojas. "Hey man, nice to meet ya," I said. Then I slowed my voice down, real cool and easy, and said, "Loved that bass track you did on 'Let's Dance.'" Inside, my music fan's voice screamed inside my head: "*Ahhhhhh!* Carmine Rojas from David Bowie!"

After that, I met the New York guitar legend Eddie Martinez. I had once talked with Eddie on the phone when he was hanging out in an office at EMI. A girl I knew from a band I was producing, The Pandoras, worked at EMI. She called me and put me on the phone with Eddie. He was the king of rap-rock guitar, creating the signature backing sound for the group Run-DMC. In L.A., I was playing a lot of rap rock as well, and some people were calling me the young Eddie Martinez.

Eddie remembered our talk, and that made me feel cool because I saw that the New York musicians in the room—Tony, Eddie, and Carmine—thought I was OK. The New York session guys had a harder vibe than the Los Angeles musicians when it came to recording in the studio. Their approaches were as different as the two coasts they came from, and these guys were street-hard New Yorkers. (More on them later.)

I wasn't from New York; actually, the furthest thing from it. I grew up surfing in North San Diego County. However, I felt and related to their New York ways and sound more than the L.A. guys.

As I looked around, the pedigree of these musicians raced through my head. Besides playing with Bowie, Tony Thompson had filled in on drums for Led Zeppelin at Live Aid, their first appearance since John Bonham died a few years before. Tony also played on hybrid funk-rock tracks like "Some Like It Hot" by The Power Station and "Upside Down," Diana Ross's number-one hit. Eddie Martinez performed on "The King of Rock" with Run-DMC and "Addicted To Love" by Robert Palmer. Then there was the bass line Carmine Rojas played on "Let's Dance" . . . like nothing I had ever heard before. You didn't hear playing like that on a Don Henley or Toto record!

I knew their music and found it pretty amazing to be in the same room with them. One thing about me: I'm as much a fan of music as I am a guitarist, songwriter, producer, or performer. I always was and always will be a fan. I never lose sight of that, which is why I'm probably a lot more approachable and into hanging out and jumping in on club gigs when my friends ask.

I plugged in my guitar. Next thing I knew, Tony kicked into a beat on the kick and snare—*plap plap plap boom*—and we all just started rockin'. I was in heaven! We jammed for quite a while, playing my favorite style, a combination of funk and rock, along the thematic lines of Rod's new record *Out of Order*. We also studied each other, figuring out how we meshed . . . or, should I say, Tony Thompson, Carmine Rojas, and Rod studied *me* to see if I meshed with them. I wasn't thinking anymore; I was lost in the moment, jamming with a few of my musical heroes. I hoped the audition would go on. Rod started ad libbing, coming up with one-liners out of nowhere, definitely not from any of his songs. *Holy shit!* First things first: I kept cool.

The appearance of cool is everything with the big boys, and luckily, I had that instinct. Here's an example of how it pays to be cool . . . or else. In 1993, I walked into a New York City restaurant late one night with my dear friend, Canadian rocker Sass Jordan, whose work I produced and played on. If you don't know Sass's music, get to know it. She's awesome. If you've watched the movie *The Bodyguard* with Kevin

Costner and the late Whitney Houston, then you've heard Sass's power-ful voice; she accompanied Joe Cocker on the title song.

When we arrived, the doorman stopped me. "Sorry, sir, it is a private party," he said.

"I know. I am Stevie Salas and I am here for Keith Richards's fiftieth birthday." Only one problem: I wasn't on the list.

Just then, Keith's assistant, Tony Russell, came up to me. "I am here to meet Bernard Fowler," I said. (Bernard has toured with The Rolling Stones as a backup singer for the past twenty-five years. In addition, I've played and recorded with him many times.)

"Hmm, I heard of you," Tony said. "Come on in."

Now here is when you really gotta be cool. Except that it almost became uncool right out of the box. I bumped hard into a table where supermodel Naomi Campbell and Eric Clapton were sitting . . . *Keep cool . . . keep coooooool . . .* I didn't make a big deal about it, but just nodded my head and kept walking. It was almost uncool, but no harm, no foul. Then I spotted the guys I knew were the coolest of the cool, Bernard Fowler and Ivan Neville. We hugged each other and talked.

All this time, Keith Richards was checking it out from afar. He walked up to Sass and me. "Happy birthday," I said. "Nice to meet you."

We engaged in a little small talk, then Keith, being the King of Cool, hugged me and walked off. As he walked away, I smiled inside and out and thought, *I did it; I'm on the inside.*

What I didn't know was that Keith walked up to Bernard and asked, "Who the fuck is Salas? Is he cool?"

"Yeah, he's cool," Bernard replied in his calm, collected way.

Later, Keith walked up to Ivan and asked, "Who the fuck is Salas? Is he cool?"

"Yeah man, he's cool."

Only then was I invited to sit at Keith's table to indulge in vodka and conversation while a very lovely Kate Moss sat next to me . . . Now that's cool!

As we continued jamming, all seemed good at the studio. Even though I was auditioning to join a band of veteran musicians, it felt a lot more like friends cutting loose than me nervously gutting it out under the watchful eye of the bandleader. We really had fun playing together.

Towards the end, Rod said, "Let's try 'Hot Legs.'" It was the only Rod Stewart song I played during that audition. I strapped on the Stratocaster that had served me well since my teen years playing for This Kids, hit the opening chords, and joined the band to play one of the signature anthems of Rod's career. What a rush to see him next to me, singing as I played! Even though we never covered "Hot Legs" with This Kids, I knew it enough by ear to get through it.

After a bit of small talk, I said my good-byes to Rod and the boys, feeling really good about the past hour.

The next day, I headed to San Francisco for two days to produce another eclectic band, The Tubes, for Columbia Records. I got a call from Randy Phillips, who later became the president of AEG. "Stevie, you did it! You got the gig!"

"What?" I made him tell me again, because I didn't believe my ears.

I couldn't get Randy off the phone fast enough. I went bananas, calling my San Diego pals Allen Carrasco and Dale Lawrence. It had only been three years since I left my high school pals, This Kids, and the comforts of my parents' Oceanside home. It had only been three years since I drove past the San Diego Sports Arena and vowed I would play with Rod Stewart, Mick Jagger, and David Bowie. Even in the 1980s, you just didn't get from there to here in three years.

Randy told me to block out April 13 on my calendar, the date full rehearsals would begin.

As it turned out, I learned a valuable lesson: *Don't tell anyone anything until you sign the contract.*

I didn't have the gig, after all. The guys all loved me and Rod said I had it. Then, reality hit them and they realized that I was almost a clone of Eddie Martinez. Furthermore, I sucked at slide guitar and had no acoustic guitar experience, which is vital for songs like the all-time classic "Maggie May," which lives or dies by acoustic guitar.

They decided to look for a seasoned musician that possessed the skills I lacked. That turned out to be Jeff Golub. How could I blame them? The Out of Order Tour would be a giant stadium and arena tour, Rod's biggest in years, with millions of dollars at stake. Your bandmates can cover missed notes and minor mistakes in concert, especially with guys as seasoned as those in Rod's band, but they can't cover someone who barely knows how to play a particular instrument. That's where I was with acoustic guitar. I was a turtle on its back.

I was pretty bummed out. Scratch that: I was *really* bummed out. However, thanks to Bill Graham Management and my other recording work and credits, I was close to getting my own recording contract and still working like crazy. Time to move on . . .

Except, I couldn't. Weeks went by, but I couldn't shake it. I couldn't get the Rod tour out of my head. It was all I could think about. I wouldn't just say I was focused on this gig—I was *obsessed* with this gig.

I am a Native American, and I experience precognition. Sometimes, I know things that are going to happen before they do. It kind of freaks me out, but it's true. I didn't consciously use visualization then, but it still seemed to happen. I had no choice. And I didn't have a choice in what I visualized this time, either: something kept telling me the Out of Order Tour was my gig.

Every week, I left phone messages with Rod's assistant, Malcolm Cullimore, and Tony Thompson. I let them know that if they needed me, I was there. Of course, they never returned my calls.

I carried a lot of confidence and a healthy ego, two very big assets when you work in the entertainment business. Normally, I wouldn't keep calling and leaving messages with people who don't return my calls, but still I called because I felt that the outcome was eventually beyond my control. I never stopped visualizing myself playing those killer Faces songs, the music of a generation, onstage with Rod and Carmine at Madison Square Garden.

Meanwhile, I was dating Christina Whitaker, an actress and friend of actress Maria Conchita Alonso, who was managed by . . . Randy Phillips. One day, Christina wanted to take a trip. "I can't leave town, because Rod's tour starts soon, and I need to be here in case they call me," I said.

Christina had had enough. She knew from Maria that the band was well into rehearsals with new guitar player Jeff Golub, and that I was not part of any conversation at Randy's office. She laid into me. "Forget this tour," she said. "It isn't going to happen. You need to wake up!"

Right then, I stopped seeing her. I had to. She never knew why I ended our relationship so abruptly, but that was why. I believed I would find my way onto the tour. She did not. I didn't feel like she had my back, or the confidence that I would make it. The likelihood seemed impossible to her. It certainly looked like it—unreturned calls, no Stevie Salas in the studio conversation, two great guitarists flanking Rod . . . but deep inside, I knew better.

At night, I tossed around to vivid dreams with Rod in them (not in his leopard-print underwear!). In one, I was at a cabin in the woods hanging out with a girl. A red Lamborghini drove up the road and stopped in front of my cabin. It was Rod. We talked about things as if we were old pals, and then he drove off . . .

I woke up thinking, *This is weird!* Remembering my dreams and looking for messages and direction from them came to me naturally. This vision and tour consumed me, so I didn't know if the dream was a message or part of my obsession that crept into the night. I was certain of my destiny, but . . . I was also secretly afraid about how I would recover if it didn't happen.

Then on June 15, less than three weeks before the Out of Order Tour's opening stop in San Juan, Puerto Rico, the phone rang. I noticed the English accent immediately. "Stevie, this is Malcolm. Can you please come to Audible Studio? Rod would like you to come and play again."

2

YOU GOT THE GIG—THIS TIME, I MEAN IT

I will never forget the words as long as I live. It was about 6:00 p.m. on June 16 when Rod looked me in the eye and said those words into his rehearsal room mic, loud enough for everyone in the room to hear. I could have died. I knew that my life was about to change and would never be the same again.

I had only ten days to rehearse and learn the *whole* set list of songs, a set list millions of people love and cherish. To a lot of people, these songs are the soundtracks of their lives, so the pressure was on! I had to play all the acoustic guitar parts, too, and let me tell you: I sucked at playing acoustic guitar.

After Malcolm Cullimore asked me to see Rod for this second-chance audition, I bought up Rod's records and spent the day before learning everything I could. I knew their big concern was whether or not I could handle the subtleties of playing acoustic guitar. Everyone knew I could bring some heat to the songs on the new *Out of Order* album, which Rod was about to tour. Since I loved the old Rod Stewart and Faces songs, I had a vibe on those, too. The Faces' sloppy party style helped me, since my lack of experience made it look like I was playing with that funky swing. Or perhaps just playing drunk. But here's the thing: with acoustic guitar, there is no faking it. When you play that acoustic guitar in a sports arena or stadium and clam it up . . . God help you.

I spent all morning running over the songs, so I could ace this God-given second chance. When I showed up at Audible Rehearsal Studio at 1:30 p.m., I was ready.

So I thought.

When I got there, Carmine Rojas greeted me and pulled me aside. Since my last audition and jam, they had made some big changes. Eddie Martinez had left the band to return to his original gig with Robert Palmer. Robert had a tour and follow-up record to produce after the success of the *Riptide* album and its huge hit "Addicted to Love," so Eddie took off and left an opening for lil' ol' me. Superstar drummer Tony Thompson had also left the band. His music director duties fell to Carmine Rojas.

After Carmine explained this to me, he sat me down and said, "I need to talk to you." He looked me in the eye. "I feel like you need to do this gig."

I nervously said, "Uhh cool uhh me too and uh . . . "

"*Stop!* Listen to what I am telling you."

Carmine said something that blew my mind: when I walked into the room on the first audition, I reminded him of his little brother, Rafael. He had carried Rafael to the hospital when they were both very young, and Rafael died in his arms of spinal meningitis.

I was frozen. He then added, "Something keeps telling me that you need to get this gig, I just feel it in my heart, so don't blow it!"

"I won't, Carmine . . . I promise. Thank you."

I walked into the rehearsal room and met all the new guys: Nick Lane on trombone, Rick Braun on trumpet, Jimmy Roberts on sax, Chuck Kentis on keyboards, Jeff Golub on guitar, and . . . *Oh my God, that's Tony Brock from The Babys!*

When I was in sixth grade, a dozen years before, I had an older friend named Roy Tuck. He and my brother-in-law, Steve Cottrell (who built my first electric guitar), liked to go fishing, race motocross, and listen to cool music. We all loved The Babys. Their two big hits, "Head First" and "Midnight Rendezvous," were showstoppers for This Kids. In fact, we used to talk about how great the drummer was.

This is nuts. I'm gonna be in the same band with him?

It gets deeper. My San Luis Rey school buddy, Jeff Smith, and I spent a lot of our year rocking out to Rod Stewart's *Atlantic Crossing* album. So now I had a lump in my throat because I was going to be playing Rod Stewart songs with Rod singing and Tony on the drums . . . *what the fuck?*

I gathered myself and plugged my guitar into the wall of amps that were brought down for me to use. Were those the same white Ampeg amps I used to see on the Faces tours with Woody (Ron Wood)? I didn't want anyone to know that I was about to lose my mind, crap my pants, throw up—or perhaps all three. I did feel like break dancing. I told myself to calm the fuck down, and then I took a breath and kept it together.

Rod walked in and seemed a little distant, as if on edge. When the boss is on edge, the whole world feels like it's on edge with him. "Let's try 'Infatuation,'" he said.

Tony Brock counted it off, and I lit it up. I was a Jedi, and the band sounded insane, like we had been together forever. I knew it was special, and by the end of the song, I could see Rod loosen up a little. We then played "Lost in You," and again it sounded like muscle. I noticed Rod growing even looser, throwing his head back like a motherfucking rooster fresh out of the coop and ready to rut. As we finished, the vibe in the room went from uptight to right on.

Then came the moment of truth: Rod needed to hear me play acoustic guitar. He said, "Let's try 'You're in My Heart,'" but right before we started, Carmine rushed over to me. "Hold on, guys, give me a second." He grabbed the acoustic guitar and took me to another room. This was one of Rod's greatest ballads, and I couldn't screw it up. He then asked me to play "You're in My Heart" for him privately, which I did. "Play it again."

I played it for Carmine once more. "Do me a favor," he said. "Go home and *really* practice this one, as well as 'Maggie May,' and come back in two hours and let's try them with the band."

That's what I did.

(As it turned out, I was playing it wrong. I kept on playing it wrong until the L.A. Forum gigs two months later. That's when the great Jimmy Cregan, Rod's music director on the 1976 world tour, wrote down the proper intro chords on a napkin. After one of the Forum concerts, Rod had said to me, "Jimmy Cregan says you're bollocksing the intro to 'You're in My Heart,'" and then handed me the napkin. How could I be wrong? Jeff Golub had originally taught me how to play the chords and notes of the intro on my audition day, before Carmine pulled me aside and made me go home to practice it.

I learned what was on the napkin. That's when I discovered that my hero, Jeff Golub, taught me wrong . . . the first of many "hazing" episodes I would endure with this band!)

I returned to Audible at 4:30 p.m. and plugged in the acoustic guitar. I had to borrow one of Rod's, since I didn't own one. It wasn't talked about, but we all knew everything was riding on this moment. Again, the angels smiled on me. We played the songs, and they felt and sounded great. The pressure in the room released, and I noticed Rod really coming to life. He must have been stressed out to the max, with no concrete band and the tour starting in less than two weeks. It was a big relief to him that I pulled it off, but I also know that the appearance of the familiar Tony Brock, his long-time drummer, must have brought him comfort, too.

We finished "Maggie May," but I still stressed, wondering if I was good enough. After all, I had already been told once, by Randy Phillips, that I had gotten the gig, and then . . . (Yes, this is the same Randy Phillips who is now the head of AEG, the giant entertainment management and production agency, so prominent in the 2013 Michael Jackson court case.)

I took off the acoustic guitar and grabbed my electric. While the guys were talking, I focused on dialing in my tone. To test it, I ripped into the Jeff Beck riff from "Infatuation," pinching out a mean harmonic squeal. It sounded raw, full of energy. Rod lit up again like a rooster, looked at the band, and said, "That's what we need! We need that edge!"

After a short pause, he turned to me. "You got the gig . . . and this time, I mean it."

The words that changed my life.

I acted cool, but deep down I could have broken down and cried. I thought of all the nights I starved with no money, along with the months of hell wondering if I was ever gonna make it. I thought of my parents and friends who believed in me, and all my visions. I knew this was my destiny, even when no one believed me!

Then, I thought about someone no one was thinking of: Malcolm Cullimore. He had always kept me in his back pocket. He was my secret ambassador of *kwan*, indeed. Malcolm later told me that he, too, had a feeling that I was right for this gig. He even spoke to Rod, saying, "Look, I know he hasn't the experience, but this guy will kill for you."

He was right: I would kill for Rod. To this day.

My other secret ambassador of *kwan* was the number-one baby-kissing, vote-getting Puerto Rican badass, Carmine Rojas. He walked over and gave me a look that said, *I love you, little bro, but you'd better not fuck up.* I nodded my head to both thank Carmine and let him know I understood.

Rod finished off the afternoon with something I would hear him say a lot: "C'mon boys, it's off to the pub."

3

OMG, THAT'S ROD STEWART!

On June 17, my alarm blew up just before 8:00 a.m. Time to wipe the crud out of my eyes and get cracking! That afternoon, my first rehearsal as an official Rod Stewart band member would happen. I needed to be ready.

I turned on my old Sony stereo. I'm talking an old-school, seven-power-button, graphic equalizer, turntable on top with speakers half as big as my wall Sony stereo. It made Rod's *Gasoline Alley* LP sound the way God meant it to sound. That got my blood moving.

I grabbed my guitar and started my crash course, learning the chords to thirty or so Rod Stewart songs that might be in our two-hour-plus concert set. Even though some of the songs were not in the rough set list I had picked up the day before at rehearsal, I still listened to everything I could get my hands on, from the Jeff Beck Group's debut record *Truth*, which in 1968 introduced the world to Rod Stewart, to the new 1988 *Out of Order* record. That's twenty years of music!

I was so excited to be alive. The night before, my manager, Morty Wiggins from Bill Graham Management, had negotiated a chubby tour salary for me. Soon, my pockets and bank account would be stuffed full of fresh, tasty lettuce, making me financially stable for the first time in my life. I was in such a great mood as I listened to Rod's music, all of it sounding so good to me . . .

Well, almost all. Try as I might, I just couldn't get through the *Every Beat of My Heart* record, which preceded *Out of Order*. As a fan of Rod's, I could listen to songs from different eras like "You Wear It Well" and "Tonight I'm Yours." Even though they were recorded years apart with completely different musicians that sounded nothing alike, there was still a common thread—Rod's power. When I put on the song "Love Touch," the main single from *Every Beat of My Heart*, the connection was lost. That song bugged me, because I felt like Rod was selling out for the sake of a hit, and you never want to see your heroes sell out! The more I heard it, the more I wanted to sock someone. I asked the rock gods to not let this song end up in our live concert set.

It worked—sort of. During the tour, Rod would sometimes look at us and say, "Play 'Love Touch,'" then Tony Brock would count it off and Chuck and I would play the intro. The band would kick into the first verse and Rod would sing the first line, then he would glance back and wave us off with this funny look, saying into the microphone, "Stop boys, stop! Nah, nah, that one's bollocks. We can't do that." Then we would count into some rocker. It never failed to make me laugh my ass off every time Rod did that, but I must admit to feeling a little guilty, since my pal Gene Black, who now plays guitar with Joe Cocker, co-wrote that song.

The afternoon rehearsal went well, and I was focused on the task at hand. However, since no one knew I had landed the gig with Rod, music people assumed I was still open for business. During a break in rehearsal, I checked my phone messages, and heard one from MCA A&R VP Michael Goldstone. (It was the same Michael Goldstone who later would sign a little Seattle band called Pearl Jam and their lead singer, Eddie Vedder, who like me grew up surfing in North San Diego County. Years earlier, he also signed a very young Austin guitarist, Charlie Sexton, who went on to become Bob Dylan's guitarist for most of the past quarter century, and is now my neighbor in Austin.) Michael wanted me to produce one song for Jetboy, a band he had just signed. *Hmm, I could squeeze in some late-night sessions for Michael and Jet-*

boy and work with Rod all day. "OK," I said, and asked him to call Bill Graham's office and work out the business.

Not thirty minutes later, Randy Phillips walked into our rehearsal room at Audible. "Stevie, you're not gonna take that MCA job, right?"

"Huh?"

"That Jetboy production job for MCA."

"Noooooo, are you kidding? I am so busy learning these songs there is no way I could do that."

I knew Randy could tell I was full of shit. "Great," he said, and walked away.

Dang, I really wanted to do that job—not to mention collect an easy ten thousand dollars plus royalties. I sheepishly called Michael Goldstone with my ass tucked in like a dog who was in trouble and told him I had to back out.

Randy was right. I didn't need any distractions. After all, I was learning the guitar parts of some of the greatest songs in pop music history, parts first played by some of the greatest guitarists in pop music history. I was indeed in over my head.

The next day, I walked into the rehearsal room around 1:00 p.m. All of a sudden, a truck pulled up to the open gate door and the crew started unloading a bunch of big boxes. "Stevie, it's your birthday, mate," Malcolm Cullimore said in his strong British accent.

It wasn't my birthday, but it sure felt like it when I realized that this was the moment every young guitar player dreams of . . . no . . . "dream" isn't big enough. I mean, if a guitar player was gonna masturbate to a fantasy that didn't include a sexy person, this would be the fantasy.

Standing in front of me were eight brand-new Marshall one-hundred-watt amplifier heads with new speaker cabinets . . . for me! I also received all new anvil road cases. The guys pulled the amps out and put them on my side of the stage, and then it hit me: *How the hell do I set all this shit up?* I didn't have my own guitar tech yet, so some of the crew helped out by setting up the amps for me. Then with much pride and *huevos,* I started rocking through my new gear.

Rod walked in. To my surprise, he didn't like the sound as much as the old Faces amps. To tell you the truth, if I was doing Rod's gig today, as a seasoned veteran musician, I would use those old Faces white Ampeg amps. But since sixth grade, when I saw KISS and their stacks at the San Diego Civic Center on the Dressed to Kill tour, I'd dreamed of having my own wall of Marshall stacks. Their opening act that night was Rush, and they also had Marshalls. Kids like me had held those dreams since the mid-1960s, when Pete Townshend of The Who and London instrument shop owner James Marshall first figured out how to stack Marshall's works of master craftsmanship, his amplifiers, to create earth-shattering walls of sound. Sure, these were stereotype amps, but they were out of reach for most kids in 1988. I was determined to keep these Marshall amps, so I kept dialing in the sound as we played. Soon it got better, and my guitar tone flew off Rod's radar.

Two days later, we moved to a bigger place for production rehearsals. A bigger place? Than Audible? Were we not already doing production rehearsals? What the hell *are* production rehearsals?

I found out. We started rehearsing on a big soundstage at MGM Studios in Culver City, where they filmed *The Wizard of Oz* and where I secretly taped four episodes of the lame TV series *Fame*. I was in actor Jesse Borrego's TV band called—get this—Albondigas. That's Spanish for "meatballs." Jesse was Mexican. Not too racist, right? The money I made on *Fame* kept me alive, and a lot of great musicians worked their way through that show. They included Jack White's solo drummer, Carla Azar, who actually got me the gig.

However, being on *Fame* was like riding a moped—lots of fun to ride, but you don't want anyone to see you. The image the show projected did not match the image of a young rock 'n' roll guitar player in L.A. I did my utmost to keep my participation on the show a secret.

Still, I was excited to be back on the MGM lot, with all the big movie stars walking around. There is never a dull moment when you eat in the cafeteria of a big studio, between running into starlets and other movers and shakers. While working on *Fame*, I entertained fantasies of running into sexy star Victoria Principal, who I used to see on the lot filming *Dallas*. I could never walk up to her and say, "Hello, I am Stevie Salas and I am working as a glorified extra on *Fame*," but perhaps I could walk up to her and say, "I am Stevie Salas, lead guitar player with Rod Stewart," and perhaps get somewhere. Don't laugh; that shit really works!

After we arrived at MGM, I found out *Dallas* wasn't filming on that particular soundstage. Instead, I saw bizarrely dressed people walking around from the movie, *Spaceballs*, which was in production. Hardly the same thing.

When I walked into our soundstage, I was blown away by the giant stage made of metal, with a huge octopus-shaped light set up above it. *Man, this is awesome!* I found my way to my gear setup, feeling the whole time like I was moving around in a spaceship.

Soon, we started playing. Right away, we realized we couldn't hear our amps. Although the stage looked supercool, it wasn't the most functional. The metal grating was blocking the amp sounds. I walked over to grab some water, and Carmine and I stood there with Rod. (I was indeed guilty of following Rod around a lot, and the boys sometimes called me his little mascot, but I didn't care, because the sun was always shining brighter where Rod was, and God knows I love the sun.) Rod was frustrated about the stage, mumbling things under his breath.

Malcolm Cullimore walked over. "They dropped a big bollock on us, didn't they, Mal?" Rod said in a very British accent.

"Excuse me, what did you say?" I asked.

Rod looked at me very dryly. "The stage, Stevie boy. They dropped a big bollock on us."

Malcolm and the crew got to work, cutting some of the steel away from the stage. After that, they moved our guitar and bass speaker cabinets onto the main stage.

We spent the next eight days rehearsing. I didn't have a lot of free time, since I had to learn so many songs. It was a colossal task. Sure, "Twistin' the Night Away" is simple, but try playing "I Was Only Joking" and that acoustic guitar solo. Drop one clam there, and the whole arena smells.

I also needed to get my tour wardrobe together. My list included custom cowboy boots, which were made at Leather and Treasures on Melrose Boulevard. After all, I was now flush with cash and could spend like a sailor, but here's the cool thing: now that I was in Rod Stewart's band, I couldn't pay for anything. "You want some free Nikes?" "How about these shirts?" "A new Body Glove jacket? Take this surfboard, too." It was awesome.

For my stage wardrobe, I wanted something unique that would really stand out. Since I was skinny then, wearing size twenty-eight jeans, I could pull it off. My soon-to-be A&R guy at Island Records, Steve Pross, took me to a new underground clothing company called Lip Service. One of my longtime guitar heroes, Joe Perry from Aerosmith, wore these all-black, shiny suits. *That's killer*, I thought. *That's what I want.* The owner was excited to know I played lead guitar with Rod Stewart and was getting ready to play before many thousands of people, so he emptied the racks for me.

This stuff looked like patent leather, but it was crazy plastic. Did it stink! After every show, I would have to hand-wash the pants with Woolite in my hotel room. Our trumpet player, Rick Braun, and trombone player, Nick Lane, would soon dub my clothes "chunderwear." Which meant I could barf on myself and one of the boys could just hose me down and all would be fine.

On June 27, production rehearsals ended. All of our gear was shipped to Puerto Rico. We would play again in San Juan, on opening night of the Out of Order Tour. I had two days to get my life in order, because when I left on the thirtieth, I wouldn't be home again until sometime in August.

I spent those two days doing anything but rock star stuff. I took my new plastic pants to my bro, Winston A. Watson Jr., the drummer in my band Colorcode, and he hemmed my pants. Winston could sew and design his own clothes, fix cars, build model planes, train animals, and build anything electronic. I also visited the dentist to get my cavities fixed. Having a big steady paycheck to cover the costs made it a lot less painful. Sure, doctor, why not? Give me a cleaning, too.

A funny aside: Six years later, in 1994, I discovered a young drummer named Taylor Hawkins. I hired Taylor for his first world tour with Sass Jordan, and he had *so* many cavities. Once he got paid, I stayed on him about fixing his teeth . . . flash forward to 2013. While leaving Taylor a message, I said, "Brush your teeth and go to the dentist." As the drummer of the Foo Fighters, he can afford it now!

After I fixed my cavities, I fulfilled one final prior commitment, a guitar session in L.A. at Powertrax studio, where I worked as a staff producer for David Kershenbaum. The session was for my dear friend, Columbia Records A&R exec Jamie Cohen, and a Swedish band he was signing, NASA.

I then drove ninety miles south to my dad's house in Oceanside, and dropped off my old Porsche. He was going to watch it while I toured, to make sure nothing happened. (He didn't do the best job. I found out both of my sisters, Sandy and Rachel, took their friends joyriding in it.)

After saying good-bye to my San Diego County friends, I hitched a ride back to my Hollywood Hills house. My girlfriend at the time, actress Lynn Oddo (*Hero, Dead On, 3000 Miles to Graceland*), helped me pack. At 5:00 a.m., a limo arrived to take me to LAX. Lynn and I were both excited, but we both knew my life was about to change forever, and things would never be the same.

En route to LAX, I realized I was carrying way too many bags. I had one bag full of shoes, one full of shirts, one full of condoms, one full of jackets . . . something like eight bags in all. The only person I ever saw tour with more bags was Sananda Maitreya (the artist formerly known as Terence Trent D'Arby), when I was his guitar player and music director on the 1993 Duran Duran tour. He may have had fifteen bags, which included the biggest suitcase he could find. He filled that suitcase with books that must have weighed two hundred pounds, and cost the tour a fortune in overweight baggage costs every time we flew commercial. I always felt bad for his female assistants, who had to hump that bag around.

When my limo arrived at LAX, an American Airlines employee awaited me. "Hello, Mr. Salas," she said.

How the heck do you know my name, lady? "Am I in trouble?" I asked.

She smiled an odd smile that suggested, *No, you greenhorn stupid dumbass kid.* "I am here to take you through the back way."

Before I knew it, someone grabbed my things, and she whisked me through the doors.

When I reached the gate, our tour manager, Henry Newman, handed me my first-ever first-class plane ticket. Inside, I giggled like a child, but on the outside, I rubbed my wild hair and kept my lame rock star pout while all the passengers looked at me, trying to figure out who the hell I was.

Back then, rock stars really looked different. People would always say, "Oh, you must be in a band." Sometimes, they would ask if I was a hairdresser. I didn't like that much, but when you were in a band, you stood out—for better or worse. When you saw Rod Stewart, David Bowie, or Steven Tyler, you knew they were something different. If you wanted a big gig, you projected some kind of image. You couldn't be fat with a big muffin top hanging over your pants, or a goon. You had to throw off some kind of vibe, because the gigs were few and far between and the competition was brutal.

Today, it's not like that. A guy could be standing next to me with the number-one record in the country and I wouldn't know him from the guy next door. It sucks. Even when I surf, I can't tell if the dude with the goatee, bald head, and tats is a badass biker who surfs, or just a dork trying to look like a badass.

I got onto the plane and sat in my big first-class seat. Jimmy Roberts sat next to me. Like all the other seasoned rock star band members, except perhaps Rick Braun, he was used to this treatment. Jimmy went way back; he'd worked with the great Otis Redding. I was so excited . . .

but no one seemed to share my enthusiasm. I must have looked to them like a hyper puppy jumping around the older dogs.

I was annoying as hell. The Spanish flight attendant asked me and Jimmy in a thick Spanish accent, "Wooooould jew like a peeeeelow?"

Like an idiot, I started laughing and asked Jimmy a thousand more times, "Would you like a peeeeelow?"

What I didn't know until later was that other band members were a little pissed off about me. Everyone else had worked through the ranks to get to the top—which is where Rod Stewart sits. You couldn't climb much higher. Meanwhile, this was my first big-time gig, and since I paid exactly zero dues, it didn't sit well with the boys. Plus, I was annoying, cocky, and overconfident. I think I used that as a shield to hide my fears and insecurities . . . truth be told, I was scared shitless.

After we landed in Dallas to change planes, they must have talked with Henry Newman. He said to me, "I need to see your boarding pass." He took my pass and handed me another one. "There was a mix-up on this flight," he said.

When I boarded, the band sat in first class. Of course . . . but I was in coach. It was hazing time . . . like being a rookie in the NFL . . . *fuck this!* I wanted to knock someone out. The boys all got a kick out of it, but I didn't.

The next few hours from Dallas to Puerto Rico proved to be a long, humbling experience. I vowed that this wouldn't happen again (even though it did). In the future, when they tried it, I would sweet talk the girl at the flight desk into upgrading me. Once, I even promised to get a girl an autographed Rod Stewart photo. I always felt badly that I never sent it.

The first couple times I pulled this off, Henry would see me walk into first class. "What are you doing here?" he asked. I foiled their haze-the-rookie plans, and I loved it. One of the first things I learned on this tour was that if I didn't have thick skin, I wouldn't survive.

We landed in San Juan, and I could tell right away this was my kind of place . . . white sand and tropical weather. We checked into the coolest hotel I'd ever seen, the Old San Juan. Rod and his managers, Arnold Stiefel and Randy Phillips, arrived before the band. While walking past the casino, I noticed Randy having fun in there.

At 7:30 p.m. on June 30, 1988, I walked into my first rock star hotel room. It looked like a palace to me. After all, I was still sleeping on the floor with a futon mattress at my Hollywood Hills house. This room sat on a beautiful beach, so I opened the sliding glass doors to take a look at the turquoise water and white sand. After a few minutes, I noticed everything in my room was covered in condensation, and I was sweating, so I closed the door and waited for the air conditioner to do its job. It wouldn't work. I tried everything, jiggling the switches and moving the dial, but my room dripped water on the walls, and the windows were completely fogged.

I called the front desk. The man came up and looked at me like I was an idiot. He walked over to the sliding glass doors and closed them properly. The A/C kicked right on. "Oh, I didn't know . . . sorry," I said.

Then I laid down to rest, since my day had started at 4:30 a.m. California time.

A message was shoved under my door to meet Rod and Carmine at the bar at 10:30 p.m. I set my alarm and got some kip. At 10:30, I walked to the lobby and met with Rod and Carmine—and, not to my surprise, a couple of *superhot* six-foot-plus models. Rod and Carmine greeted me and bought me a drink. "Let's go," they said. I had no idea where we were going, but since I was the tour virgin (so to speak), the pros would take me out and show me how it's done. We jumped into a big limo and pulled out.

The girls were all laughing and drinking champagne. Rod and Carmine were carrying on. Meanwhile, I was going into shock. Only a few years earlier, a Carmine Rojas poster hung on my bedroom wall at my dad's house. I listened to the David Bowie "Let's Dance" record until the grooves wore out. I watched Carmine on HBO Live in Concert with John Waite. Carmine was a hero to me. He still is.

Meanwhile, I played it cool with the girls, sharing some fun conversation, but they were *so* beautiful. One Puerto Rican model who was down from NYC had the longest legs I had ever seen, not to mention a short skirt and killer heels as well. I said to myself, *calm down, Stevie old boy, you have seen this moment in your mind a million times.*

I stopped looking at her legs and peered out the limo window. We passed some beautiful lit-up fountains, so gorgeous. I started to say something to Rod . . .

Then it happened. I looked across the seat. For the first time it hit me: OH MY GOD, THAT'S ROD STEWART! WHAT THE FUCK AM I DOING HERE? I instantly felt like someone was sitting on my chest and squeezing the breath out of me. We were so busy getting ready for the tour that I'd never had time to digest how massively my life and career had instantly changed.

I will never forget that moment. It can happen a lot when working with superstars. A few years later, when I was Mick Jagger's guitarist and music director, I brought a second guitar player into the band, Nick Lashley, a seasoned pro. We had worked together with Sass Jordan, and he also played with Alanis Morrisette for many years. You would think he would be cool, right?

Not exactly. As we rehearsed one night at SIR Studios in L.A., Mick wanted to do some improv jamming. Mick ran around the stage, playing harmonica. Then he got up into Nick's face as if to say, *let's riff.*

All Nick could do was look at the ground or look away. Jagger kept egging him on, but was getting nothing in return. Nick couldn't look him in the eye; he just kept staring at the ground.

The next morning, Mick called me. "Can Nick get rid of some of his guitar peddos [British slang for effect pedals]?"

"Why?" I asked.

"Look man, I was like 'c'mon, let's jam,' but all Nick could do was stare down at his peddos!"

"Mick, maybe he is just freaked out. After all, you are *Mick Jagger*," I calmly and respectfully said.

"I know, I know, and I try, and I know he is a quiet guy." He paused for a second, then said excitedly, "Mick Taylor was a quiet guy, too, but when it came time to jam, *he would jam!*"

Later that day, I talked with Nick about trying not to get freaked out when Mick wanted to rock with him. I also told him, "Whatever you do, don't look down at your peddos!"

Nick stayed in the band.

We parked in front of the entrance of a packed club with hundreds of well-dressed people in line. Someone figured out Rod was in the limo; all of a sudden, people started surrounding it. They grew louder and louder, screaming "Rod! Rod! Rod!" then shaking the limo. Some even tried to crawl onto the roof. Instant pure madness!!

Our driver started freaking out. "Let's get out of here!" he yelled. He inched forward, but the crowd wouldn't budge. They kept chanting Rod's name and bouncing the car up and down, but our driver kept inching forward. Soon, we were able to escape.

WOW, that was insane. I was a bit afraid, but I loved it . . .

I then looked at Rod and Carmine. They didn't even flinch; they were cool as cucumbers. Meanwhile, my heart tried to thump right through my shirt.

The next stop was a bit calmer. Our driver summoned security, and they arranged a table for us, along with a team of security guards. We walked into the club and sat at a table with a fresh bottle of champagne.

Here is where the night grew weird. The table sat in the middle of an open area, with velvet ropes and security guards surrounding us. Around those ropes were hundreds of people, covering all 360 degrees. They snapped photos and stared at us. The girls loved it, and Rod and Carmine kept laughing and chatting away, but I was freaking out. I felt like an animal in the zoo with people piled up staring at us. After a few drinks, I got over it.

I noticed a commotion in the crowd. A big fella and his date were working their way to our roped-in area. It was Toto's keyboard player, David Paich. He sweated profusely, looking like a heart attack ready to happen, but a heart attack with a superhot chick. That helps to balance out a sweaty, disheveled look. David sat down, grabbed a drink, and jumped right in. He was awesome, too . . . what positive energy!

After a while, we decided to take off. We said our good-byes to David and told him we would see him tomorrow at the gig, since Toto was our opening act. An L.A. band, Toto was still very popular, but not as much as when they summited to the top of the charts in 1982 with *Toto IV* and its three massive hits, "Hold the Line," "Rosanna," and "Africa." It was now 3:00 a.m. and I was hammered, so we slid into the limo and headed back to the Old San Juan.

I should have slept in, but I was so excited about playing my first baseball stadium. At around noon, I jumped into the taxi with our tour accountant, Baron Jonathon Kessler (later the manager of Depeche Mode) and headed to Hirum Bithorn Stadium for a walk around. When I got there, the Toto band members were already done with their sound check, but their lead guitarist, the legendary Steve Lukather, was there with his technician, Bob Bradshaw. Bob is the guitar electronics wiz behind the Bradshaw switching system. I had met Bob before, so he introduced me to Steve, who became a dear friend to this day.

(However, something happened on my first trip to Kenya in 2003 that pissed me off. I sat on the beach in Mombasa to listen to an *authentic* African band, and the first song they played was "Africa"—by Toto. I e-mailed Steve immediately.)

It was really stormy in San Juan. When I got to the stage, Malcolm Cullimore was drilling the local promoters and their workers for a bunch of stuff they did wrong. Mal was a little guy, but he could lay down the wood; I made it a point to never get on his bad side. A big tarp hovered above the stage like a parachute to block the rain, but it was filling with water. I decided to get my American Indian ass back to the hotel. As surely as the day I was born, a big wind blew as I left the stage, and water drenched everything.

I came back later with the band for sound check. I didn't know how loud my amps should be, since I had never done anything like this in my life. I cranked my Marshalls up to around 6, *ungodly loud*, loud enough to take your head off if I was to hit a power chord while you walked past. It sounded killer to me, and no one told me to turn it down.

I played on the same side of the stage as Carmine, who had his own PA system for a bass setup. He had shipped it fresh from the David Bowie Glass Spider Tour, which he'd played in 1987. If you were suffering from bad constipation, all you needed to do was stand in front of his speakers for thirty seconds . . . I am talking bowel-shaking low end with monster-truck force. I then walked over to Jeff's side of the stage, and he was loud as hell, too. Later on the tour, our volume would become a big problem, but Rod wasn't at sound check, so we had nothing against which to gauge our volume.

After sound check, we went back to the hotel to gather our things and eat a little, but I couldn't eat a bite. I was too nervous and pumped up, like an athlete ready for a big game.

We headed to the stadium. When we arrived, Toto was already finished, but still no sign of Rod. Most of the baseball field was fenced off, with thousands of people pressed up against an eight-foot-tall chain-link fence. The grandstands were packed. We hung out in a baseball dugout converted into a dressing room. I put on my plastic pants, my cut-up Big Fun T-shirt, and my super-low-cut black suede and python cowboy boots, ready to destroy all comers. I then walked out onto the baseball field, and people started screaming. To my surprise, I saw our six-foot Puerto Rican model friend and her pals, so I invited them into the dugout for a drink.

A few minutes later, Henry came in. "It's showtime, boys!"

Out of nowhere, a helicopter whisked over our heads as we walked out of the dugout, landing on the grass field. There he was . . . our singer. The campy hit song "The Stripper," which became wildly famous in the 1960s Gillette razor TV commercials, started blasting through the huge stadium's PA system.

As we ran across the grass infield, I felt like The Beatles at Shea Stadium. The crowd roared. I knew this was my destiny. I had been preparing for this moment since I first picked up a guitar when I was fifteen.

We jumped into the back of an empty semi truck–trailer that was on the side of the stage. Rod gave us some type of pep talk, but I only heard thousands of people screaming and the "The Stripper" music.

We jumped onto the stage and grabbed our guitars. The place went bananas as I hit a couple of power chords to test the amps. That's when I noticed something weird. I looked at the chain-link fence, maybe forty yards from the stage, and saw thousands of kids going nuts. *I hope no one gets crushed.*

As I thought that, Tony Brock yelled, "1-2-1-2-3-4," signaling me to hit the massive D-chord guitar-intro riff to "Lost in You." While the riff pumped with Tony's kick drum, the chain-link fence started to shake . . . then convulse . . . then explode to the grass. When the band kicked in and Rod yelled, "Hey baby, you've been on my mind tonight," thousands of people ran at full speed towards the stage.

The hair spiked on every part of my body. For a second, I thought the people might knock over our massive stage. It was pure pandemonium.

We played our stadium festival set, which lasted only an hour and a half counting encores. Every one of those ninety minutes was a blur to me.

After the show, we met at a hotel restaurant. Rod toasted to a great show, and Arnold Stiefel told us to order whatever we wanted, so I enjoyed lobster. My Puerto Rican model friend sat with me at dinner (notice I said *my* . . . because after that set, she gave me *that look* to let me know it was on).

Every dream was coming true. I had money, I was in a superstar band playing stadiums, and now I had my own gorgeous model (don't blame me for being stereotypical. It was fun, I was young—and after all, I was of weak character!).

After dinner, I went out with the horn players and Carmine. Since Carmine was the king of Puerto Rico, we had no problems scooting around town with our car full of women and cocktails. This had to be one of the greatest nights of my life.

And it was only the first show.

4

WHAT'S A HOOTERS GIRL?

Our second gig was set for Tampa at the Buccaneers' football stadium, otherwise known as the Big Sombrero . . . my first U.S. stadium concert, by the way. Now that's a mouthful.

Some of us partied late the night before and were really tired as we left the plane. We jumped onto a tour bus for the hotel. It was still early in the day, and since we were headlining, we wouldn't play until late that night, so everyone wanted to rest . . . except me.

My morning began with trouble at the Old San Juan Hotel. At about 5:00 a.m., my beautiful six-foot Puerto Rican gal pal left my room and went back to her house (she was in San Juan visiting her mother, so she couldn't stay). As I kissed her good-bye, I saw a very professional piece of paper under my door. It said:

Lobby Call 8:00 a.m.

What the hell was a lobby call? No worries. I would just sleep for a minute and pack when I woke up.

I set the alarm and passed out. At 7:30, it blasted me awake to a wicked hangover, so I crawled into the bathroom thinking I might barf. Then looked at myself in the mirror and smiled. *I'm A ROCK STAR.*

After showering, I heard the phone ring. It was Henry Newman, our tour manager. "Let's go!" he barked. Now I was scared, because I didn't want to be in trouble. Then I saw my eight unpacked bags. *Oh shit for real* . . . I threw everything in them and shot down to the lobby as fast as I could, only to find everyone in the vans waiting for me. Boy, did I feel like a jackass.

Thanks to me, we barely made the flight to Tampa. The "treat the new kid like shit rule" was in full effect, and I got stuck in coach while the others sat in first class. This time, the excuse was, "There was only one seat left and they flipped a coin and Rick Braun won." I knew it was bullshit, but I felt like such an idiot for being late to my first lobby call. So I stayed quiet and took my seat.

When we reached the hotel in Tampa, all the boys went inside, but I asked the driver to take me to Tampa Stadium. Chicago and Hall and Oates were our opening acts, and I wanted to check them out.

I arrived backstage and walked to our dressing room, where I noticed the cool, free stuff—sandwiches, soda, and booze. I took photos of everything. Then I heard Chicago starting, so I walked out to the back of the stage to check it out. I looked out at the thirty thousand or so people already there and just melted. This was my dream . . . and here I was.

While watching Chicago, I noticed these young girls backstage dressed in orange shorts and little T-shirts—staring at *me*. "Hello," I said with a smile.

"You're him? Aren't you?" one of the girls shouted.

I had no idea who they were talking about. "Yes, I am . . . who?"

"You're that young kid Stevie in Rod's band, his new guitar player he discovered."

Now I smiled. "Yes, that *is* me! How did you know?"

"We heard Rod on the radio talking about this being your first tour," one of them said.

Then I looked at their skimpy, look-alike outfits. "Why are you all dressed like that?"

"We're Hooters girls!"

Hooters girls? "What's that?"

"Haven't y'all ever heard of the restaurant Hooters?"

"No, they don't have those in L.A. or San Diego," I said. Funny outfits or not, these girls were hot. "Let me get you a drink."

The next move was a gift straight from the gods. There was a guy backstage, lugging a keg on a golf cart. I asked to borrow the cart. "Here, take it," he said.

I got into the cart and pulled up to the girls. "Hop on!"

Soon, we were cruising backstage in the cart, grabbing more Hooters girls and having a great time being young and stupid. The girls were easygoing, almost like college girls, so I felt really comfortable around them.

Then I noticed something that made me change course—one of the most beautiful, sexy blondes I had ever seen. She looked like the devil herself.

I pulled up my golf cart to investigate. We shook hands and said hello. She asked me to take a photo with her . . . *is that what I think it is?* She had on a tiny white skirt and *no underwear.* (I know this doesn't sound shocking nowadays, but in 1988, it floored me! I was too young and dumb to know it then, because I never had a chance to be around girls like this, but she was what veteran rockers called a "rock mattress"—a superhot sex bomb that can slay dragons backstage as she hunts down rock stars and rich guys. I would learn to spot these girls right away.)

As much as I wanted her, I was smart enough to know she wasn't for me, since I don't like easy kills. Once naked, her Florida tan would be impressive, but . . . even though I acted cocky and confident, those gals kind of scared me a bit. Plus, there was no sport in it. After all, the chase is half the fun.

I grabbed my golf cart, my keg, and my pack of Hooters girls, and drove off to continue socializing and watch a bit of Hall and Oates, who had just taken the stage. When they played their megahit, "Maneater," I flashed back to my rock-mattress girl who I'd just met . . . remember the one with no undies? This song could have been written about her . . . God bless her! Later, while Daryl Hall did his "take one word and soul sing it 'til you want to stab yourself in the head" rap that he does at the end of every song, I thought back to a couple years earlier at the San Diego Sports Arena . . .

It was the night my buddy Kenny Gilmore and his date went out with my then-girlfriend, Suzanne Beveridge, and me. We rented a white limo to see Hall and Oates. We were sitting in loge-level seats, which seemed good at the time, but were still a mile away from center stage.

Now I was on the stage watching them while sitting in my own golf cart, transporting a keg along with a bunch of hot girls who dressed funny—at a concert my band would be headlining.

Madness indeed.

While Hall was still riffing (on the same word, I think), I decided to get my shit together for the show, since we would be going on next. I said my good-byes to the girls, grabbed a few kisses, and then asked, "How many of you Hooters girls are here tonight?"

"About seventy-five," one said.

"Okay. Do me a little favor. When you're watching the show, and we get to a nice quiet spot, get all the girls and scream, as loud as you can, 'WE LOVE YOU STEVIE!'"

They said, "Sure thing."

I walked into the dressing room, and the band was there. Rod came in and wanted to practice a couple songs and segues before the show, so we walked into an adjoining jam room set up with drums, amps, keyboards, and a PA system, and got to work. Later in the tour, we would often learn an entire song and play it that night in concert, but this time, we focused on the small details of our stadium set.

Then Henry walked in. "It's showtime, boys."

Everyone ran into the bathroom for a last-minute nerve pee, and then we walked out to nearly sixty thousand screaming fans as "The Stripper" music blasted through the PA at a bazillion decibels. I felt like a warrior going into battle as I grabbed my guitar and lit up my four Marshall one-hundred-watt half-stack amps with a power chord. The boys looked at each other, Tony Brock counted it off, the lights exploded, and my first U.S. concert was in full swing.

I looked at the crowd from stage left. What happened to my Hooters girls?

About halfway through the set, I grabbed my twelve-string acoustic guitar and started the soft opening chords to "The First Cut Is the Deepest." Out of nowhere, I heard a gang of female voices yell, "WE LOVE YOU STEVIE!"

I instantly regretted it. Rod looked over to me with the most puzzled expression on his face, undoubtedly thinking, *how is this possible?* After all, I was a complete unknown who nobody in Tampa had heard of until he'd mentioned me on the radio that morning.

I looked back at him with a puzzled look and shrugged my shoulders. *I don't know, man.*

5

EVERY GOD NEEDS A DEVIL TO STAY IN BUSINESS

Every god needs a devil to stay in business. I discovered this the hard way many times.

At 7:31 p.m. on November 17, 1962, I jettisoned from the peaceful safety and warmth of my mother's womb into the static of a cold, hostile world in Oceanside. I entered this world literally fighting for my life. I was born with my umbilical cord wrapped around my neck, strangling me. It caused a little commotion in the delivery room, making me a shit stirrer from the very beginning. As I lay there with my face turning fifty shades of blue, my subconscious mind gave me the decision to live. Or die. There would be no middle ground.

As I came into the world, I had my first negative experience. Right out of the box, I was forced to fight. This fight enabled me to also have my first empowering positive experience shortly after the negative . . . my first finest moment. By winning the fight and taking my first breath, my subconscious mind experienced victory. That proved to me that no matter the odds, if I fought hard enough, I could be successful.

I would experience life's highs and lows with no middle ground. I would forever feel the ever-present static of being the underdog, fighting for my life. I knew if I fought hard enough I could indeed win. I am as sure of this as if it were written into my DNA.

My mother, Estanaslada Maya, was born May 7, 1934, in San Miguel, New Mexico. When she was three, her family left the desert sand and headed west to the sleepy beach town of Carlsbad, just south of Oceanside. My mother was led to believe that she was Mexican . . . but there was a family secret. When I was a little boy, my uncle, Raymond Maya (who we all called Uncle Bobby; I have no idea why), had a portrait of Geronimo, the fierce Chiricahua Apache warrior, painted on a wall at his house. Whenever Uncle Bobby drank, he would say, "This is who we are!" He took offense when we were called Mexicans. My cousins Gilbert, Ralph, Little Ray, and I knew we were Apache, because my grandpa Cruz Maya, who we all called CuCu, used to tell us all the time.

While nearly one hundred years old and on her deathbed, my Great-Aunt Consuela told my cousin, Gilbert, the truth about the secret. Her sister, my Great-Aunt Louisa, who was strongly connected to the Catholic Church, sat next to them, denying it by saying over and over, "I am not a savage!"

My father, Hilario Salas, was born in Fort Collins, Colorado, on May 10, 1934. He grew up outside Cheyenne, Wyoming, near a small place called Ozone. His grandmother was kidnapped in New Mexico as a child and sold to a Mexican hacienda (in those days, Indians would steal and trade Mexican children, and vice versa). The man who stole her was an Indian outlaw who later went to prison for killing a man. As the girl grew up, the same man stole her *again*, this time to marry her. Later, they migrated to Kansas, where a group of Apaches lived. My grandmother's parents told everyone they were Mexican, because Indians were the lowest people in society in those times. How far did this deception go? Check this out: when my father was born, his birth certificate did not say he was Mexican, nor Indian. It said he was *Caucasian*. Oh, my Great White Father!

My dad's father was a light-skinned Mexican man, descended from a family that migrated from Spain to Guadalajara, Mexico. My grandfather made his way into the United States by working for the railroad. My father held a great love for his dad, but he had issues, too. When

away, his head down. "She died at birth . . . your mother almost went with her."

John was crushed. I had never seen him like this. I was too young to know how to digest this news or these emotions, but I knew I had been born while dying and that I somehow made it. My little sister was not as fortunate.

When mom returned home from the hospital, our happy home quickly went from vibrant color to black and white. I didn't know it yet, but soon the dark days would be coming for me. No matter how fast I ran, they were going to hunt me down.

Mom was no longer herself, as she fought her depression with daily doses of prescription drugs. My stepfather also tried to rise out of his depression after losing Shawnie, but he couldn't. Soon, he quit his band. Not long after that, he quit me.

One day, I was out playing wildly with my neighborhood friends, Carl and Johnny Thames and Danny Cobian, when I ran into the house and slammed the front door a little too hard. The pane glass in the door exploded everywhere, but it didn't seem like a big deal, so I cleaned it up and told mom I was sorry. Later that afternoon, John came home, and I saw him ask mom about the broken door glass. It must have been the last straw. His head dropped, and he walked out of the house. That's the last time I remember seeing him.

Now that I am a father, I get it. If anything happened to my boy, Shane, my whole world would crumble. When you're down that low, it doesn't take much to pull you under.

It grew lonely at my house. I missed John so much. We fell into dire straits, living on welfare cheese and powdered milk. Mom couldn't work, since she was severely depressed after losing both her child and husband; plus, her prescription drug use hit an all-time high. I started hiding them from her. Once, I asked my grandpa CuCu Maya to help me by talking to her, but it didn't work. She was either asleep in her room or visiting the bars at night. Sandy found peace by hanging out with her boyfriend, Micky Cobian. I had my neighborhood buddies to play with.

Thank God for dad, who always came around and checked on me, bringing me clothes or a new baseball glove. He was a rock I could depend on. Dad knew things were bad, and he was now trying to gain custody of us, but it wasn't working out.

One day, he came over. "We are going to court, and all you have to do is tell the judge you want to live with me," he said.

The only way the court would grant my dad custody would be for me to take the stand. I was in fifth grade, but I was willing to do it, because I was already going down the tubes. I was rebelling and starting to steal things at stores, so I agreed to testify to live at his house.

When mom found out, she broke down, crying her eyes out, and looked at me. "You don't want to leave me, do you?"

All I could say was, "No, Mom, I won't leave you."

My poor mother was in hell, and I was on my way. Still, no matter how unhappy I was, I couldn't do it. She had been through so much.

Shortly after that, my mom took up with a new boyfriend, a dirtbag wannabe thug named Richard Hernandez. He was a Mexican American who thought he was a badass. His nickname was Dickey, but it should have been *Dick*, because that's what he was. Sports became my only outlet with a purpose, so I sank myself into Pop Warner football and Little League baseball. I hated being at home with Richard, so I stayed with my friend Randy Folds and his family.

Randy was a tough guy, a scrapper. No one dared to mess with me, because Randy was the toughest guy at Bobier Elementary School in Vista, the neighboring town to Oceanside. A lot of tough kids liked me, including Jamie and Tim Wynn (years later, Tim would become the bodyguard/roadie for This Kids). I was a good fighter, but with Randy, Jamie, or Tim always looking after me, God help anyone who messed with me.

The Gallegos brothers tried. I'd known Frank and Fernie since first grade, but one day, they came up behind me while I was shooting hoops. For no reason, Frank, who was a lot bigger and older than me, cracked me in the back of my head and knocked me to the ground. Out of nowhere, Jamie Wynn appeared and *bam*! He laid out Big Frank.

"Don't you touch Stevie again!" The Gallegos brothers eventually ended up in jail.

At home, Richard and mom spent a lot of time partying. One night, they took me to my Grandma Maya's house to spend the night so they could head to some party. They came back late, really drunk. My sister Sandy was there with her boyfriend, Micky.

For some reason, Richard went nuts and started beating up mom. Micky tried to stop him, but Richard chased him out of the house. Then he resumed his beating of mom. Sandy, who was four foot eleven and ninety pounds, also tried to help. Richard turned around and belted her in the face, knocking all her front teeth out. Later that night, mom and Sandy showed up at Grandma Maya's house, and my grandma looked after them both.

I saw what happened, and it unleashed the anger of my ancestors in me. As the days went on, it grew stronger and stronger. Richard was nowhere to be found, because my uncles wanted to kick his ass, but I knew his punk ass would be back. I wanted to be ready for him. I took out my bow and arrows, set up a target in the front yard, and started shooting arrows into that haystack like a crazed kid on a mission. My mind became set: *I'm gonna kill this man.*

About a week later, I came home after playing outside. Richard sat in my living room, drinking with mom. Sandy had now moved out and was living with my dad, so it was just us. And Richard. I saw red, but said nothing as Richard tried to buddy up with me while giving me a half-assed apology. I ignored him, went into my room, and shut the door. Only two years earlier, my life was at an all-time high, but somehow, here I was again with that umbilical cord strangling me.

Richard walked into my room to talk to me, tell me he was moving back in, things were going to be different, etc. etc. Even though I was young, I always had a great sense of sussing out people. I knew he was a loser. He sat next to me on my bed, talking and trying to be nice, but I looked at him with death in my eyes.

My look finally caused him to snap. With his *choont* Mexican American wannabe bad-guy accent, he said, "Okay, so you wanna be a badass, huh? You want to hurt me?" He pulled out a knife. "Go ahead, take the knife if you think you're such a badass."

Before he finished his next word, I grabbed that knife, jumped up, and pressed the blade onto his neck. He froze, looking at me with his eyes wide open. Then he said, "Go ahead. Kill me."

Time stood still as a vision came over me. I knew I had been here before, in this position, as though I was living in another dimension. I was a warrior in the desert fighting for my life, which meant I was forced to kill a Mexican. I knew this moment. I had seen it in my dreams. I had seen it in my nightmares.

It dawned on me how easy it would be to take a man's life. All I had to do was push the knife.

Another voice entered my head. "If you do this, your life will never be the same," my angel told me.

A crazed look filled Richard's eyes. He knew this shit had seriously escalated out of his control. The second voice in my head was right, and I knew it. I dropped the knife, and Richard left my room. I never told anyone about what happened in my room, but it has lived with me ever since.

I grabbed my things and went to stay at Randy's house. Not that I had many clothes, but since I didn't want to go back home, I wore the same clothes to school every day, which made me feel like a loser. I started making up stories to friends, saying I had many pairs of jeans with the exact same patchwork. They knew it was a lie. I couldn't stay at Randy's forever, so I sucked it up and went home.

When I opened the door, there was no sign of my mother or Richard. I ended up staying home by myself for two more days.

On the third afternoon, I kicked around a football in my front yard, feeling pretty lonesome. I had lost my stepfather, my mother was nowhere to be found, Sandy was living at dad's, and my baby sister Shawnie had died. My life sucked. I walked out to the street and was kicking my football over the electric wires above the telephone poles when a car drove up . . .

Dad! He looked like a knight in shining armor. When he stopped, a puzzled look crossed his face. "Where's your mom?" he asked.

"I haven't seen her for days."

"Get in the car."

I never went back.

When I moved in with my dad and Sandy, the sun started shining again. He took me to the Value Fair department store where he worked and bought me new clothes. He worked up to five jobs at a time to support us, with a schedule that makes me tired just writing it: civil service from midnight to 8:00 a.m.; Value Fair from 8:30 a.m. until 4:30 p.m.; then cleaning three different banks until dinnertime. After dinner, he would sleep until 11:30 p.m., wake up, and do it all again, night after day after night after day.

My sixth-grade school year began. I quickly made friends at my new school, San Luis Rey Elementary in Oceanside. I also owned a little Honda SL 70 motorcycle that my dad bought me. Behind his house were thousands of acres of farmland on which to ride, so every day, I jumped on my bike after school.

There's a story behind this Honda SL 70 that involves the power of visualization. I would later visualize playing with Rod Stewart and Mick Jagger, but in sixth grade, I wanted that Honda. I rode my bicycle every day to a shop in downtown Vista to look at the used Honda SL 70 for sale. There was no way I could come up with the three hundred dollars to buy it, but the bike possessed and consumed me. Every day, I would sit on that bike and dream . . . and then I would go home and dream about it some more. I was nuts!

Over a period of weeks, I told my dad about it. Again—and again—and again. After hearing me talk about this dang motorcycle so much, he finally drove me down to the shop so I could show it to him. The bike was always parked out front, so I never went inside, but after dad saw it, he walked into the shop to ask about it. I remember the man and woman who worked there saying, "Oh my God," and then the woman tearing up.

"We see him here every day, just sitting on that bike and staring at it, I am so glad you're here," she said. "Tell me you're buying it for him."

Ever the cool cat, dad laid down the cash and bought it, even though he couldn't afford it. I freaked out, jumping for joy, and then the lady looked at me and started weeping because she was so happy for me.

As it turned out, the motorcycle became a very important part of my future.

I rode the motorcycle in the fields every day, making friends with other guys in our neighborhood that owned bikes, like Rick and Jim Weldon and Marshall Spencer. They were older than me and really cool, but there was another guy riding who was much older than us and really fast. He would change my life forever.

My dad, Sandy, and I lived in a trailer park. Down our street lived that older guy with the really fast motorcycle—Steve Cottrell. He was a racer with piles of trophies from all his victories. He always tore his bike apart on the front porch of the mobile home he shared with his mother. He would always say hello and talk to me about our bikes, but one day, he didn't want to talk about motorcycles . . . he wanted to meet Sandy.

I introduced them. Next thing I knew, they had gotten married. I now had a big brother who raced motocross, a father who would never leave me, and a sister to nurture me. Life was wonderful again.

Steve also built boats and surfboards. Soon I was surfing and deep-sea fishing off Oceanside, and sometimes in Mexico. Steve was really into cool music, too, and he and Sandy took me to my first concerts. I was only in sixth grade, but I saw Black Sabbath with Black Oak Arkansas at the Long Beach Arena, and KISS on their Dressed to Kill Tour with Rush opening. (Okay, here's how cool life can be: I would later become friends with Paul Stanley from KISS, jam with Alex Lifeson of Rush, do session work with Black Oak drummer Tommy Aldridge, and sit in a room and talk guitars with Tony Iommi of Black Sabbath, who told me how he created the sounds on those great early Sabbath records.)

These concerts blew my sixth-grade mind. Once, I was with Sandy and Steve at a Foghat show with Rick Derringer (former guitarist from the Edgar Winter Group) opening. Rick's bass player was Kenny Aronson, who was best friends with my fellow Out of Order Tour guitarist, Jeff Golub. If you were a sixth-grade kid and saw the bass player onstage with a big-time band, would you ever think, "In fifteen years, I will party with that guy in another country and surprise him for his birthday with naked girls in a hotel hallway knocking on his door"? That's what Jeff and I did for Kenny in Toronto in 1988.

While watching that Foghat show, I saw a career possibility. I could be a roadie! I thought the coolest thing in the world was when the guitar techs walked out before the show and tested the amps by hitting power chords. I could do that!

Steve helped make my life wonderful. Besides the fishing, surfing, motocross riding, and concerts, I still played Pop Warner football and Little League baseball. Team sports were very important to me.

Later, I would take what I learned from team sports and use those concepts for bands. I think that's why Rod and I connected. Early in the tour, we struggled like a team starting its season. We were filled with talent, but not running on all cylinders. We worked on the fundamentals of the music and sweated out the small details, finding a way to win. You can have a team with superstars, and they can lose often. Just ask LeBron James, who played on several underperforming teams filled with stars before finally winning two NBA titles with the Miami Heat. In the same way, you can have a band with virtuosos that sounds like crap. I could name a lot of jazz bands in that category, but a team and a band need to have people who push and pull to make it work.

Rod could have seen my lack of skill as a liability. Instead, he realized that my raw, reckless rock energy balanced nicely with Jeff Golub's massive skills and more mature approach. When Jeff and I left the band in 1989, they hired two great guitar players, Steve Farris from Mr. Mister and Todd Sharp, who worked with artists like Hall and Oates and Mick Fleetwood. Steve and Todd are great at what they do individually. Both played Rod's music just fine, but that version of the Out of Order band didn't have the magic. The two didn't mesh. Jeff and I made Rod's band roll like Magic and Kareem on the Showtime Lakers, while Steve and Todd made Rod's band feel more like the L.A. Clippers pre–Blake Griffin and Chris Paul. I also used my sports musician/player approach when I was a music director, putting musicians together behind Mick Jagger, Terence Trent D'Arby, and a variety of *American Idol* finalists, Chris Daughtry, Jordin Sparks, and Adam Lambert included.

My brother-in-law had one more thing up his sleeve. Steve made a guitar, which he gave to me. It was a Fender Stratocaster copy.

You could say it was a life-changing gift.

At first, my neighbor, Pat Roman, and I would only use the Strat to play air guitar to Led Zeppelin and Aerosmith. As the guitar sat in my room, it ended up in my hands more and more—and not just for playing air guitar. My fishing buddy, Robert Mann, swapped me a few lessons for a fishing reel and taught me some basic playing fundamentals that remain part of my foundation today. Suddenly, one day I could play the riff to Bachman Turner Overdrive's "Roll on Down the Highway." The rest would soon be history.

Now do you see why that Honda SL 70 was so important? It blows my mind, because I was obsessed with that motorcycle, and it set off a series of events that changed my life forever and revealed my destiny. Nuts, isn't it?

The other way dad kept me out of trouble was to make sure I kept playing organized sports, where I was responsible to teammates as well as myself, both in my skills and my fitness. That continued in high school. During my freshman year at El Camino High School in Oceanside, he wanted me to join the wrestling team because I was a little chubby. I was thinking about girls now, but I couldn't land dates with the cheerleaders because I was too chubby and not studly like my friends Allen Carrasco, Jeff Smith, Jerry Jones, and Eddie Binder, who the girls loved. When I joined the wrestling team, I was four foot eleven and weighed 117 pounds. When the season ended, I was five foot three and 103 pounds. *Now* the girls were checking me out!

I really wanted to play sports and fit in at El Camino High School for other reasons. El Camino was a new school, with far fewer hoodlums and losers than crosstown Oceanside High School, which had more gang-style kids. After what I experienced with my mom in Vista, I didn't want to be around those kinds of people anymore. (It has since cracked me up to see rich white-bread people wanting to live in shit-hole dangerous neighborhoods because they feel it gives them street cred. I grew up in that, and I am never going back.)

As I entered tenth grade, everything was awesome until my hot temper got me into trouble. Since I lived in an area outside the El Camino High School district, there wasn't a regular school bus for me to take to school, so my sister would give me a ride, or I could catch this small van bus that kids cruelly called "the retard bus." I was always a fight-first kid, not a good thing, but necessary in the places where I'd lived before. One day on the bus, a kid said something I didn't like. I slugged him.

This happened during the time dad was teaching me to drive. Dad believed in the "practice makes perfect" principle; how could I practice driving to pass the test for my license if I didn't get out there and drive? *Alone?*

One night, I was hanging out at the house with Cathy Quill, my dear friend who I loved so much, and my best pal Eddie Binder. When it came time to go home, dad decided to chuck me the keys. "Go ahead, son, you drive them."

I was only fifteen and still hadn't taken driver's education class yet. Eddie was also fifteen, while Cathy was sixteen. I acted cool on the outside, while on the inside, I was screaming LOVE YA DAD!

We jumped into the car. Neither Eddie nor I had driver's licenses or permits, but we drove down the street and pulled over because Cathy had decided it was time for Stevie to not be a virgin anymore. Don't think badly of her. I thank God for her for having mercy on me. So Eddie, who was also a virgin, started driving. Cathy made Eddie and me promise we wouldn't tell anyone at school. Of course we agreed! Cathy took me into the back of the Datsun B210, and we did our thing. I had no idea what I was doing, but Eddie kept looking back and screaming, "Oh my God!"

"Keep your eyes on the road!" I yelled back.

Eddie almost crashed twice in the minute or two it lasted, but I felt amazing!

All of us guys and girls from high school were beyond close and remain that way. To this day, we love each other and hang out, except for our dear Cathy, who we lost years ago.

Because of dad's trust in me driving, I was able to drive myself to school once they banned me from the bus. It was an important early lesson in self-reliance—and watching my temper.

One day near the end of the first semester, we ran into a problem. Someone at my school found out that our house wasn't in the El Camino High district; we were in the dreaded Oceanside High zone. My dad lied and used a friend's address as our own so I could continue attending El Camino.

Shortly after that, I was in wrestling practice when the coach, Dayle Mazzarella, pulled me out. Coach Maz started chewing me out, saying, "The school district found out you lied about your address!"

The year before, we had won state. If the California Interscholastic Federation powers that be found out that I was on the team, they could have stripped that championship. Coach Maz was not happy to think he could lose the state title over me. I was a shitty wrestler to boot. I was not happy, because I *loved* all my friends at school.

The shit went down. I got kicked out of El Camino and was forced to spend my second semester at Oceanside High. This turned out to be much cooler than I expected. During the beginning of each school year, it's exciting and you're meeting and dating all the new girls, but by the second semester, you settle into a routine. When I showed up, I was like the new kid on campus and already a little popular from surfing and sports. I knew a lot of the kids from Jefferson Junior High, where I had gone. I was fresh meat for all the girls, *plus* I was playing guitar now and had formed a little band, Revolution, with Jerry Jones and Ronnie Sarkisian.

My dad was really concerned about my high school problem. He also had just married the new woman in his life, Helen, which gave me a new stepmother and a little sister, Rachel. Dad thought we needed a bigger house, so he bought a house up the street from my best friend, Allen Carrasco. It happened to be in the El Camino High School district. Just like that, I was out of the mobile-home park and next to my best pal in the world.

When I started eleventh grade, this guitar thing was getting serious. I was obsessed, practicing three hours a day in my bedroom with my amp cranked up and driving my parents nuts. Allen used to sit in my room, buzzed, and listen to me rock out, playing along with my stereo to Aerosmith, Led Zeppelin, Montrose, Van Halen, Ted Nugent, David Bowie, The Ramones, and other 1970s rockers. One of my favorite records to play to was Aerosmith's *Rocks* (which most longtime hardcore Aerosmith fans consider their best release). Good thing, because many years later, Steven Tyler said in his scratchy voice, "Stevie, get up onstage and jam 'Last Child' with us!"

"I know that!" I said.

As I jammed with Aerosmith at the National Stadium in Costa Rica, I went back to being fifteen years old in my bedroom, where I learned how to play that song. "Last Child" was an early funk-rock classic, and funk rock would become my forte, my ticket to a major-label recording contract.

After I turned sixteen, I saw an ad in the local *Blade-Tribune* newspaper. A band was looking for a rhythm guitar player. Their set list included all the bands I loved, plus Rush and UFO, both killer bands. When I called, Greg Hammond answered and invited me for an audition. When I asked around, I found out that Greg was the premier drummer in Carlsbad and could play Led Zeppelin and Rush songs beat for beat, so I was really excited.

I showed up and met Greg and his fellow band member, Don Ayala, in a mini-storage building in San Marcos, where they and a lot of other bands had set up music rooms to jam. It felt magical! These guys were so good! I got the gig and started spending all my nights out there, jamming and making new musician friends. There was Rick Gould, who years later would become a professional photographer for all the big music magazines; he even shot a spread on me for *Guitar Player*. There was Jay Jardine, who could fix any guitar and play any instrument. Later, he would become my introduction into Hollywood, getting me my first professional recording session as a guitar player.

All the bands in that mini-storage possessed a healthy balance of competition and togetherness. Those guys really helped to create my foundation as a young musician.

After jamming all winter and spring, it was time to play some summertime parties on the beach. Greg, Don, myself, and a new bass player named Paul Mukomela booked a gig. We played our first backyard party, and I made my first bit of cash playing guitar. We collected twelve dollars in a jar. *Yo! Three dollars of that is mine!*

I was hooked. When we jammed, and I saw all the girls from high school there, I noticed that they looked at me differently. I felt like the king of the world. I had great friends and was popular in school, I was in a rock 'n' roll band, and my home life was happy.

I owed it all to my dad. He really saved my life. Never again would that umbilical cord find its way back around my neck. So I thought.

6

THIS KID

Even though my first two bands had already come and gone, I started to feel the possibility of a career in music. My first group, Revolution, with Jerry Jones and Ron Sarkisian, wasn't really a band, but This Kids, with Don Ayala, Paul Mukomela, and Greg Hammond, sure felt real, especially when we were playing those summer beach parties.

Before I became addicted to my guitar, and these pie-in-the-sky thoughts entered my young brain, my plan was to graduate from high school and then join the Coast Guard. My main love was the ocean, where I spent most of my time surfing and fishing. Now, I was cheating on my main love by practicing my guitar three hours a day, as if nothing else mattered.

The first version of This Kids broke up after the summer, because Don and Greg acted like an old married couple that couldn't figure out how to get along. Greg was about the greatest drummer I had ever seen play . . . and that includes drummers in big national acts. Greg studied the greats like Tommy Aldridge of Black Oak Arkansas and the Pat Travers Band (many years later, I would do a recording session with Tommy and Richie Kotzen for a beer commercial and talk to Tommy about his days with Pat Travers). Like every other drummer, Greg loved Neil Peart from Rush and could play his parts note for note, but what set Greg off from all the other great local drummers, like Robert Munger of Seraphim and The Neat, Mikey Quiroz from The Incognito

Rockers, and the versatile Danny Campbell, was that Greg loved and understood the oddly amazing style of Stewart Copeland from The Police. He was ahead of the curve because he understood that music was changing and going in an alternative direction.

In 1980, an edgy mentality reigned, thanks to punk music. Yes, Greg got the name This Kids from a UFO song we all loved, but that's not why we named the band This Kids. We used it because of the odd word combination. It reminded me of Mitch Easter's band, Let's Active, a cool underground group of the day. The name made no sense, yet was perfect for a band that didn't want to be a rock dinosaur. I hated bands like The Eagles, but I was into Elvis Costello, Joe Jackson, The Police, and The Ramones, as well as Led Zeppelin, Aerosmith, and Van Halen. The real reason I loved The Ramones was not because I wanted to be a punk rocker, but because Johnny Ramone had the sickest power-chord rock guitar sound. Engineer/producer Ed Stasium really knew how to draw out the tones. Like many talented people I admired while growing up, Ed would enter into my life years later. Makes you wonder if there are any coincidences . . . or is this whole thing called life planned in advance?

When I say I hated The Eagles, I mean no offense to Joe Walsh, who is a very nice person. However, I was a surfing, skateboarding hard charger, and The Eagles were the Mellow Mafia; I couldn't skate to that shit. While in Rod Stewart's band, my personal Eagles issue would come up again. While at an Academy Awards party at the Le Mondrian Hotel on the Sunset Strip with my new friend, MTV VJ Nina Blackwood, I spotted *Growing Pains* actress Julie McCullough, who was also a *Playboy* centerfold. Someone introduced us while Julie was sitting outside. I felt like a big rooster strutting in the barnyard; after all, I was a lead guitar player in Rod Stewart's band, with a chubby major-label recording contract with Island Records to boot. Julie smiled at me. When she smiles, her eyes sparkle, and the effect was like fairy dust on me . . . I was smitten.

We started talking. Soon, it felt as if no one else was around us. We were talking and talking, and my mind was saying . . . *Oh my God, she is not only beautiful, but she is sweet!* I was positive she felt the same about me. After about an hour, I was convinced she was in love with me and would be my new girlfriend. The recording artist and the actress . . . a true Hollywood story.

In the middle of my stereotypical fantasy, she got a page. She looked up at me. "I gotta go."

"Huh? You gotta go?"

"That was my boyfriend. He's picking me up outside."

"Huh? Boyfriend?" *Who the hell could this small-time boyfriend be? Certainly not the lead guitar player for Rod Stewart!* "Who's your boyfriend?" I asked.

"Don Henley from The Eagles."

At my high school, Andre Teitscheid was a great singer, a little older than me. His sister, Renee, sang for the coolest and most popular band in North County, The Incognito Rockers. Andre had started a band with Dave Judy, the best musician in our school, and some guys from nearby Vista. I was invited to see them jam. My girlfriend, Judy Carpenter, and I drove to their gig to watch them play. They were pretty cool. I knew the bass player, Paul Martinez, and rhythm-guitar player, Pat Pinamonti, from my younger days, when I lived with my mom in Vista. Paul Martinez's father was my mailman, and Paul's little brother, Rico, had played Junior Pee Wee Pop Warner football with me on the Vista Chargers.

While watching the band, I could easily see that Andre had total control. He was a natural, and Dave and I thought the band sounded pretty good. Then Andre took a break from singing, and Pat Pinamonti sang the Queen song "Tie Your Mother Down." Most guys couldn't sing a high vocal like that, but Pat nailed it. He was also a really tall, slim, good-looking guy. I started thinking, *this guy could be a lead singer.* Only one or two potential problems: I heard he was a little shy, and he was a super stoner . . . I'm talking wake and bake. I wasn't sure if he would be up for the center-stage spotlight. I mentioned my idea to

Dave, who laughed in my face. However, Paul thought perhaps it could work.

Paul was really ambitious and kept on me about jamming together, which of course I was keen to do. However, I couldn't get Greg to jam with us. Greg was a bit of a musical elitist, but I knew there could be no great band without a great drummer, so I worked on him, calling him over and over again. I kept telling him how talented and cool Paul Martinez was. Finally, just to get me to shut up, he placated me and agreed to have a jam. When we first jammed, Pat was on a family hunting trip, so he wasn't able to come, but Greg, Paul, and I played. It was magic.

When Pat returned to town, he jammed with us—not as a rhythm guitarist, but as our lead singer, taking center stage. He was a little uncomfortable and insecure at first, but once we started playing, we knew this was something special.

That day, I learned something very important that I still carry with me when I produce or music direct a project: When you start with the right pieces of the puzzle, everything that follows seems effortless. Don't spend time trying to make a square piece fit into a round hole. Spend the time to find the right players, because when you do, it works without effort. I am not saying you still don't have to work your ass off on the tiny details to be great, because you do. For example, with Terence Trent D'Arby, I auditioned exactly fifty drummers, some of the best in the world, including the drummers for Stevie Wonder and Michael Jackson. They were all very, very good. I ended up hiring an unknown named Stevo Theard, because his fill worked perfectly with the rest of the band. (He was also from New Orleans, and Terence had a psychic that told him a musician from New Orleans would change his life.)

Following our jam, Pat, Paul, Greg, and I went to work on the tiny details. After three solid months of rehearsing, we thought we might be ready for a gig, so when our friend Joe James asked us to play a party in his Carlsbad living room, we said, "Okay."

All the local surfers and musicians packed Joe's house, not to mention all the beautiful North County girls, so we were a little nervous. When we finally played, the energy was thick. We opened up with the Tom Petty and the Heartbreakers rocker "I Need to Know," then moved into The Babys' great hit "Head First." Instantly, the place was going nuts. We were *so tight*!

Our gig ended as quickly as it started. The cops showed up right away and broke up the party, but the cat was out of the bag. The town was abuzz about our new band. Funny thing to think about as I write this: Our first-ever live song was a Tom Petty and the Heartbreakers rocker. Years later, their bass player, Ron Blair, would move to Carlsbad and live just down the road from me. We are great friends, and once in a while pop into local bars together to jam when I'm in town. The second song we played that night, "Head First," was by The Babys, whose drummer was . . . Tony Brock, our drummer in Rod Stewart's band. Again . . . is this all a coincidence?

Within a month of that first gig, we were huge in North County, even though we still didn't have a name for the band. Why not? For the same reason many bands break up; we couldn't agree on anything. Greg and I wanted to keep This Kids, but Paul and Pat didn't want the baggage from the old lineup to follow them. For a minute, we went by the name Emerald. Lame, I know. Even worse, it was my idea. We played a couple of high school dances with that tentative name, but we knew it sucked. Bookings lined up quickly, and we couldn't wait anymore, so we finally agreed to stick with This Kids.

We played a ton of backyard parties and high school dances, including one at my high school, which made me and my friends feel beyond cool. Why? Because our band was really good . . . not the kind of good where people say they like you but could really care less, but so good that our gigs became the only places for any cool person to show up, with girls screaming, crying, and carrying on like we were Duran Duran. With Pat's killer high voice, we could play songs by The Police, who were becoming huge. Most other local vocalists couldn't touch the stuff.

For the lower-range material, like Elvis Costello and The Rolling Stones, Paul could kill that style, so we had the sound of the day sorted out. (In 2001, I was getting ready to go onstage with Mick Jagger when longtime friend and legendary San Diego DJ Halloran called me live on 91X, the first San Diego station to play alternative music in the early 1980s. He asked me what it was like playing with Jagger. "Tonight, we are going to play 'Respectable' from the *Some Girls* record. I play it exactly the same way I played it in backyard parties with This Kids, but instead of Paul Martinez from Vista singing, it's Mick Jagger.")

With This Kids, we knew the cool set list, and the four of us were okay looking but nothing to lose your mind over. However, when we played, big crowds turned up, with the girls packed in the front. Everyone knows that where the girls go, the guys follow. I was the youngest in the band and still had peach fuzz on my upper lip . . . I hadn't even had a shave yet! It had only been seven years since my dad picked me up at my mom's house and brought me home to live with him. Back then, I almost didn't care if I lived or died. Now, I had the best friends in the world, and I was in a band. I was again at an all-time high.

We spent a couple years being a big local band, playing all the proms, dances, and backyard parties. One of the top North County promoters, Big Beat Productions, got us steady gigs in front of larger audiences by combining us with bigger bands like Romeo Void, 20/20, The Penetrators, and Felony. "Of all the shows we did, you knew Stevie was going to make it big, because he always had an entourage of hangers and friends that wanted passes and followed him to every show," Big Beat producer Scott Threlfall recalls. "Stevie was a rock star, right out of the gate."

Eventually, we thought we should make our own record. My dad helped us by cosigning a bank loan of ten thousand dollars, and we went into a recording studio in San Diego and made our first EP, *This Kids— Let's Have Fun*. We faced problems from the start. The first was that our singer, Pat, met a hot girl named Lisa and decided he had reached his musical goal, which was to be in a band and get laid as much as he could until he found a superbeauty to marry. Lisa was that superbeauty.

Remember, Pat was shy before he was in This Kids, and I don't think he had much luck with the ladies. Once he was in This Kids, girls threw themselves at him. After Lisa socked it to him, he was done. Just like that, he quit.

A singer named Randy joined the band for a minute, but he was just too different personality-wise from us small-town boys. It didn't work out at all, but his photo ended up on the record, even though Pat, Paul, and Dave did almost all the singing.

The other problem we had with the record was the artwork. It was so ugly! The art director designed the mock-up in a cool silver, but when the record came out, the silver looked like flat battleship gray. One girl I talked to at a gig said, "I like your record a lot, the one with the butt-ugly cover."

The record came out and sold really well, with help from a lot of local radio play on 91X and KGB-FM. It didn't take long to pay off the bank loan my dad arranged for us. However, we still needed a singer.

We used to play big concert/dances at Del Mar Fairgrounds, where the famous horse track is located. All the big bands from San Diego and sometimes L.A. would play. These dance parties were huge, the crowds never less than five thousand. In our first gig, we opened for the Surf Punks (who got covered in spit during their set). In another, we played with Gary Myrick and The Figures, who were getting airtime with the radio hit "She Talks in Stereo." Most of the cool bands were leaning towards a New Wave or punk vibe. After a while, promoter Paul Lukas realized he didn't need to bring in the bigger out-of-town bands, because just as many people would come to see local bands. Plus, he could pay the locals peanuts by comparison.

Paul had plenty of bands from which to choose. Besides This Kids, the hot San Diego bands included Aircraft (fronted by Rob Lamothe, the most amazing singer I had ever heard), The Snails, Four Eyes, The Incognito Rockers, The Neat, RV and the Hubcaps, and a cool band called The T-Birds that was fronted by a tall blond hipster singer named Marty Wimer.

Marty was looking for another band, because the guitar player in The T-Birds was also in the biggest San Diego band of them all, The Penetrators. They were getting gigs in L.A., which meant The T-Birds had to constantly work around The Penetrators' schedule. Marty knew This Kids played at colleges throughout the Southwest, and he wanted more gigs, so Marty joined This Kids, and we kept up our popularity without missing a step. He didn't have the best voice, but he had a unique sound, along with mad star power and charisma. Greg had also decided to leave the band for a while, so now we consisted of Paul and me, Brian Weiss on drums, Marty on lead vocals, and Dave Judy on keyboards and sax. Dave would come and go as he pleased.

We spent the next few years playing across San Diego County and the southwestern United States at big university parties and clubs. We had a blast! We even made another EP, this time on colored vinyl, and that prompted some major record labels to check us out.

I also caught the Hollywood buzz. My longtime musician friend Jay Jardine started inviting me to hang out there with him and his actor buddies from the *Superman* movies, Marc McClure and Jeff East. They were working with Steve DePatie, son of Dave DePatie, half of the legendary cartoon production team of DePatie Freleng. How cool was DePatie Freleng? Try *Pink Panther* cool; that was their biggest cartoon franchise. Marc, Jeff, Jay, and Steve were working on the soundtrack for a new Saturday-morning cartoon for CBS, *Meatballs and Spaghetti*. They invited me to help on the recording sessions, along with Alan Meyers, the outstanding drummer for the great band Devo. It was the early 1980s, and *Meatballs and Spaghetti* needed an authentic alternative-music style. The pro session players were too slick. Steve DePatie's idea of having non-studio pro musicians like me, Marc, Jeff, and Jay, along with pros like Alan Meyers and himself, worked well. You could say it was a perfect mixture of great and shitty, which proved to be a winning combination.

By now, people were getting to know my name, between radio play and my gigs with This Kids. One time, the eclectic producer of The Runaways, Kim Fowley, called my parents' house, asking about This

Kids and also about me specifically. Kim had a forty-five-minute conversation with my stepmom, Helen, but a lot of it was not about my band. When I returned home from wherever I was, Helen said, "That guy Kim that called was weird!"

I was sure This Kids had the goods to make it big. That changed one day in Tucson, Arizona. We played an outdoor gig at the University of Arizona, and the state's biggest unsigned band was playing with us, Gentlemen after Dark. Man, did they have star power! Their singer was a regional superstar, but couldn't sing well enough to pull it off at the next level. However, their drummer, Winston A. Watson Jr., played at another level. His combination of drum power and star power was over the top. I realized two things that afternoon: (1) I had to be in a band with Winston; and (2) if I really wanted to have a chance to make it in music, I would have to leave This Kids.

It was a long, depressing ride back to San Diego for me.

I started calling Winston a lot. Although he was always pleasant, I could tell he wanted little to do with me. I kept calling. Luckily, Winston's girlfriend, Patty, thought I had something and gently pushed Winston in my direction. Plus, they were planning on moving to L.A., and so was I. They moved into this cool, funky Hollywood neighborhood with Sharine, a musician and sometimes substance abuser with a rich dad. She had some really good songs, and they had a cool jam room in the house. Another girl musician named Mary lived there, too. They decided to let me move into the small walk-in closet in the jam room for seventy-five dollars per month.

On Jan. 1, 1985, the closet was mine. It was just big enough for a single mattress, and since there were no windows, I would have to set the alarm to wake myself up. It was pitch black in there.

A cool singer kid I knew back in Carlsbad, Jimmy Jon Jackson, had moved up to L.A., along with Kevin Pat, a bass player Winston knew from Phoenix. Before we knew it, Winston and I had an L.A. band. We called the band Colorcode, and soon we were playing all over Hollywood.

When I got to L.A., I weighed 153 pounds, but within a couple months of starving with no cash flow, I shrunk to a good rock 'n' roll weight of 132 pounds. Chalk that up to the lack of Mother Helen's home cooking in Oceanside. My on-again, off-again girlfriend Deirdre, the rich stepdaughter of country-music superstar Tammy Wynette, was always there to help me with an occasional meal. However, we both knew it was important for me to embrace the struggle and make it on my own. (Deirdre remains one of my dearest friends, as well as a lawyer who still works with me.)

In L.A., we quickly developed a buzz. A lot of people watched us play for free at places like FM Station and Madame Wong's. Some people said we sounded like an alternative funk version of Van Halen. One night after a show, a guy we considered a real rock star talked to me about us being his backup band. His name was David Pahoa, but people knew him as David O, the bass player in the Plimsouls. This Kids used to play a couple of Plimsouls songs, so for me, this was cool. David also worked at a recording studio on Sunset called Baby O (that's why they called him David O); soon, I was hanging out there with him.

Since I was now beyond broke, I started putting ads in *Music Connection* looking for side work as a guitar player. One night, I got a call from an odd programmer producer named Zeo. He was working on a record with the well-known Robert Margoleff, who had produced Stevie Wonder, Jeff Beck, and Devo (he produced Devo's *Freedom of Choice* record and the hit song "Whip It," the favorite record of my buddy Eddie Binder and mine one summer).

Zeo and Robert were in their Crystal Sound studio in Hollywood when Zeo called me. "It's 1:00 a.m. You wanna come down and cut some tracks, or is it too late?"

"I will be right there," I said.

We started recording as soon as I arrived. I guess Zeo loved my odd style, because he introduced me to Robert Margoleff. Zeo owned a Fairlight, one of the first digital sampling synthesizers, used by artists like Herbie Hancock, Thomas Dolby, and Peter Gabriel. He was way ahead of the dance-music curve in L.A. He and a DJ from the UK, Paul

Oakenfold, were creating some really new kinds of dance music, and I loved it.

Just like that, we were making a record.

This is where it gets strange: my new world with Zeo and my other new world with David O soon would crash together. In August 1985, I had to move out of Sharine's house, so David O talked Baby O owner Rick Perrotta into letting me clean up at the studio and rehearsal room they owned. In exchange, they would pay me a little money and let me sleep on the couch. Coincidentally, Zeo and Bob decided to record the Zeo record at Baby O, so this worked out well for me.

It gets better. Many superstars recorded at Baby O, including Gene Simmons, Ricky Nelson, Vinnie Vincent, and Keel. I would always say hello and tell them, "Hey, if you ever need a guitar player . . ." They would all tell me to fuck off in their own subtle ways.

Well, not all of them. Ron Keel and Mark Ferrari from Keel were always nice to me. I started making friends with a couple other people there, like a very young Matt Sorum, then a struggling musician like me (and later, my very good friend and the drummer for The Cult, Guns N' Roses, and Velvet Revolver). I also met a supercool soul singer, Gloria Jones, who cut the original Motown version of "Tainted Love" and was the widow of the late, great Marc Bolan . . . as in T. Rex, the band that launched the glam-rock movement. (Remember the megahit "Get It On [Bang a Gong]"?) I also met another fantastic lady, Terry Costa, widow of the late great Frank Sinatra producer Don Costa.

One night, funk legend George Clinton, the mastermind of Parliament Funkadelic, came into the studio. I knew that he knew Zeo, who was working with him. Again, I dropped my "if you ever need a guitar player" thing.

To my surprise, at 3:00 a.m. that night, George and David Spradle, his collaborator and the cowriter of "Atomic Dog," woke me up and asked me to play on a track called "Hurray for Our Team." They were recording the R&B *Skeletons in the Closet* record.

Just like that, I played my first major-label guitar session and received a check from Capitol Records for $212. It was my first session check, but it wouldn't be my last.

I would soon spend a lot of time working with Zeo and George on that record and meeting a lot of the P-Funk guys, like Gary Shider and Amp Fiddler. One day, I met the main mug masher of all, bass player Bootsy Collins, who loved me like a little brother and took me under his wing. Terry Costa was around a lot then, too. Once she found out I had no place to live, she offered me her guesthouse, which I gladly accepted. The couch in Baby O was a drag. Keeping all my clothes in garbage bags sucked, too.

The guesthouse was really Don Costa's old home studio, later converted into a guesthouse behind the main residence in the very cool Trousdale Estates in Beverly Hills. After I moved in, I found old one-inch master tapes. "Donny Osmond," the labels read. That's big! I also looked after Terry's young high school daughter, Nikka, from time to time. Nikka was an ex–child star and an amazing singer, and would later show the world that she was much more than a child star when she released her first adult CD, *Everybody Got Their Something*, on Virgin Records.

Terry was beautiful and loads of fun. So was her best friend, legendary actress Connie Stevens, who hung out a lot. When Connie and Terry were buzzed, I often drove Connie home. One night, while I drove Connie home, she gave me a Hollywood history lesson, telling me some incredible stories about when she was young, including a great tale about her and Elvis.

One night, the girls were having a fun party night at the house when I couldn't resist doing a little wind-up on Connie. Since she and Terry had such great personalities and were always fun, I figured it would be okay. I told Connie how much I loved her in *How the West Was Won*, and how I loved those songs she sang. She stared at me with this odd look as I kept rambling on about the film, until she finally said, "Stevie, you idiot, that wasn't me. That was Debbie Reynolds!"

In 1987, Connie did a huge favor for me. My San Diego friends Dale Lawrence, Pat Pinamonti, Matt Allan, Allen Carrasco, and I were off to spring break to hit Pompeii, the hottest club in Palm Springs. It was almost impossible to get into Pompeii during spring break unless you arrived super early or stood in line for several hours. Connie called her buddy that ran the place. When my friends and I got there, we received the royal treatment! It was another of many valuable entertainment business lessons I learned: a powerful Rolodex is almost as important as talent itself.

Yes, these were indeed hard times because I was so broke, but they were exciting times.

After a couple years of constantly making friends and connections, things picked up for me. Soon, I was cutting Colorcode demos for A&M Records. Then one day out of the blue, the phone rang. It was Zeo, who had moved to London earlier that year. He was working with a group of people that included an amazing young soul singer named Terence Trent D'Arby. "I need you to come to London right away to record," he said, "because there are no guitar players here that play like you."

His manager bought me a plane ticket. A week later, I found myself in London.

7

WELCOME TO MIAMI

While running from the Tampa Stadium stage to my waiting limousine, I realized there would be no way to explain to my friends and family exactly how I felt after just rocking nearly sixty thousand people. Even after the car doors shut and the police escort hit its lights, I could hear screams echoing off the giant cement walls with massive reverb as the crowd chanted for another encore.

I had just played my first U.S. concert as a truly professional musician, and I was lit up like a Christmas tree. All the cocaine in the world couldn't match this high! My already massively wild, thick Apache hair was even bigger than normal, as though it had been teased with pure electricity. At that moment, the reality of my situation almost made me break down and cry.

I always knew in my heart that my visions never lied. I knew this day would come. I still couldn't believe that it actually had.

Our concert act was not yet slick or polished, but our band possessed a street attitude and a pure, raw energy that could not be denied in a massive stadium setting. On top of that, Rod's incredible stage act blew me away. I felt like I witnessed something truly special in his God-given power and presence. He looked like he didn't even have to try. The whole stadium fed from the palm of his hand.

I was also proud of the fact that we had just blown both our opening acts off the stage. Not that it was too hard. We were a true rock band, while Hall and Oates and Chicago, though legendary, were both pop bands. Our triumph was important to my competitive spirit.

When we arrived at the private airport, a pretty cool big brown private plane awaited us. I had just played my first giant U.S. football stadium, and now I was going to fly in my first private plane. Could it get any better? I asked Randy Phillips if this was our plane for the tour. "No, ours is much bigger. We borrowed this one from Sting."

"Oh, this is Sting's plane? That's pretty cool," I said.

Then I thought about it . . . *STING FROM THE POLICE?* Three years earlier, I had played his songs with This Kids in front of a few hundred people. Now, I flew in his plane after blowing away a crowd of sixty thousand. Who would've thunk?

Rod arranged for a big spread of sushi on board, but before we could eat, he poured the saké and we toasted to a job well done. It was a short flight from Tampa to Miami, but long enough for Rod to get into some trouble. I was sitting next to Rod and Tony Brock at a long, beautiful wooden teak table, eating sushi, when Rod took a fork and started carving it into the side of the wood. He then asked Tony to get him a knife. Perhaps it was the fact we had just played the Tampa Bay Buccaneers' stadium that made Rod start to behave like a pillaging pirate. Or it could have been the mixture of saké and adrenaline. I'll never know for sure, but an ornery look crossed his face, and I knew something was about to go down.

Rod sat up in his seat. "String takes himself far too serious!" he protested loudly. (For reasons unknown to me, he called Sting "String.") He slid down and proceeded to dig the knife into the side of the wooden table, carving like a semidrunk master wood carver. When his masterpiece was finished it read, "STRING . . .YOU MISERABLE CUNT WHERE'S YOUR SENSE OF HUMOUR?"

When the plane landed, the pilots and flight attendant didn't look too happy about the carving in Sting's table. However, when you are a rock band who just headlined a football stadium, one gives little fuck about such trivial issues. (That's not really true, but it sounded so cold-blooded I couldn't resist typing it.) Word was, Rod's carving started a miniwar between he and Sting, with Sting striking next by dead-bolting the gates to Rod's house. Or something like that. I wish they'd still been fighting in 1993, when they and Bryan Adams recorded that lame "All for Love" song. I prefer to see our hero as the king of heavy soul.

We checked into suites at the swanky Alexander Hotel on South Miami Beach. Carmine had a little party waiting for us in South Beach at Woody's, the club owned by Rolling Stone guitarist Ronnie Wood. So we hit it.

After I woke up late the next morning, my bro Dale Lawrence showed up from San Diego to spend the Fourth of July weekend with me. Dale and I traveled a lot together, mostly because we got along great, but also because he was my only friend who made enough money to afford the travel. Only a year before, we had flown to Holland together while I was recording, and we partied in Ibiza, Spain. Dale was the light man for This Kids, but he didn't do it for the money. He did it to get laid—and he got laid a lot. In 1985, when I was a starving musician trying to make it in L.A., Dale was kind enough to take me on an all-expenses-paid trip to Hawaii. As far as I was concerned, when I made it, Dale made it, too.

We jumped in Dale's rental car and took a drive down the beach to get some sun and cocktails. We had no idea where we were going when these two really pretty girls pulled up next to us. "Where's a good place for a drink?" I asked.

"South Beach. Follow us."

We followed our new friends, Beth (a blonde) and DeDe (a brunette). They were supercool. We stopped at an outdoor café and ordered a bite and a drink. I told them I was in a band. "Oooh, really? Who?"

"Just a small band you never heard of, but we have a gig tonight."

They looked at each other. "We're kind of busy, but maybe we can go. Where's it at?"

"Joe Robbie Stadium."

Their expressions said it all . . . *huh*? "Who do you play with?" one of them asked.

When I told them, they freaked out.

That was the first time I pulled that gag, and man, was it fun! We told the girls to meet us after the show at our hotel. Dale and I split so I could chill a bit before the big headlining concert.

When we reached the hotel, it was already a madhouse. The place was packed with beautiful, suntanned Miami supermodels. They weren't real supermodels, but there was something about the tan skin and the blonde hair (even the Latin girls had blonde hair) and the way everyone looked so healthy.

Now you're going to think I'm lying, but I swear, what you're about to read is true. Until this point, this kind of stuff had never happened to me, nor anyone I knew.

Dale and I walked into the elevator, followed by several beautiful girls. I told them I played guitar with Rod. Within a couple floors, they'd peeled their tops off. I had to take photos, because I knew no one would believe me.

"Why did you do that?" I asked. They said they were on a secret wild weekend.

When we stepped out of the elevator, it looked like a lot of people were on a secret wild weekend. There were girls everywhere! A few came into my suite. Within minutes, I was in my room with two sisters, while Dale was in the living room with some other girl . . . at three in the afternoon. After shooting more photos, I said good-bye to my new sister friends and Dale's friend (please don't think I am a total pig; I was just as baffled, so I needed to document it to make sure it really happened).

I walked up the hall to talk to Carmine. When I arrived at his suite, he had a ton of gals in there, too. The old spooky tooth was on fire! I went back to my room and opened the door to find Dale with what had to be a six foot three Amazon girl spread-eagled on my coffee table. *Hello!* She jumped up and ran into my room to hide, while Dale giggled like a little boy . . . this was crazy!

I was excited to get to the gig early, like I did in Tampa, and check out things at the brand-new Joe Robbie Stadium. (Our show was the first concert held there.) Dale brought a movie camera, so we played some stupid gags for his local TV show. We found the highest, furthest seat on the opposite side of the stadium and framed a close-up. I said into the camera, "When you play lead guitar for Rod Stewart, you get the best seat in the house." Dale panned the lens out, showing me to be about a mile away from the stage . . . yuk yuk. Next, I had Dale follow me with the camera while I walked up to people with Rod Stewart Out of Order Tour books. "Can I look at that?" I asked. After they handed it to me, I opened the page to my picture and said, "Isn't that guy good looking?" When they realized it was me and freaked out, we'd run away.

Later that night, I had about ten girls in my room. This crazy gorgeous, but crazy as in *truly cuckoo* girl said to me, "Tony Brock said you're really immature."

"Tony Brock's right . . . would you like another piña colada?"

Yes, I could be immature. Then I rolled my eyes while thinking, *the great Tony Brock said I was immature?* Perhaps one shouldn't cast stones. Earlier that night, I walked out of the main lobby of the Alexander Hotel and saw Tony peeing into a flowerpot.

Dale had a familiar look, one that led people to always believe he was someone famous. When we were young, we drove to Palm Springs during spring break (our VIP treatment at Pompeii, compliments of Connie Stevens, happened on one of those trips.) Dale's VW carried a personalized license plate that said "NU ROCK." For Palm Springs, he would rent a Mercedes Benz SL convertible, and then replace the plates with his VW plates, so it looked like the Mercedes was his car with its own rock star plates. He started telling people he was Bryan Adams, and everyone believed him . . . even to the point of Dale signing autographs. I kind of looked like John Oates, but I wasn't prepared to go there. Don't get me wrong, John Oates is a super nice guy, but . . .

In Miami, Dale's hair was dyed blonde and all spiked up, making him look like Rod if you squinted your eyes. You could say he looked like Rod's little brother, but I mean "brother," like Dale being Fredo and Rod being Michael Corleone.

We walked from behind the stage to take a look at the bazillion people already packing Joe Robbie Stadium. When they saw Dale standing near the side of the stage, they started going crazy. We looked at each other, and then tried to see what everyone was screaming about. I grabbed Dale and pulled him behind the stage. The screaming stopped. They thought Dale was Rod Stewart! He poked his head and half his body out really slyly, and the crowd went nuts again. When he pulled back, they stopped. Soon, he was jumping and dancing around out there, waving like an idiot and making everyone crazy, thinking he was Rod . . .

That is, until our eighteen-foot-tall, mean-as-hell stage manager Nick Kotos walked up and grabbed Dale by the scruff of his neck. He yanked him up with his feet dangling in the air like a rag doll and threw him on the grass behind the stage. I got my ass handed to me for letting my friend get out of line, but I was like a spoiled child and Rod was my rich dad and everyone knew they just had to deal with me. I needed to grow up, but I was now too full of my own shit to notice.

Well, guess what? Payback can be a bitch. In 2007, I was working my second season with 19 Entertainment and *American Idol*. My job that year was to music direct the winner, Jordin Sparks. I played with her while she was still seventeen, with a plan to hire my replacement when she turned eighteen. We were performing at Madison Square Garden, and the Jonas Brothers were on the bill. There were a million little brats running around backstage, driving everyone crazy. They would walk into the dressing room and say, "Ohh, hello, I want Jordin's autograph." Or, "Do you know where the Jonas Brothers are?" I was like, *"Close the door, you little brat!"*

I spoke to the people at 19 Entertainment, who told me that these kids belonged to the heads of Disney, or the heads of Viacom, or some other heads. In other words, we couldn't do shit. We had to take it, while the kids' parents were off in VIP rooms being fabulous. From this experience, I realized that in Miami, Dale and I were acting like king-sized versions of those kids, and I was pushing my luck.

1. A Revolution Is Almost Born. (L to R: Me, Eddie Binder, Tom Kerr, Jerry Jones; photo: Steve Jones)

2. This Kids. (L to R: Paul Martinez, Pat Pinamonti, Greg Hammond, Me; photo: Allen Carrasco)

3. Rock Star in Training. (Photo: Allen Carrasco)

4. Broke and Homeless at Baby O. (Courtesy of Stevie Salas Archives)

5. Stand by This Man. (Courtesy of Stevie Salas Archives)

6. We Want the Funk. (L to R: Gary Shider, Me, George Clinton; courtesy of Stevie Salas Archives)

7. "We're Hooters Girls!" (Courtesy of Stevie Salas Archives)

8. The Wind Cries "Maggie!" (Photo: Dale Lawrence)

9. Madre Mia Maria! (Photo: Dale Lawrence)

10. Sake Party on Sting's Private Plane. (L to R: Kelly Emberg, Don Archell, Rod, and Tony Brock; courtesy of Stevie Salas Archives)

11. Our Home Away from Home. (L to R: Tour Manager Henry Newman, me, Carmine Rojas; courtesy of Stevie Salas Archives)

12. Every Picture Tells a Story. (Photo: Bruce Kessler)

13. Nice Selfie. (Courtesy of Stevie Salas Archives)

14. Once More for Me Ol' Mucker. (Courtesy of Stevie Salas Archives)

15. Spongy and Me. (Photo: Bruce Kessler)

16. A Rock 'n' Roll Rite of Passage. (Courtesy of Stevie Salas Archives)

I didn't know it yet, but hell was coming to dinner.

A few months earlier, I had broken up with my girlfriend in L.A., Christina Whitaker, for not believing my dream of playing with Rod. Shortly after that, I started dating actress Lynn Oddo. Now, Christina's best friend, Maria Conchita Alonzo, was sitting sidestage, on my side. It was fun to see her again, superpeppy and funny as always (unless you're Sean Penn . . . I hear they don't get along so well).

The band was rocking. Between songs, it was fun to goof around with Maria and Dale, as we were all in awe of the massive crowd. I felt like I was an equal to Maria, a bona fide star. This was where I belonged.

Everything was going smoothly . . . or so I thought. I had no idea, but I was on the radar of Rod and the band. Among other things, I still had problems with my acoustic guitar playing. Yes, it's true that Rod can rock, but part of what makes him such a great artist is the way he can blow up a rocker like "Infatuation," sing a beautiful, sensitive ballad such as "A Reason to Believe," and then bring the extra dimension to the folk songs like "You Wear It Well." That night, when I started playing "Maggie May," I didn't perform that beautiful, majestic twelve-string intro with a gentle touch. I was so pumped up that I was strumming it like Pete Townshend playing "Pinball Wizard." Rod was not happy. This problem really was on Carmine, since he was our music director and should have heard what I was doing wrong and told me to correct it long before it got to Rod. For all I know, Carmine and the boys could have been waiting for me to hang myself.

The other big fuckup that night was directly due to my immaturity and lack of professionalism. As I started the acoustic-guitar intro to "The First Cut Is the Deepest," I happened to look across the huge, lit-up stadium. Directly across from the stage stood the biggest, most colossal diamond-vision TV screen I'd ever seen. (I wasn't alone; it was the largest in any professional sports stadium in 1988.) I looked up midway through the opening chords and saw a giant, sixty-foot Stevie Salas and stopped dead in my tracks. I then lifted my hand up and sort of pointed at it, mouthing the word "f-u-c-k" like I was in a slow-motion dream. I quickly woke up to see everyone looking at me, wondering what the hell was going on. I restarted the intro chords and all seemed okay.

When we left the stage, I felt like the king of the world—until Rod ran up next to me, yelling, "You can't play 'Maggie' like you're pounding through a rock song! And another thing: I can't believe you stopped the intro of 'First Cut' to wave at a girl. You need to be a pro!"

"No Rod, I swear I didn't stop and wave at a girl," I said. "I just freaked out when I saw myself on that TV screen."

"That's even worse!" he screamed. Then he ran off.

Did I feel like shit. Now I was nervous, too. Had I just gotten myself fired? The band was not happy with me. Not only did I not pay my dues and earn the right to play with these guys, but I was not playing to their standard. I knew I was capable of rising to the occasion, and I believe Rod did, too. That's why he took a chance on me. However, I was putting all the rock star bullshit ahead of the music. For a real musician, that is the ultimate sin.

8

PLEASE DON'T FIRE ME BEFORE SAN DIEGO

After exactly seven days on my first major tour, we boarded our private plane that would serve as our home away from home for the rest of the year. It was a big, beautiful vintage orange-and-white four-engine Vickers Viscount. I got nervous when flying in planes, so the four engines helped to calm my nerves, since our pilot told me that the Viscount could fly on just one engine if there was a problem.

I needed to deal with my fear of flying issue pretty fast. We flew a minimum of twice a day, three to four times a week. At first, I got a little freaked out, wondering if I was pushing my luck flying twice a day, but I needed to nip my anxiety quickly. I told myself, *look, you committed to getting on the plane. If the plane is going crash, it's going to crash, and all the worrying and anxiety in the world won't stop it, so you might as well relax and enjoy the sights, because Stevie, there is no way in heck you're going to quit this tour because you're afraid of flying!* Many a musician has lost a gig due to travel issues, whether claustrophobia on a tour bus or the need to medicate before flying. I would not become one of them.

Our plane was a British flagship of luxury. The inside was decked out with big leather couches and huge seats that almost made me feel like I was at home in Oceanside on my dad's La-Z-Boy. This plane also flew at lower altitudes, which helped with pressurization and dehydration issues. Due to the amount of alcohol we were consuming, we were already dehydrated enough.

Nevertheless, I was still bouncing off the walls like a hyperactive, superpeppy Jack Russell terrier, yapping, snipping, and barking at everything around me. My older, more seasoned bandmates were growing tired of my childlike exuberance. Don't get me wrong: in many ways, these guys were very immature at times, Rod included, but I was *way* more immature than them.

There's a basic and important difference between being immature, or childish, and being childlike. I think being childlike is a blessing if you're going to be in a rock band, because it's a young man's game. Once logic gets into your head, it can mean the death of creativity—and a career.

Logic happened to me about fifteen years later. While in my late thirties, I woke up one day and thought about my life. I had a lot of money and a couple of homes, but all of a sudden, I felt I was wasting my life traveling the world yet walking in circles. I thought, *I have to go to London tomorrow and get onstage and jump around like a monkey; that's no life for a grown man!* These thoughts are pure poison to an artist, because we must stay open-minded, curious, and young at heart in order to keep the cosmic channel open and the messages coming.

This inner struggle would continue to rage in me until I started working with Mick Jagger. In 2001, Mick was almost in his sixties, yet he had more energy, chased more women, finished more business, and worked harder at rehearsal than anyone I have ever seen before or since. He really inspired me, letting me know that I wasn't too old to have fun rocking.

Rod was in his mid-forties when I was in the band. Sometimes, I would look at him and think, *Man, he is old . . . I don't want to be doing this when I'm in my forties!* (Oddly enough, I'm still doing this in my early fifties!) It's much different now than it was in 1988, with people keeping physically active deep into their sixties. It's also different from when I was a little kid in the 1970s, when most people in their forties looked like Ben Franklin or the dad on *Happy Days*. Rod still looked amazing, really fit and incredibly fun to hang around with.

He used to like to play silly games with the band, too. If we were in a limo, he would open the sunroof, and we would take turns sticking our heads out, with the wind blowing our hair back. Then we would see who could make the stupidest possible face. Rod's always closed the game with his squinty-eyed, bucktoothed face. He and the band, especially Tony Brock, used to prank people riding with us who were either too drunk or overly annoying. He would somehow get them to take their shoes off, then sneak the sunroof open and place one shoe on the roof of the car. The limo driver would close the sunroof, pinning the shoe outside. We would arrive at our destination and jump out of the car, but the person missing the shoe would be still inside, going nuts looking for his or her shoe. Then we bailed. Once, we were driving through Central Park in New York, and Carmine's date was a rude diva. She was so rude that Tony convinced her to take off her cowboy boots, and then he snuck one on the roof while the boys distracted her. She was such a pain in the ass that Tony opened the sunroof ever so slightly, and as we rounded a corner, her boot slid off somewhere in Central Park. When we arrived at the China Club, we ran inside as she frantically searched for her missing boot. Later, I saw her and Carmine in the club; she was walking around in her socks.

Rod also taught us how to steal a limousine. That's right—you read it here. Rod was the king of the limo heist. Here's how he did it: He would ask the driver to pull over at a store. Or, if we were approaching a club, he'd ask the driver to get out and tell security he was in the car. When the driver walked far enough away, Rod would climb through the boot between the passenger cab and driver's cab and drive off. If you were graced with agility and speed (or jacked up on cocaine) and the limo was really long, you could test the limits by slipping and sliding from back to front while the driver walked back to open your door. Then, you would tear out before he reached the car. Only the skinny guys in the band could do this. The chubby ones risked getting stuck in the boot.

So yes, I was immature, but look at the big brothers that I idolized.

It was 11:00 a.m. when our new private plane left Miami, bound for our next show in Pensacola. I assumed everyone was grumbly because it was so early in the morning (11:00 a.m. was indeed the crack of dawn for this band). For years, Rod toured with a band that included his longtime dear friends, Jim Cregan and Robin Le Mesurier, who gave him a certain bit of comfort and security. He was used to things feeling and sounding a certain way with those guys. Plus, they knew each other inside and out, so Rod could lay into them or freak out and it would be no big deal. For the Out of Order Tour, Rod knew he needed to reinvent himself, and the management wanted a newer, more powerful modern sound, so they went to New York City and found the best talent.

New York musicians are a lot different than L.A. musicians. Guys from New York City didn't take any shit. If you popped off at the mouth, you might get your ass cracked. L.A. musicians were a lot more like, "Hey, cats, the downbeat's at 11:00 a.m . . . we're playing a monster shuffle groove." The New York musicians would say, "That's some old bullshit you're playing there . . . play your shit right or get the fuck out, you country muthafucker!" The New York sound and attitude was harder, which is why I recorded my first solo album, *Colorcode*, in New York.

Rod didn't know the New York guys that well yet. Perhaps he didn't feel comfortable flexing his power and weight yet. After all, he was still feeling out the new band. He may not have known it then, but he commanded great respect from all of us. His distinctive voice and massive collection of hit songs as a solo artist spoke for themselves. Not to mention the work he did with The Faces and The Jeff Beck Group, dating back to 1968.

After three shows, the band was good, but not great. Yes, we had just blown away a couple hundred thousand people in our three gigs, but our musicians (with the exception of me) were top dogs whose greatness was measured on a different scale. Consequently, the vibe was thick on the plane, and not in a good way.

Then it hit me: I was the big problem. I had no idea what I was doing onstage for half the songs. Damn! Why did I just spend the past three days in Miami partying with Dale and all those naked women parading in and out of my hotel suite? *I should have been practicing!* What good is being a rock star if you can't back it up on the stage? That attitude may be okay nowadays, with all these nonplaying fools in pop bands, but in 1988, you had to possess skill above all else.

I'd forgotten the rules. I'd allowed the environment to intoxicate me.

Not anymore. I grabbed a guitar on the plane and started working on my parts. All of the boys in the band were feeling the heat of the hot seat, so Carmine and Jeff stopped babysitting me. They had to make sure they knew their own shit; after all, Carmine was music director, the glue that held the rest of us together. I was now on my own, sink or swim, and that was okay by me. I have always been good under pressure, and I have always been an overachiever . . . I wasn't about to let this gig beat me. I was going to rise to the challenge.

I believed it—but I was still scared shitless of being fired.

It made me think back to fourth grade, when I started playing Little League baseball. I was put on a beginner-level T-ball team called B Minors. I worked superhard all year on my baseball fundamentals, so when I tried out the next season, I was certain I would jump to the A Minors—or maybe even make the majors with the eleven- and twelve-year-olds.

After tryouts, I got a call from a coach. "You were put on my B Minors team again," he said.

I freaked out. *I'm better than that; I deserve to be with the bigger kids, not these scrubs!*

I reported to my team, but the whole time I kept bothering my mailman, Mr. Martinez, about this issue. Mr. Martinez was also the Little League commissioner where I lived (his son, Paul, became the bass player for This Kids). Mr. Martinez was getting tired of hearing my fifth-grade mouth complain about my lack of status, so he arranged for me to try out for two A Minors teams. Yes, I got bumped up, yes, our team went to the championship game, and yes, I was a starter.

I knew, as with baseball, that if I worked hard enough and pushed myself, I could rise to another level and hold my own on the Out of Order Tour. Keep in mind: going from This Kids to Rod Stewart's band wasn't like jumping from the B Minors to the A Minors. It was more like jumping from a high school baseball team to the New York Yankees. Just the same, I made it, and I wasn't going to leave without a fight.

After landing in Pensacola, I headed straight to my hotel room to practice, with a bad feeling in my stomach. Even though all the higher-ups in Arnold Stiefel's office had told me at rehearsals in L.A. that my wild modern approach and energy was exactly what the band needed, I knew that if I didn't play the music great, nothing would save me from getting sacked, not even all the novelty and energy in the world. I needed to come correct and in a hurry . . .

Was it too late?

We met in the hotel lobby to drive to the Civic Center Arena for sound check. The lobby was loaded with people drinking and getting ready to cross the street to our concert. When we got out of the elevator, we got mobbed! I was cutting in and out of people when this wild, pretty girl grabbed the arm of our keyboard player, Chuck Kentis. She pulled his arm really hard to get him to stop and talk to her, but Chuck wasn't having it. He yanked his arm violently. "Let me go!" he yelled. But she wouldn't; she gripped him tighter. Chuck then walked into the rotating glass door of the hotel. He made it, but the girl's arm got caught between the door and the post, almost snapping it in two.

"Oh my God!" I yelled.

She screamed, pulling her arm to her side as if she'd broken it. I didn't know what to do other than run past her as fast as I could, but that made a tense vibe feel even worse. It wasn't Chuck's fault at all. It was just an unfortunate event.

As we got to sound check, I was conflicted. I still held a lot of anxiety about the bad energy within the band, but I was also very excited, because this would be my first time playing in a sports arena. I'd dreamt of this moment for most of my life, but the dream didn't include a double-edged knot in my stomach. I certainly didn't want my first arena gig to be my last, so I quickly refocused. Sound check wasn't going well, because this was the first gig with our own sound and light production, and there were a lot of kinks to work out. The room and stage were filled with continual feedback from the house speakers as well as the monitors. The band was also too loud onstage, and because of that, as well as the feedback, Rod couldn't hear his own voice.

When a tour starts, the stress often causes musicians to try to overlisten. Your nerves create a false chaos that fills your head with static, tricking your mind and making it hard to hear detail. In this situation, the first thing a musician often does is turn up the volume, so they can hear themselves better; that starts the landslide. A drummer might not realize he or she is gripping tighter and hitting harder than normal, breaking sticks, cymbals, or heads and getting blisters. Guitarists pick harder without realizing it, often busting strings. That started happening to us because we knew Rod wasn't happy, and we were all on edge. My Marshall amps were almost on ten! (By the end of the tour, when I was no longer a stressed-out rookie, my amps were on three and a half. They never changed, and I heard everything just fine.)

I wasn't the only loud one. Everyone was loud, and Rod was melting down. In the dressing room, he was really distant with us—and me in particular. I thought he was distancing himself so it wouldn't be so hard when he fired me.

We played well that night, but the feedback was awful. That helped me in a way, because the microscope switched from me to the total production. Now the whole band and crew was in the hot seat.

After the show, I talked to Rod on the flight to Atlanta. He told me he was seriously considering canceling some dates and changing the band and production, in a voice made hoarse from not hearing himself correctly onstage. He was frustrated in a way that went much deeper than anger. He seemed deeply depressed about the situation, which made me feel worse, since I knew I could be playing better.

If anyone was going to get fired, it would be me. I was an easy target, because I was new and the band had already been hazing me in an innocent sort of way. Now that everyone was in trouble, my overconfident, louder-than-life personality was getting on their nerves.

I'd already caught Carmine throwing me under the bus. He did this a few times on the tour, and later I would find it funny, but not during this sensitive time. Carmine had a superdeep sense of outside melody and harmony that worked perfectly with his last gig. David Bowie would often create tension and mood by mixing thirds and fifths into the root notes of his songs, which in the 1990s would become very popular. If you're playing a dark alternative cut from David Bowie's album *Diamond Dogs* or Soundgarden's *Superunknown*, those notes are magic. However, if you're playing "Maggie May" or "Baby Jane," those notes sound like some sort of jazz odyssey, not pop music.

During the Pensacola show, the band was going into a big vocal breakdown. Carmine played a beautiful buildup with Tony Brock, but when we stung the note for Rod's vocal, Carmine didn't hit the root note. He hit some alternate note like a G sharp over the E major, and when Rod turned around . . .

Let me rephrase that. Rod snapped around and glared at our music director with an expression that said *what the hell was that?* Carmine slyly nodded his head and eyes in my direction, with a little covert point of his hand, telling Rod it was the dumbass new kid. (Thanks, Carmine!) Rod looked at me funny . . . and not in the *ha! ha!* way. His instincts told him that it wasn't me that hit that clam, but it was almost easier to go ahead and believe it, to just make me the scapegoat.

Afterwards, I sat on the plane with a lump in my throat, depressed. I thought about my friends in San Diego who, the year before, had bought tickets to see me play with Duran Duran's Andy Taylor, who was opening for the Psychedelic Furs at the San Diego Open Air Amphitheater—only to be let down when I got fired a few days before the tour started.

I looked out the window into the darkness and kept thinking *please, PLEASE* don't let me get fired before the San Diego show. I couldn't let my family and friends down again. I just couldn't.

9

I DO DECLARE, THIS IS THE DEEP SOUTH

Why were we going to Atlanta? My tour book said we weren't playing the Omni Arena until October 29, so I was confused. I asked Randy Phillips, and he explained to me that Atlanta was a satellite city. "Oh, okay . . . what the hell does that mean?" I asked. It meant we would stay in one major city and take day flights to other cities in which we were playing, then return to the satellite city after each show.

That kind of sucked. Everyone knows that after a big concert, the hotel and local club after-parties are the best for musicians, since all the girls know who you are. Rod then chimed in, agreeing with me before explaining why it was better to have a satellite city. "We move into a plush five-star hotel and make it our home for a week or two. We never have to pack and unpack our bags, and we get to know all the local spots, making the city like our new home."

I soon figured out that two weeks in town was a perfect amount of time to make friends, learn about the best clubs and restaurants, and perhaps have a few wild love affairs. Anything after two weeks was no good, because then we would run the risk of everyone figuring out what a bunch of assholes we really were.

We arrived in Atlanta and checked into the Ritz Carlton in Buckhead. When I reached my room, I was not only stressed out from the Pensacola show, but also plain exhausted. Since the tour had started seven days earlier, I had not enjoyed a single good night of sleep. Still, I was stoked to have this big corner room that would be my home away from home for the next nine nights. I shut the heavy curtains and passed out.

My phone rang. I looked at the clock: four in the afternoon. I jumped out of bed in disbelief . . . I never sleep that long! When I opened the curtains in my pitch-black room, the sunlight blasted me like a laser beam. I went downstairs to grab a bite and saw Chuck Kentis sitting at a table. When I told him what happened, he started laughing. "You always gotta leave a small crack in the curtain, otherwise you'll sleep all day," he said.

Hmm, cracking the curtains. You learn something new every day on tour. I never had blackout curtains before, so what did I know? At my Hollywood house, my bedroom curtains were old beach towels hanging over the windows with cheap bamboo screens.

Since things had been a little tense with Rod, we decided to blow off a little steam on our night off. Rod didn't join us, so our second in command, Carmine Rojas, a.k.a. Spongy (his famous nickname, honoring his very unique Afro), set up some spots for us to hit. Our first stop was The Limelight. This place was huge and loaded with fun people that all seemed to know Carmine. I'm not kidding when I tell you I have never seen a more well-known or loved person in my life. We hung out until about 3:00 a.m., when we walked next door to a place called Club 112. Why so late? Because the place didn't open until then! As you can imagine, there were some dubious characters in there, as well as girls that looked like custom-shop funny cars with boobs that went *blam* and booties that said *pow!* Just like the *Batman* fight scenes on TV when I was a kid. (Well, not quite.) They all knew Carmine. Of course. I thought I would cut out before I started to get myself into trouble.

The next afternoon, we played our first satellite gig, leaving Atlanta at 2:30 p.m. for Charlotte, North Carolina. The band was really trying to get it together, and I thought we played well, but when we jumped back on our plane to fly back to Atlanta, Rod was in a shit mood. We indeed played better, and were off Rod's radar (for the moment), but the crew still caught hell because Rod continued to have feedback problems with the monitors. Deep down, I knew it was partly our fault, because we were still pretty loud onstage, but I wasn't going to open my mouth unless asked. I had enough heat on me already.

When we got back to the hotel around midnight, no one was in the mood to party. We called it a night, hoping for a better gig tomorrow.

The next couple of gigs, in Chapel Hill, North Carolina, and Norfolk, Virginia, progressed from good to great, which meant our singer was starting to get back to his fun self. During the gigs, Rod started kicking soccer balls into the crowd. In the South, a lot of gigs still used what they call open seating. With no chairs on the whole arena floor, ten thousand people would smash themselves towards the front, which could make chasing after flying soccer balls kind of dangerous. Rod kicked these balls with considerable power, and people dove for them and got crushed!

I noticed a man with a little girl on his shoulders, maybe five years old, and he kept trying to get closer to the front. I thought he was nuts, because not only was the volume insanely loud, the people were bananas up front, taking their tits out and screaming . . . definitely no place for a little kid. The man and the girl were now on my side of the stage, about twenty yards back, and he was rocking out. He had a tight grip on the little girl's ankles, so she looked pretty safe. That is, until a hail of soccer balls starting flying into the crowd. What happened next still upsets my stomach when I think about it. Rod kicked a ball that flew straight at the guy and little girl. It was soaring well over their heads, but for a split second, the man reacted to the ball—and released the girl's ankles. When he jumped for the ball, he launched the little girl about five feet in the air above him. *OH MY GOD!* Her little dress filled with air like a mini-parachute, and her little arms and legs stretched out as she flew up and behind him, as if in slow motion. The last thing I saw was the bottoms of her little shoes as she disappeared into the crowd behind her dad. I always wondered and hoped someone behind them caught her, but I never found out . . . it still gives me the willies.

I also got into a little trouble during the set when I walked up to the front of my side of the stage during one of Jeff Golub's solos. With the monitor problems, I couldn't hear what the fuck Jeff or anyone else was playing, and it didn't help that some of those old southern arenas were giant echo chambers. Regardless, I was locked into the rhythm, feeling the groove. Problem was, Jeff had stopped soloing, and the band was set to break it down, but I was still up front dancing and grooving, carrying on like a madman. My ever-perceptive third eye woke me up from my personal celebration, and I turned my head to the right.

I wanted to die. Rod, Carmine, Jeff, and the whole band stood together, looking at me. Seems the boys were waiting for quite a few bars of music while I was off in my own world, my eyes closed and head rocking back and forth . . . I must have looked like such a fool! If this were James Brown's band, I would have been hella fired, because everyone needs to watch everyone.

I should have known better. I was so embarrassed and mad at myself, because it was a rookie move, and I was better than that. In the end, Rod and the boys didn't get that mad at me, because I looked like such a dumbass that they couldn't stop laughing at me. Yep, they wore me out, for sure.

Now that Rod was in a great mood, we started to party like mad. We met tons of strippers at Club 112, so we decided to visit them at their work—The Gold Club. When we walked into a strip club with Rod Stewart, it was like the scene from the Jerry Lewis movie *The Nutty Professor* when Buddy Love first enters the Purple Pit. Everything stopped, the record scratched, and everyone froze, all eyes on Rod. Instantly, we were in a private area with a million girls on us. Back then, you didn't have to tip but a dollar, unlike now, where fools give away hundreds for a three-minute dry hump in the back room. I was by no means a strip club expert, but back home, Dale Lawrence and I would hang a bit at our own purple pit called Dirty Dan's.

Rod and the boys seemed to have it down. At first, I watched and tried to pick up some pointers. However, Nick and Rick, the horn players, were not teaching me anything. They looked like Heckle and Jeckle bouncing off the walls, most likely on blow, but the third man in the horn section, Jimmy Roberts, was something else. He sat back in his chair like a cold-blooded killer, completely disinterested. Then he did something pretty dope. A naked girl came up to him and chatted away. While she was in mid-sentence, he looked at her and put his palm up as if to say *stop*. When she froze, he handed her a fifty-dollar bill, then politely shooed her away with a hand gesture. He never said one word during that whole transaction. Jimmy Roberts was laid-back in the cut.

A minute later, I saw a super beautiful petite blonde that was mind-blowing fine, so I went to her table and decided to watch her. A diva stripper who knew she was red hot, she had a wolf pack showering her with a constant flow of cash and bad rap. She looked at me and knew I was in Rod's band, so she decided to give me some ice to put me in my place.

I then thought about the book *The Art of War* by Sun Tzu. I worked up a plan to get this girl. If it worked, cool. If it didn't, at least I would have a good time playing some mind games. I sat at the table where she was dancing, then ignored her, looking around and acting like I was in deep thought. Right when I sensed she was thinking I was a rude asshole, I turned and said something really nice to her. Which confused her. I did this for about an hour, and every once in a while, after totally ignoring her, I would give her a big whack of cash and a compliment. Now she was definitely off-balance, trying to figure me out. Soon, she stopped paying attention to all the other guys and got off her dance table just to talk to me.

Then I dropped the super rap. "You know, I totally know how you feel in this place, these people shower you with attention and love, but they don't really get you and your incredible talent," I said. "It's the same for me when I am playing at arenas, and they all yell and go crazy, but they have no idea what's going on in my mind. You're an artist just like me, and as much as I loved watching you, I don't want to be like all those other dudes who were going nuts. I respect your talent; therefore, I don't want to disrespect you . . . "

The next morning, when we both woke up at my hotel, it seemed I'd turned from the spider to the fly. I found myself getting tricked. She was so cool that I really liked her. Everyone knows you don't fall for strippers, but sometimes they're magic. Once my friend Adam Duritz, the lead singer of the Counting Crows, told me and Bernard Fowler that he too knew not to fall for strippers, but sometimes, they have a way of looking through your eyes and straight into your soul—where no secret is safe. I'm no expert on strippers, so when she told me she was from Malibu and only in Atlanta to strip as a way to make money for her college tuition at Pepperdine, I believed her.

My game the night before was so tight, but now as she walked around naked in my room watching TV at two in the afternoon, I was turning into a smitten goon. We decided to walk to the Lenox Mall for a bit, and on the way back, we were actually holding hands. That's when I heard, "Ahh, Ol' Stevie boy's in love, is he? You two look like two shirts fluttering in the wind on a clothesline" (whatever the fuck that meant).

It was Rod and Don Archell, his valet . . . who by the way is about the coolest older English cat on the planet. While sitting in a limo, they saw us and couldn't resist driving up slowly with the windows down, taking the piss (that's British for teasing me).

After hanging out with my tiny dancer in Atlanta, I called her when I got to L.A. later in the tour. That's when I realized she lived in L.A., all right, with a full-on boyfriend—and I don't think she went to Pepperdine, either. So in the end, the one good thing I learned was that my "We Are Both Artists" rap worked without fail, but I also learned that I needed to not be such a sucker.

We jumped on our plane late that July 12 afternoon for a short flight to Nashville. I was excited because my old flame, Deirdre Richardson, used to take me to Nashville to hang out with her dad, stepmom, and stepsisters, and I was looking forward to seeing them and playing for them on the big stage. Deirdre's stepmom was Tammy Wynette, the legendary country singer, and they used to take me all over the country years earlier when Deirdre and I dated. I loved hanging out with Deirdre's dad, George Richey, because he was like a redneck rock star. He and Tammy were good to me right up to her death. Rod found out I knew Tammy and really wanted her to come to the show. I invited her, but she wasn't feeling well, so Rod said we should get a car and drive to her house. He *really* wanted to meet her, but it was not to be. That's when I learned about Rod's deep love of old-school country music. Rod told me that, when he was recording songs like "You Wear It Well," with the fiddle accompaniment, he was attempting to write country music. It all made sense to me.

The show went great until feedback squeals started in the monitors. *SHIT . . .* Rod had been in such a great mood, too. He took out his soccer balls and started kicking the crud out of them into the crowd. I winced as I saw balls exploding off people's heads. One girl yelled, "Hey Rod! Hey Rod! Kick one to me!" then *WHAM . . .* he missed that gal, but the guy holding the two beers next to her didn't have a chance! Carmine and I looked at each other. *Ohhh, man!* Rod had a strong foot, developed from many years as a soccer player (one who was good enough to try out for a professional British club). He could kick that ball to the other end of the arena.

The monitor squeals were picking up. Rod gave our poor monitor man David Bryson that "I can't hear me voice" look, and then the ball whizzed by me en route to the monitor board, as if kicked by Maradona himself . . . *Blamo!* A straight one-hundred-mile-per-hour shot! David ducked and weaved, shucked and spun, his eyes bugged out of his head, but he kept his hands on the monitor faders, trying to get rid of that feedback. I once looked down at David when he was under fire from the boss, and all I saw was fingers on the board. He stuffed his whole body under that desk while Rod was kicking ballistic missiles at him. I felt bad for David, but it was awesome to behold.

My nine days in the Deep South were coming to an end. Just one show to go. We left Atlanta at 3:30 p.m. and soon landed in Birmingham, Alabama. I hope I don't offend anyone, but I grew up as a Southern

California surfer in an area that included people of many ethnic backgrounds because of the nearby Marine Corps base at Camp Pendleton. I always thought that in places like Alabama, guys like me with wild hair that were not white might have trouble with the locals and the law, so I was a little paranoid.

One of my best friends from Carlsbad, Libby Monet, was studying in Birmingham. Libby was not only gorgeous, but also supersmart, and as wild as me when it came to dancing and partying. We shared many great adventures growing up, and I was really excited to see her. She had a couple of days off, so she planned on driving the two hours to Atlanta after our Birmingham show (which she attended) to spend a couple days with me. I didn't feel great about her driving alone, so I decided to go with her. Our tour manager, Henry Newman, wasn't sure about me not flying back with the band; after all, I was a greenhorn kid who, in two weeks, had managed to get himself in plenty of trouble. However, Rod said it was okay, and the plane left without me. Before the others took off, Rod looked me in the eye and said, "Be careful."

I was really freaked out about being alone with a white girl in the Deep South, especially dressed like a late 1980s rock star with crazy hair. I thought I might meet the kid in *Deliverance*, or worse, end up like the Ned Beatty character. If you've seen the movie, you know which scene I'm talking about. I wouldn't even stop to pee on the side of the road!

Libby and I tore down the highway, just having a good ol' time chewing the fat, when all of a sudden lights flipped on behind us . . . *Oh my God, a Smokey!* I looked at Libby's speedometer as she started slowing down; we were going almost one hundred miles per hour. *Shit.* We were somewhere in the middle of nowhere in Alabama, and I was a Native American with a white woman. To a person who had never been to L.A., London, or New York, I could also look gay with my wild clothes and hair, which could be dangerous in the 1980s. I was absolutely positive that *Walking Tall*'s Sheriff Buford Pusser himself would walk up and hit me with that big-ass stick of his.

I was really worried. If I got arrested and Henry had to come get me, Rod would fire me for sure.

The officer approached us calmly. "Ma'am, do you know you were going almost one hundred miles an hour?"

Ever the charismatic one, Libby wiggled and giggled as she handed the deputy her license. After glancing at it for a moment, he said, "Ma'am, do you realize your license is expired?"

I was ready to stroke out. She wiggled and giggled a little more, and then he walked off. Now we were both freaking out, with visions of jail rape dancing through our heads.

The officer returned, this time to talk to me. "Sir, do you have a license with you?"

"No, sir, I don't." All my stuff was in Atlanta.

He walked back to his car again. We sat in Libby's car for what felt like an hour, even though it was only five minutes before he came back.

"Ma'am, I was gonna let your friend drive, since your license is expired, but since he doesn't have his license, I can't recommend that, so I'll tell ya what I am gonna do. I'm gonna let you off with a warning, *but* you gotta promise to get your license renewed right away, and you gotta slow down."

"YEAH!!!!" we both screamed.

We couldn't believe our luck. The officer turned out to be supermellow.

We left the scene of the crime and made our way to Atlanta. We arrived a couple hours later, but it was really late, so we headed straight to Club 112. As soon as Rod and Don Archell saw Libby and me walking through the door, they yelled "Hey!" The boys had the whole club rocking on another level.

When we finally walked out of there, the sun was shining. While all of us were stumbling through the parking lot, an incredible feeling washed over me. I felt like I was starting to connect with Rod and the boys. They truly cared that I made it back safely. I could tell that they were a bit worried about me driving and not going with them. That felt really good.

10

THE LOST SPIRIT OF ST. LOUIS

Wherever we traveled, we always checked into the best hotel the city had to offer. It was no different in St. Louis, where my usual corner room was, as always, fantastic. As I packed my equipment for sound check and the gig, I paused and took one last look at my boss room. *If I get a gal back here tonight, she won't have a chance, because this room is magic.*

Some of the magic dissolved when I got to the Purina Checkerdome. The place was as old as dirt! I flashed back to a few hours earlier, when I was on our plane looking out the window at downtown St. Louis, and noticed the big building with the Purina Dog Chow logo on the roof. That's when it hit me: *We're playing the Dog Chow Arena!*

I can't stand the corporate takeover of America, especially the changing of arena and stadium names. When I was a kid in San Diego, I used to watch the Chargers and Padres play at Jack Murphy Stadium, and I watched a ton of concerts at the San Diego Sports Arena. Now, Jack Murphy Stadium is called Qualcomm. Poor old Jack got thrown out with the bathwater for a few corporate bucks! And what the hell's the deal with the Valley View Casino Center? You can't tell me that sounds like hallowed ground for rock 'n' roll. Even though it's sponsored by my Native American brothers, it still doesn't make it cool. What's next? Will Madison Square Garden be called the Yahoo! Square Garden?

I went into my dressing room, where Rod asked me about my progress on my chord chugging. I had trouble getting it just right, and I knew Rod was not happy about it. The last thing I wanted or needed was for him to be upset with me. He took a big chance by hiring me, and I didn't want to let him down.

Rod Stewart songs like "Hot Legs" and "Twistin' the Night Away" have a specific way they are picked by guitarists to get that "chugga chugga" feel. If you listen to the rhythm guitar on Chuck Berry's "Johnny B. Goode," or The Rolling Stones' "It's Only Rock 'n' Roll," and think that it's all played the same, as if it was just an old-school rock 1-4-5 R&B jam, you're wrong. They are not the same if you really listen. While in The Faces, Ronnie Wood's interpretation of that old-school rhythm guitar created Rod Stewart's signature feel that you hear on "Twistin' the Night Away" and "Hot Legs," among others. Rod wanted that feel; in fact, he demanded it. Even though Woody didn't play guitar on "Hot Legs," Rod made sure the song had the same chug. He was right; that rhythm chug was almost part of the composition. If I was going to play these songs like one of the big boys, I had to get that rhythm right, but I was having trouble getting that rhythm right. It pissed me off that I wasn't experienced enough to fake it, or get it right on my own. I had no idea that the woods used to make the bodies of guitars could make such a difference in electronics. I never thought about why a mahogany guitar sounded different than an ash guitar, or why a super-distortion humbucking pickup sounded different than a P-90 pickup. To tell you the truth, until that point, I never gave a shit. There was no reason to care.

Well, I was learning on the fly. I figured out that some of my more modern rock 'n' roll–sounding guitars with high-gain pickups sounded great on songs like "Infatuation," but had too much power and size to get that tight-picking rhythm Rod needed. Once I tried it on my old-school trusty Fender Stratocaster with single-coil pickups, things started to click. This was the very same black Strat that came from Joe Orndoff's Musician's Exchange store in Carlsbad when I was in high school. Who would've thunk that a guitar that cost me nothing would work in a big-time pro situation?

I have hundreds of guitars now, but I have used that old black Strat on over eighty recordings during the last twenty-five years, including Justin Timberlake and TI's recent hit "Dead and Gone," which was nominated for two Grammy Awards, sold two million copies upon its release, and has since added three million digital downloads. That old black Strat has never let me down!

Even with my Strat, I was having trouble getting the rhythm just right. That night in St. Louis, Rod gave me the opportunity to learn it properly from Billy Peak, the guitarist who actually played "Hot Legs" as recorded on the *Foot Loose & Fancy Free* album. Rod walked into my dressing room with Billy, who came to see the show.

Rod left us alone, and I showed Billy how I was playing the rhythm. Right away, he knew what I was doing wrong. In his slight country drawl, Billy said, "Stevie, the trick is, to get that sound and feel, you must stop that up-and-down strumming and down-pick it."

I tried it. *Voila!* There it was!

It was the smallest little adjustment, but it made the biggest difference. Soon, I was a down-picking fool! In fact, I got it so down that by the end of the tour, I could mix in other strumming patterns. Rod was *so* happy that I got it, and I was so proud to get it right for him, because I didn't want to disrespect his music.

Years later, this issue would come up again, but I switched from being the student to the teacher. In 2006, I started a four-year run at 19 Entertainment/*American Idol*, working as a consultant and a music director. My first act was Chris Daughtry, who many picked to win season 5 (the highest-rated season in the show's twelve-year history) until he finished fourth. Daughtry's debut record had a specific rock feel and mean attitude, and the playing was very disciplined, but one of the guitar players that I brought to the band, my dear friend Josh Steely, was playing it all wrong. He was strumming a loose, happy up-and-down strum, as though he was playing an acoustic guitar on the beach. Although it was subtle, it was important to the feel and tightness to get it right. The song sounded nothing like a Rod Stewart tune, but it was played using the same down-picking technique.

I drove Josh crazy in just the same way Rod drove me crazy, but it was worth the struggle. Once Josh got it, Daughtry's music carried the right feel and attitude, in very much the same way as Rod's music did when I got it right. It was nice to be at a point in my career where I could give back some of my knowledge, and, in Josh's case, help out a fellow Carlsbad local. Josh hated my guts at first for riding him so hard, but when I brought him to the band, he had nothing; now, he owns a big house. I'm sure he now understands that the little details pay dividends.

I couldn't wait to rock that rhythm for Rod in front of twenty thousand fans. I used to grab my Strat before we would play the Chuck Berry song "Sweet Little Rock 'n' Roller" and do a little chugga chugga picking before the band started and Rod would light up. I remember seeing a film in which I did it, and Rod said, "I like that one! I like that one!" Once I did that, Jeff Golub and I kicked into the intro, and that's all she wrote. The concert went great.

I jumped into the limo feeling on top of the world. We pulled up to the hotel, and in the lobby, I spotted two beautiful girls, Katie and Kim. One was a very sexy tall blonde, while the other was a very sexy redhead. Not that orange Raggedy Ann red hair, but the dark, deep European red hair that looked like money and smelled like honey. I said hello and invited them to have a cocktail with me. They smiled and said yes.

These girls were really nice, not groupie, slutty types. They were very educated and classy, but like college girls who came from money, still knew how to have fun. In every town, I would want to see the sights, since everything was so new to me. I asked the girls to take me to some fun drinking spots. Did they ever!

We tore up the city and closed all the spots in downtown St. Louis, but we were having a blast and not ready to stop. They drove me across the Mississippi River to an after-hours spot in Illinois. We were having so much fun, but I couldn't figure out which girl liked me more, and I wasn't feeling a threesome vibe from them. I didn't have a lot of those three-to-five naked girls in my room sex-party things happening. It was rare in 1988, and wouldn't come into vogue until much later in the 1990s.

It was nearly sunup when we returned to my room. I still wasn't sure how the night would play out. All of a sudden, the tall blonde grabbed me, kissed me, and said good night—and the redhead invited herself in and took off her clothes. My mind screamed, *I love being a rock star!* It was awesome to see her naked in my magic room.

After a fair amount of slap and tickle, we were laying in my bed, laughing. I thought to myself, *I could really fall for this girl . . . she is something special.* She was smart, elegant, funny, and could drink like a fella but handle her booze like a lady. She had great hair, knew how to dress, *and* wore great shoes! (I think shoes say a lot about a woman's personality.) The best thing was that we could just talk, and it felt like I knew her from another lifetime. It was really beautiful.

A few hours after we fell asleep, the alarm clock blew up. Time to get my bags packed, not only the ones for my clothes, but also the ones under my eyes. We were a little hungover, but happy, both feeling good about being together . . .

That's when it happened. I thought I saw her put something on her hand. No, it couldn't be . . . "Is that a wedding ring you just put on your finger?"

She looked at me, and her smile went away. "Yes," she said very sheepishly.

"You're *married*?"

Her half-confused expression suggested, *what's the big deal?* "Well . . . yes . . . I am married."

This may sound crazy. Sure, I was a wild rock 'n' roller to the bone, but I did have some rules. One was, I didn't mess with married women.

I instantly felt sick to my stomach. "Where is your husband?" I asked.

"He's at home. With my kid."

"Your *kid*?"

Boy, was I a sucker. The girls I knew back home in Oceanside and Carlsbad, and even in Hollywood, would have never done that!

I was more sad than mad. I was also angry and ashamed for letting myself down. She could tell I wasn't happy. When she left, we didn't kiss. I just said good-bye and watched her and her beautiful red hair walk away.

Downstairs at our lobby call, I told Rod and the boys my traumatic story. None of them seemed to give a shit, nor think it a big deal. These seasoned touring musicians were all so much older than me, and this lifestyle was normal to them, while I was still in fantasyland. I felt like such a loser for sleeping with a married girl, and Rod could tell. He pulled me aside. "It wasn't your fault; you didn't know," he said.

I sat in my regular seat on our plane and looked out the window, feeling guilty as hell. I worried that I somehow had changed, wondering if I would ever be the same young kid again. Then I looked around and noticed the comforting sight of my bandmates. Carmine was passed out with a banana in his hand. Jeff Golub was passed out in a robe with green hospital scrubs and black tennis shoes, his hair in a rat's nest.

Life would go on. Although I got stung a little, I remained the same kid I was the day before.

11

PURPLE HAZING

The first time I ever saw a gun pulled with violent intent happened at the Oceanside roller rink, where my elementary school friends and I used to skate and eat junk food on Friday nights. I was waiting in line when a car screeched around the corner. I looked up to see a guy with fear in his eyes jump from the moving car. He ran right past me as another chased him with a gun. This was a rough area, part of the reason Oceanside used to be nicknamed "Ocean-crime."

Years later, my former brother-in-law, Steve Cottrell (who is still a brother to me), bought the rink and ran all the hookers and drug dealers out of the area. Today, the land is worth a fortune (no one from Oceanside ever bothered to thank him for cleaning up the place, which really sucks).

At the rink, my personal favorite skate song was "American Band" by Grand Funk Railroad, an accurate tale of life on tour for a rock band. Grand Funk definitely knew that life, since they were one of America's most successful bands and outdoor acts in the early 1970s (in 1971, they broke The Beatles' attendance record at Shea Stadium in New York). In the song, they tear up hotel rooms and party down from town to town. They also sing about Sweet Sweet Connie, a woman from Little Rock.

I had no idea Connie was a real person until Jeff Golub introduced her to me.

We landed in Little Rock on July 16 to play the Barton Coliseum. The backstage area of the old, crusty arena wasn't very nice. After sound check, I walked over to catering for some food. Jeff sat with this older foxy cougar gal, so I joined them. Jeff was poring over some photos intensely and didn't notice me, but the woman said hello. "What are you guys looking at?" I asked.

"Some modeling photos. Do you wanna see them?"

"Sure!"

She passed me the photos—wild, sexy naked shots of herself. I didn't see that coming. "Oh wow!" I exclaimed. "This is you?"

Jeff looked at me with a *you dumb little fucker* look. "Stevie, this is Sweet Connie from Little Rock."

Instantly, I flashed back to the sixth-grade version of myself rocking to the song "American Band" on my roller skates. "You're a real person?" I blurted out.

As it turned out, Sweet Connie was a world-famous old-school groupie. She looked at my baby face and was ready to tear me apart. When you get right down to it, I was afraid of her, so I laughed and kept my distance, but a lot of the people on our crew were sure excited to see her. After the show, Rod asked on the plane, "Did anybody have fun with Connie?"

A year and a half later, I played a big theater in Little Rock with my band Colorcode, opening the Joe Satriani tour—and there was Connie, hanging out backstage. She told Winston, C.J., and me that she was a part-time schoolteacher. She was supernice, and we were in no way judgmental. I have met many a churchgoer or important politician that had nothing but hate or greed on their minds; conversely, Connie wasn't hurting anyone. She loved life. Later that night, C.J. flat-out asked, "Connie, so what it is exactly that you do?"

To C.J.'s surprise, she looked him dead in the eye and said, "Honey, I suck dick."

After the Little Rock show, Rod's plane landed in New Orleans. I wanted to go out and see the place, but I was still getting the cold shoulder from the boys. Since our tour-opening trip to Puerto Rico, when they stuck me in coach, the boys had been giving me the rookie treatment. They fucked with me whenever they could. I understood where it was coming from, and like a good soldier, I took it.

All of that changed when we played a gig a week before Little Rock in Norfolk, Virginia. One minute, the band members acted like my bros. The next, they gave me ice. They were practicing the art of war *on me*. I have always had thick skin, plus I looked up to these guys so much that I dealt with it, but after our Norfolk show, it went too far.

After the concert, we did a runner straight to the plane. When we took off, I started to clean up and change out of my sweaty stage clothes, but when I reached into my travel bag for my clean clothes, I noticed they were sticky. I looked into my bag to see a ton of squished fruit all over my clothes. I have never backed down from a fight, and there were times I wanted to pop some of the guys in the band for pushing my buttons. I always kept my cool, because I knew they were making me pay my dues.

This was too much. I exploded. I stood up and screamed, "FUCK YOU GUYS!" I picked up my bag and threw it wildly in the direction of the whole band, nailing poor Chuck Kentis directly in the face. I then held up my fists. "C'mon, right now! I will kick all your asses! C'mon, motherfuckers! LET'S GO!"

Everybody freaked out. I must have looked like a maniac. I sure felt like one. Of all people, Rod stood in the aisle, watching me with a smile that, in my mind, was telling me, *Yes, Stevie, stand up for yourself.* All the boys calmed me down, but I was seeing red. I really lost it. I was done with their bullshit, and I told them so. "I don't need to be your friend, and if you have a problem with me, let's go right now."

I could tell the boys felt bad. I sat back in my seat. To my surprise, they took turns sitting next to me, one by one, and told me they were sorry and that I was indeed their friend.

Later, Rod talked to me, letting me know he understood why I blew up; in a way, it felt like he was proud of me. "Stevie," he added, "you're too wound up. When's the last time you got a massage?"

"I've never gotten a massage in my life."

"I get three a week, and you should do the same."

He told Randy Phillips to book an appointment for me at the Ritz Carlton in Atlanta and put it on his tab.

I felt funny when I had to lay there naked with a grown man rubbing me down. The massage therapist told me he had just given a massage to Bon Jovi drummer Tico Torres, and he spent the whole time rubbing out his glutes . . . in other words, his butt cheeks. He added that the next day, Jon Bon Jovi came in, looked him in the eye and said, "Whatever you do, you're not rubbing my ass."

My massage was not enjoyable. It hurt like hell. Randy Phillips told me that the massage therapist called him and reported he had never worked on anyone with more knots in his body than me. I have always been a little too uptight. In 2012, my friend Danny Torres ran into my old pal Sammy Hagar. When my name got mentioned, Sammy said, "Man, Stevie is too uptight."

Sam might be onto something. I'd better work on that.

In New Orleans, the band ran off without me. Although they didn't say I couldn't join them, they also chose not to invite me. That really hurt my feelings. I thought that after our big fight, things would become hunky-dory, but it was not to be. I loved these guys like my big brothers, and in turn, wanted to be one of the boys. Carmine and Jeff were so much older and wiser than me, and after all, I was such a smartass. Even though I had spent a lot of time living in Europe, I was not very worldly. Let's face it: hanging around a little kid can be annoying.

It was no different for Rod. One day, he wore an amazing black leather jacket, the most incredible jacket I had ever seen. I said, "Wow, that looks expensive. How much was it, five hundred dollars?"

He just chuckled and rubbed my head like I was a little kid. Turns out that jacket cost closer to ten thousand dollars. I needed to grow up, but I wasn't exactly sure how to do that.

The next night, we played Shreveport, Louisiana, so we took the short flight from New Orleans at 2:15 p.m. Rod boarded the plane and realized he and Carmine were wearing the exact same shoes. Rod said something rather ponce like, "Where'd ya get those shoes?"

"I bought them at a shop in New Orleans," Carmine replied.

"They look a bit like mine, but they aren't really the same, are they? After all, I got these at Fred Segal on Melrose."

Carmine remained very laid-back in the cut. "They look like the same shoes to me."

Carmine put his shoe up to Rod's. Sure as shit, they were the exact brand and style. Carmine knew he had the singer right where he wanted him, all set up for the coup d'état. "Okay, how much did you pay for yours?" Rod asked.

"Seventy-five bucks."

"*Shit!* I paid three hundred and seventy-five at Fred Segal!"

Carmine looked at him with a dry stare. "What did you do that for?"

The band played pretty well in Shreveport. Our "pretty well" still killed most other bands, and on the bright side, the fans as always were beyond pleased as they screamed for endless encores. To me, it still felt like we were nine guys being nine guys, and not one unified band, one team. We had the talent, but we hadn't yet tapped into the magic. We never talked about it, but we had only played eleven gigs, and I'd only participated in a handful of rehearsals. I still felt tension emanating from Rod, which sucked, because I knew I was the easy scapegoat. All I could do was to keep working my ass off on the parts—which I did. However, I sensed Rod and the band members subtly distancing themselves from me, and it was really bumming me out. In New Orleans, my heart felt mighty low.

Little did I know it would fall lower.

After the Shreveport show, a small, frail man came up to me and said, "My name is Robert, and I *love* your guitar playing." He told me that my guitar sounded like his clarinet, and that he liked to play wild, screaming notes like the notes I would produce with the wang bar on my guitar. I didn't know who he was, but I noticed that people were nervous around him.

When we flew back to New Orleans, I was surprised to see the frail clarinet player on the flight. Turned out that he was Robert Palmer, a big-shot writer from *Rolling Stone* magazine. Along with him was a loud, very abrasive woman. She was his wife. He was so sweet and quiet, while she laid into him in front of the boys, talking rudely. I felt bad for him. So did the boys. Problem was, we were all drinking. The more everyone drank, the more her king-sized rack of chi-chis seemed to soften her hard edges. Soon, she, Carmine, and the horn players were flirting like mad. She was overtly sexual, and Robert didn't seem to notice or care. She wasn't just talking shit to her husband now, but also barking at everyone on the plane.

Our saxophonist, Jimmy Roberts, an old-school brother with a "fuck with me and I'll cut you" vibe, wasn't having any of it. "What's wrong with you, woman?" he said. "Why are you talking all that shit? Sit your ass down right here!"

She sat her ass down right next to Jimmy. I'm not kidding.

After a couple minutes of some kind of cold-blooded, old-school jazz-player rap, she was under his control as though in a spell. Jimmy was the mack, and because of that, we didn't hear a peep from her for the rest of the flight. I thought it was awesome, but I wasn't sure how Carmine, Nick, and Rick felt.

When we landed, none of us were sure what to do about Robert, because it was obvious his wife was now the slave of one Jimmy Roberts. I thought fast. I really wanted to see New Orleans, and Robert had been telling me about it, so when we arrived at the hotel, Robert and I split straightaway. He proceeded to give me an incredible all-night tour of the French Quarter. I never brought up his wife, even though we both knew she was in Jimmy's room singing James Bond theme songs . . . *Nobody does it better / Why'd you have to be so good?*

Robert and I stayed in touch. When my first album came out, he really liked it, and he was a big fan of my producer, Bill Laswell. Robert was a gentle cat, and I always liked him. I think he respected not only the way I played my guitar, but also that I was there for him when his wife was doing her thing. In 1993, Robert ended up relocating to the very same New Orleans hotel that he showed me, and he resided there until he died in 1997.

It became really obvious the next day: no one wanted to hang out with me. Jimmy Roberts found me in the lobby, looking lonesome. He thanked me for covering for him regarding Robert and his wife. He said he couldn't take her rudeness anymore and felt he needed to break her down a little. Jimmy Roberts is an angel of a guy and an incredible musician, but that doesn't change the fact that he is a straight-up pimp and not one to be trifled with. Jimmy knew the boys were having fun without me, and he could tell I was really down about it. I was hurting, feeling lower than low, and I needed a friend like I never needed one before. Thank God Jimmy had mercy on me. "C'mon, man. I am taking you to the movies."

He bought us a big bag of popcorn and did something I had never seen before. He dumped a box of Raisinets into the popcorn, and man, that tasted like *some more*! Jimmy knew I had something going on and gave me subtle big-brother advice, making sure that I understood where I was fucking up, but also not taking away the spark that got me the gig in the first place. I wasn't sure if he knew it or not, but his words of wisdom gave me some much-needed strength.

After that afternoon, I knew I could fix this problem with the boys. It was a long, tough day for me dealing with all the dejection, but a necessary day, something I needed to experience and grow from. I never forgot Jimmy's kindness. On my first record, *Colorcode*, under the special thanks, it says "Jimmy 'Save Me in New Orleans' Roberts."

12

A REASON TO BELIEVE

When Nine Became One

We sat on the airport tarmac for two hours, bored out of our minds. The band, travel party, flight attendants, and pilots were all getting crabby in the New Orleans summer heat. Our singer was late to the lobby call and nowhere to be found, but we still drove to the plane as scheduled.

I always found it funny how people talk shit about those in charge when they are not around, but then puss out when the person is present. Or, worse, kiss ass. Where I come from, that's cause for an ass kicking. When someone shot their mouth off, you could bitch slap them or even get into a punch-up. The cops would come and break it up, making sure everyone shook hands and went their separate ways. Then all was cool—no lawsuits, no jail time.

Well, I heard the familiar rumblings towards our singer . . . "Where's Eagle Beak?" "What's Up with Big Nose?" "Where's the Cum Guzzler?" (When I was a kid, a vicious rumor circulated that Rod Stewart gave blowjobs to a bunch of blokes, which of course was total bullshit. A pissed-off PR person created that rumor, which spread like wildfire. Now get this: when I got the gig with Rod, my Oceanside bro Vince Bucelli told some friends he was genuinely worried that Rod would seduce me!)

The grumbling and bitching made me think. Here I was, sitting on a private plane, with my own stewardess giving me cut melon and whatever else I wanted. I had a pocketful of cash and all the girls I could ever want falling for all my bullshit. Plus, Rod was paying my ass plenty to sit on this tarmac, if need be. The other guys were big-time dudes that truly could quit the band and pick up another arena gig right away, except perhaps Rick Braun, who like me was pretty new, too. However, Rick now held some juice with a current hit song he wrote with REO Chuckwagon. (I shouldn't call them that. Their real name is REO Speedwagon, and their singer Kevin Cronin was always nice to me at parties, but what can I say? I can be an asshole).

Are you wondering how I knew Rick had a hit on the charts? Every time he got mad at Randy, Rod, or anyone, he would start mumbling under his breath, or louder, "I don't need this; I got a song on the charts with REO." At the beginning of the tour, he blasted us with that shit at least twice a week. At the end of the day, Rick didn't need the tour. He became a highly successful jazz solo artist.

Eventually, Rod's limo pulled up to the plane. After he boarded, he gave us a heartfelt apology. I was *so* surprised. Here was the main man, paying out millions in tour expenses, and the name on the plane said Rod Stewart—not Stevie Salas or Carmine Rojas—but he still respected us enough to tell us he was sorry. You've got to respect that sincerity. Believe me, I did.

I've told you about the healthy ego I carried on the tour. We all had them, but I knew that if he fired any one of us, the fans would not give a fuck about us anymore. It's not like if Billy Idol went on tour without Steve Stevens. People who saw Billy wanted to see him with Steve Stevens. However, not one fan would ask Rod to refund a ticket if he fired a band member. I'll bet if he fired me, my mom would have still gone to the concert!

The plane took off for Houston. I was excited to play the world-famous Summit Arena. When we arrived at the Four Seasons Hotel, I saw pop star Debbie Gibson in the lobby. Please don't think I'm nuts, but she was looking good to me. She was eighteen, still a little young for me (I was twenty-four), but perhaps in a few years, I could take her out for a soda pop? That mini-fantasy left my mind as soon as I met her Long Island mom, who gave me a look that said, *I'll cut you down like Amy Fisher cut down Joey Buttafuoco's wife.* I felt a rumbling in my stomach, reminiscent of being called to the principal's office over the school's PA system when I knew the paddle was out.

I grabbed my room key, but not before inviting them to the concert. They showed up.

After the show, we held a party at the hotel bar and then met some people who took a few of us to Rick's Gentlemen's Club. I'm not sure what happened to everyone else, but Jeff and I took a very late-night excursion with a couple of wild-looking girls to some food place (for some reason, strippers never get chubby, even though they eat plenty of food . . . one of life's great mysteries). After that, we went back to the Four Seasons.

We had an early-afternoon lobby call to catch our plane to Dallas, so I sent my luggage with our crew and headed downstairs. My wild, exotic new BFF from Houston had left earlier that morning, so I was alone. Thank God, because there in the lobby was Debbie Gibson . . . and her mom . . . *yikes*!

"Hello, Mrs. Gibson. Good morning. Isn't it a beautiful morning, ma'am?" I asked in my best Beaver Cleaver imitation.

"Hello, Stevie." She rolled her eyes; after all, it was already 1:30 in the afternoon.

Debbie gave me a huge smile. "Hi Stevie! I really liked the show last night!"

She seemed really excited, so I sat on the couch with her and started talking. After a bit of small talk, I noticed the rock star of the hour, Jeff Golub, walking out of the elevator in his white Four Seasons robe . . . with, to my surprise, his girl from the night before in tow. He started walking towards me, not noticing sweet little Debbie Gibson and her very proper mother. *Oh, shit.* Try as I might to covertly signal him to abort the mission, it was no use. Jeff and his girl walked over to me and straight into a bear trap.

"Hey!" Jeff said.

Then he saw Debbie Gibson . . . and her *mom* . . .

I couldn't resist. "Mrs. Gibson, do you know the other guitar player in our band, Jeff Golub?"

A look of disgust crossed her face as she eyeballed Jeff's girl up and down, knowing the girl had on last night's "party" outfit. I'm still not sure just how Mrs. Gibson knew; after all, the girl wore an elegant, deep-blue sparkly supermini cocktail dress with tons of shiny blue fringe dangling from it. The dress complemented her king-sized knockers, which were hanging in there by a very stretched thread. Oh yeah—she also sported bright fuchsia hair, blue toenails, and six-inch heels. I cringed at the rising stress level in the room.

While Mrs. Gibson gave Jeff the stink-eye, he didn't even flinch. Instead, he summoned his own inner *Leave It to Beaver*. "Hello, Mrs. Gibson. Hello, Debbie. Have you met my friend Venus?"

With that, I received another lesson on how real rock stars roll, another reminder of why Jeff Golub is the rock star's rock star and not a poser.

We headed for Dallas on that Friday afternoon, July 22, and checked into the brand-new Crescent Hotel near Turtle Creek. I was really excited to be back in Dallas, because four years earlier, when This Kids played the Tango Club, it was always over the top. While playing in Dallas, This Kids even got written up in *Rolling Stone*, so the city was good luck as far as I was concerned. (If you can find it, check out the April 1984 issue with John Belushi on the cover. It was a small mention, but for four kids from Oceanside, a *big* deal.)

I was also excited because my hometown bro, Dale Lawrence, was waiting for me in the lobby with cash and a rental car. Our three straight nights of wild womanizing in Miami had whetted his taste buds. Now he planned on spending every available penny visiting me on tour. Cool! I was glad someone from Oceanside eyewitnessed (and participated in) the madness, because back home, they still had trouble believing me.

I changed my clothes and grabbed my trusty Rod Stewart all-access pass. This was like an American Express black card; flashing it to security admitted me as a VIP with free drinks everywhere, not to mention tons of female company. Dale and I soaked up a little sun at the pool, and then we hit the bars early, just to get a feel for Big D. It wouldn't take long before we had a bunch of nice Texas gals to show us around. Everywhere we went, I would flash my all-access Rod pass, and the girls would say, "He is Rod Stewart's guitar player." Every time, the security guard at the door would greet me with, "Ohhh, you're already on the list. Welcome, Carmine." How could they mistake me for Carmine? Well, they did, but it worked for me. Carmine was on the guest list to every place in the city, and we had only arrived that afternoon! I gladly walked in as Carmine.

That same night, the band held a private party at the Hard Rock Café's Cheeze Club. Dale and I met Rod and the band there. When I arrived, a tall, beautiful blonde with a ten-gallon smile named Heather walked me into the private room, where the boys were in full swing. It looked like Rod had a crush on her, but I think it was the brown bandit Carmine who tiptoed around those tall tulips. Later, Heather would move into the house next to mine in the Hollywood Hills and become a dear friend. Many a rock star stayed at my house over the years, and Heather liked to visit just to drive many a boy crazy, including Terence Trent D'Arby, who she took special pride in teasing but not pleasing. That frustrated the singer even more.

The private room at the Hard Rock was loaded with girls, and the band was having a great time, but I could see Rod wasn't himself. He really looked unhappy. I sat next to him and we started talking . . . I mean *really talking*. Rod and I were the only jocks in the band, the only people with competitive sports backgrounds. Sometimes, he and I could speak on another level, not as guitar player and boss, but as competitive men of honor—pick up the little guy, victory always, never give up, death before dishonor. I know it sounds a little corny, but athletes will understand. In team sports, you have to rely on the person next to you to hold up his end.

Rod was still holding some doubts about his new band. He wasn't sure if he was going to keep things as they were, and I completely understood. We had great potential, but we weren't even close to reaching it.

Through my many subsequent years as a music director and producer, I have found that even the best players need to have someone kicking them in the ass. Tom Brady is one of the greatest quarterbacks to ever play football, but he still needs Coach Belichick to push him to his potential. Likewise, I think our superb musicians still needed some leadership and a small kick in the ass, but only Rod could lift up his boot. No one else could do it.

I don't know if anyone else in the band had a clue that Rod was feeling this way, but I'd known for some time. I felt a lot of it was my fault, since I was a rookie and out of my league. When I am drunk, I often get emotional, and when it comes to talking about sports and being the greatest, I get even more emotional. Even though I know it's coming, I still cry every time I see Rudy make that end-of-the-game tackle in the movie. Being over my head in Rod's band was okay with me, because I have always been the underdog fighting for what comes easy to others—just like I fought for my first breath when I was born.

I looked at Rod. "Please trust us, and that trust will bring us together. You are a great leader, but you really need to lead us."

All the time we talked, he stared intensely at me with his undivided attention. The only exception was when a happily wasted Rick Braun kept cutting in with a sweet, drunk voice, saying, "Rod, can I do your room tonight?" (He wanted to go to Rod's room and destroy it like we were The Who or Led Zeppelin.)

Rod kept waving him off. "Hold on. Stevie and I are talking."

Rick interrupted again and again. Finally, Rod had enough. "Rick, you can't tell the person whose room it is that you're gonna do his room! And you don't ask for permission . . . it doesn't work that way!"

Rick looked at us cross-eyed with this love-filled, drunk smile and went back to bouncing off the walls with our trombone player, Nick Lane.

Rod and I got focused again, talking about the band and tour. I said to him, almost in tears, "I will take a bullet for you, and so will the boys. But you gotta lead us and you gotta believe in us, and if you do that, we won't let you down."

He looked at me and said, "OK, I will. I promise." Then we hugged like athletes after winning a championship.

This turned out to be the defining moment of the Out of Order Tour. The stupid kid with no experience helped make it happen. I don't think anyone in the band even knew what went down that night, but from then on, everything changed for The Rod Stewart Band.

Well, not everything. Later that night, we were at Club Clearview, and Rod stole another limo, with the band in tow.

We were in Dallas to play the first-ever concert in the brand-new Starplex Amphitheater. Earlier in the day, Rod was invited to a ribbon-cutting ceremony, and he asked me to go. No one else in the band gave a shit about going to something like this, but me? I wanted to see and do everything there was to do, because every day was like a new adventure. There was one major problem with this new venue . . . the back wall had collapsed that morning. Thank God it happened then and not later that night at our sold-out show, because it would have been ugly.

Two years later, during my first world tour with my band Colorcode, we played in Dallas at the Bronco Bowl. While there, the whole roof collapsed into my dressing room. I started thinking, "What's up with me and these Dallas venues falling apart?"

At the Starplex, they roped off the back where the wall damage occurred. After some photos with the mayor, we made our way back to the Crescent to rest.

That night at the concert was special, because Rod was true to his word. I could feel he had surrendered himself to this band and was now really our leader. The show rocked! We received one encore after another, and I knew Rod was happy, because I asked him to please let us play my favorite song from the *Out of Order* record, "Lethal Dose of Love." He looked at me and said, "Let's do it!"

I first heard "Lethal Dose of Love" in the rough mix stages, when I was at the Record Plant studio working with Andy Taylor, who cowrote and coproduced it with Rod and Bernard Edwards. "You wanna hear a new Rod song?" Andy asked. Then he cranked up that funk-rock monster, and it really inspired me with its Power Station style and groove.

In our show, the song started when Tony Brock lit up his drum intro with an incredible loop he created. When it kicked in, the crowd went nuts! I will never forget these guys in front jumping like gorillas in the mist, almost as if having a religious experience. The band and Rod were now perfectly in synch. We never really rehearsed it before, so at the end Tony had a small fuckup, failing to turn off the loop in time. He was mad at himself, but I was like, "Dude, you're Tony Brock. You are the truth. Your fuckups are better than most drummers' best fills . . . don't worry!" He put his arm around me as we ran off the stage and into the waiting limos.

Back at the hotel, we put on a huge Texas-style party in the Grand Ballroom, and everyone was ready. The party was loaded with classic Dallas women. There were the beautiful big ol' crunchy-hair girls with enormous fake boobs, as well as the sexy tattooed alt rockers in cowboy boots and swing dresses—plus everything in between. I had made friends with a girl named Deanna. She knew a friend of mine from El Camino High School, Denise Thornton, who lived up the street from my dad. Deanna was kind of a snob, and I didn't have the patience for her, but Dale did. He had no problem spending the evening getting abused by her (she was indeed hot, and Dale had a way of taking tons of shit and letting it roll off his back until he got what he was after—and he did get what he was after). Deanna had a sweet, beautiful friend named Sandy, who was cool. We hung out as friends, because she appealed to my parental instincts that made me want to protect her from the wickedness of rock 'n' roll. Sandy watched me make an ass out of myself all week with all the girls, but she knew I was having fun and not really believing my own bullshit. She actually helped me meet a ton of girls, including a beauty from Kansas City that would tickle my fancy. Sandy remains my friend to this day.

After the party, all the girls came back to my room. For the second straight night, Dale and I hosted a slumber party. The next day, we flew to Austin and played the Frank Erwin Center, but had an underwhelming show and Rod wasn't feeling the people. Even though the crowd was screaming when we finished, he didn't want to do an encore. Not even one. That was the one and only time that happened while I was in the band.

We shook it off on the plane ride back to Dallas. When we got there, Rod wanted to meet Heather and all our gal pals at the Cheeze Club, where we rolled late into the night.

Rod was now committed to making this band work. He needed to make sure not only that the band was on point, but also that the crew was together, so he booked a rehearsal in Dallas. Rod not only wanted to hear us play the songs, but also the sounds our front-house mixer was dialing up. It was stressful for everyone, because Rod knows his shit— and he had the microscope out. Our great rock front-house mixer, John Godenzi, became the scapegoat. I loved the guy because he always treated me like an equal, making me feel like I belonged with the rest of the band. His firing was a bummer, but it might have been the best thing that happened for The Rod Stewart Band, whether it made an actual difference or not. Rod felt like the problem was being solved. This enabled us to move forward without any doubts.

Rod brought in Lars Brogaard, a person he knew and trusted (and who remains his front-house mixer to this day). Lars really has it together. When you're on a wild circus act like the Out of Order Tour, you need a solid guy like him around. Lars also worked closely with Diana Ross. In 2002, I was in New York City for a month working on a project for Clive Davis with the late, great Lamya, and I ran into Lars. He invited me to meet the superdiva Diana Ross. Truly a thrill!

After our rehearsal, we were invited to a special private dinner at the home of the Hard Rock Café's original coowner/cofounder Isaac

Tigrett, who owned the franchise with Peter Morton. (The Florida Seminole Indians would later buy the franchise, paying billions for it. My Native American Seminole brother Christopher Osceola and a few other dear friends run Hard Rock now, and are doing incredibly well.)

Isaac lived in a mansion on top of the Stoneleigh Hotel (now the Le Meridien Stoneleigh), which was out of this world. When we showed up, Isaac was sitting somewhat like a guru with all these beautiful world-class women, both around him and spread out about the mansion. I thought he was a little bananas, but he was my kind of bananas. I liked the guy instantly. The vibe in the house was a little bizarre, and in some ways felt like we stood on a movie set of a spy thriller.

While we were there, I took a private tour of the Hard Rock Café's massive memorabilia collection in the basement of Isaac's building. When no one was looking, I tried on the chrome dragon boots that KISS bassist/vocalist Gene Simmons wore in the Love Gun Tour.

Heather was there because she was tight with Isaac. She couldn't believe that all the girls were asking us to sign their boots and shirts. Isaac didn't seem in the best of moods, and later Dale would tell me why. Dale and Rod saw Isaac and his girlfriend shouting it out in the hallway, so it made sense why his vibe was a little off. He was having a rough night.

The other odd thing was that a lot of the girls were a bit like Stepford Wives, seemingly there for our pleasure. Not so much sexually, but for the total visual stimulation, as if we were all involved in a live art show. Perhaps Isaac was an Andy Warhol/Velvet Underground fan.

Rough night or not, Stepford Wives or not, Isaac was an incredible host. I was blown away. At the end of the night, he sent me off with a beautiful Playboy model who was waiting to find out if she would be named Playmate of the Year. She spoke in this soft, southern accent that made it clear I wasn't in Oceanside anymore.

I got into the limo with the beautiful Playboy model when it hit me—was I becoming a sex addict? It really is no different than being hooked on cocaine; it's just a different kind of high.

I had been on tour just over a month, and knew I was beyond my legal limit for catch and release, but I couldn't help myself. How could I say no to a woman like this? It just seemed un-American and definitely un–rock 'n' roll. As a kid, I read about rock stars like Van Halen and Led Zeppelin always surrounded by naked women. How about Jimi Hendrix on the *Electric Ladyland* record, sitting with all those naked girls? I even eyewitnessed Mick Jagger dancing on a club floor one night in Tokyo with at least forty girls. When he took his shirt off and started spinning it over his head, almost all the girls did the same. Your whole life, you're brainwashed to believe that if you become a musician, the girls come with the gig!

Montrose and Van Halen singer Sammy Hagar, also a great solo artist, told me something. When Sammy was young, he was with more women than he could remember. So why did I feel conflicted? In 1988, when you were a headlining big-arena band, the girls threw themselves at you—and not just the sluts. I am also talking regular, smart, and wonderful church-going girls.

The Playboy girl prompted me to think I might have a problem. She was unbelievably sexy and beautiful, the kind of girl a young musician who dreams of being a rock star pictures himself dating, then taking home to the Mansion in the Ferrari. After being with this girl, I felt a little empty, which caused me to realize something: the superhot ones were far from the most fun. In fact, they were almost always boring, high maintenance, and lazy, and, get this—most were really bad in the sack, too! Think about it. Men and often women line up for these girls, ready to take them out and shower them with the finer things in life, so they never have to learn how to be funny, make conversation, or please their partners. They assume that everything they do or say is awesome, because no man has ever told them differently. Guys who like trophy women usually have these girls around to serve their egos more than anything else, but the girls don't seem to know that.

I took a look in the mirror. Was I becoming a lost soul? The talk between Rod and me helped to bring the band together, so now perhaps I needed to have a talk with yours truly to get it together.

While I was tripping out, my girl started feeling insecure. "Is something wrong? Do you not like me? Don't you think I'm beautiful?"

This was starting to feel like a drag, but I'm not the kind of guy who can pull a Morris Day. Remember the song "Jerk Out"? His girl, after having sex, said, "Baby, can I stay?" And cold-blooded Morris Day said, "Baby, you can stay anywhere you like, but you got to get the hell out of here."

My brother Jimmy Roberts, our sax player, was old-school cold. He could shut a girl down in such a way that she loved him even more. That brother had real game, but I definitely did not.

"No, baby," I told the girl, "I'll be right there. I'm just flossing my teeth."

Flossing my teeth? See what I mean? Jimmy Roberts would never say that.

It was a wake-up call, letting me know it was time to watch it with all the cocktails and women . . . or else I might lose myself. I looked in the mirror and said, "Okay, I have made up my mind. I am gonna stay focused on my main love, which is music, and stop being such a dog."

When I did that, a weight lifted off my shoulders. Instantly, I felt better, as if I was a new man.

I walked back into my room and smiled, then took a few photos of my beautiful friend, who gladly posed. Then we went to sleep.

I know what you're thinking, and I get it. However, there was no need to waste a good night. I figured I would start my new plan tomorrow.

13

FIDDLER'S GREEN IN THE RED

The band arrived at the Fiddler's Green Outdoor Amphitheater in Denver for our sound check minus our singer, Mr. Stewart. It wasn't unusual for Rod to miss sound checks; in fact, it was better that he took the time to rest his voice, since he was having more and more trouble with it.

We sat around on a beautiful Friday afternoon, waiting to play as Lars, our sound man, talked to the Fiddler's Green sound cops. None of the boys cared or thought noise levels were going to be a big deal. At our sound check, we worked hard at keeping our stage volume down, but we steadfastly protected the power of the band. After all, we made it a point to perform as an arena rock band, not a wimpy pop band.

The problem with the sound started a month or so before our July 29 concert, when a series of complaints came in from the citizens of a new neighborhood built near the Fiddler's Green Amphitheater. Their complaint? Excessive volume after 9:00 p.m. Word on the street was it was our pals from Down Under, INXS, who set the record for the most complaints in one night while touring their massive hit record *Kick*. The city decided to pass an ordinance to keep concert sound below one hundred decibels, a ridiculously low level that might work for The Captain and Tennille or Paul Young, but wouldn't fly for The Rod Stewart Band and the muscle we brought to bear.

For our sound check, the city stationed a Nazi-style dude to hold a decibel meter. He was a real prick. He would complain to Lars, who would tell us to turn it down. Then we'd run through the song again. Time after time, I would see him stare at his meter and shake his head. *Nope. Not low enough.* When we finally adjusted the volume to jive with the sound-meter prick, I could hear my footsteps on the stage in the middle of a song. I'm not kidding. No matter how much we tried to keep our integrity as a powerful rock 'n' roll band intact, we were going to be screwed. Carmine, always the calm in the storm, knew it and grew a little uptight. He knew Rod wasn't going to dig this at all.

"I wish our singer was at sound check today," I said to Carmine, "because you and I both know that come showtime, Tony is gonna hit the snare-drum crack for 'Hot Legs' and instead of sounding like a cannon going off, it's gonna sound like a little popcorn fart. Rod is gonna lose his mind."

We felt the storm coming. Rod liked to dance and feel the beat when he sang, and if the beat was gone, it would most likely put him in a bad mood—which would cause him to look for a scapegoat. Or, he would nail a couple of soccer balls at two hundred miles per hour. That was never fun . . .

Sometimes the soccer ball attacks were fun to watch. If there was a problem with the onstage vocal monitors, I would always feel bad, but still laugh my ass off while watching our awesome monitor man, David Bryson, dive to the floor in sheer terror when white-and-black projectiles flew past his head.

We arrived in Denver all beat up after a couple of insane nights in Kansas City. We arrived in Kansas City pretty late, since we'd stopped in Norman, Oklahoma, to play at another sold-out arena en route from Dallas. When I reached my room, I was tired but also a little bored, wishing there was something more fun to do than watching TV.

That's when my phone rang. "Stevie boy, it's Rod. Where ya at? Come up to my suite and have a drink with the boys."

I jumped up and headed to Rod's suite. When I got there, he and Tony Brock were already completely smashed, pissed out of their heads, as the Brits would say. Also there was Rod's valet, Don Archell, the Silver Fox. He and Rod used to tell the ladies they were father and son while pulling birds singing soft shoe like Hope and Crosby. They were the Brits in our travel party, and when they got lit, their accents and conversations became almost unrecognizable. They'd start saying things like, "'Ello mam, old ya tits for ya . . . you reckon ee's a woolly? . . . A wooly woofter? . . . Ah bollocks, ee's a bleeding cunt that's what ee is! . . . Ahh ee's all right I reckon, ee just cant keep the 'ands off his block and tackle . . . Not the wedding tackle! . . . ee's gone too far . . ."

It would go on like this all night.

I walked over to where Jimmy Roberts, Jeff Golub, and Nick Lane were drinking and grabbed a cocktail. When I returned to the living room, Rod and Tony were gone. *Where the hell did they go?* I quickly forgot about them and took a seat with the rest of the boys, drinking, cussing, and telling tall tales. After about thirty minutes or so, Rod and Tony returned; soon, we were up to our old tricks, singing old songs and acting like hooligans. For some reason unknown to me, Rod fell to the ground and started to roll around like a wet dog drying his fur.

Then I noticed something weird. While Rod was rolling on the floor, a metal object fell out of his chest pocket. It looked like the round mic you would find in a hotel phone handset (with the old house phones, you could unscrew the mouth and ear ends of the phone handle and remove a round microphone piece). Rod saw it fall onto the carpet . . . and he also noticed that I saw it. He made an Inspector Clouseau face (not on purpose, mind you). He quickly grabbed the mic and shoved it into his pocket and continued rolling around with Tony.

A short while later, we said our good nights and headed off to our rooms. After all, we had just played a show, we needed to play again the next day, and sunrise was quickly approaching.

Rod and The Faces were known as a notorious party band—and it didn't stop there. The Faces formed in 1969, with Rod taking over lead

vocals after leaving The Jeff Beck Group. He was accompanied by
Ronnie Wood on guitars, Ronnie Lane on bass, Ian McLagan on keyboards, and Kenney Jones on drums. Probably their greatest hit was
"Stay with Me." The Faces are one of the most important rock 'n' roll
bands of all time, inducted into the Rock and Roll Hall of Fame in
2012. I used to read magazine stories and book accounts of crazy Rod
Stewart and Faces parties, and I know for a fact that Ron Wood kept
the tradition alive and well, since I attended many of Woody's hotel-
room parties later during Rolling Stones tours. One of the things that I
would read about as a young boy, and then hear about firsthand while in
Rod's band, were legendary stories about how rock stars would trash
hotel rooms. Well, Rod could trash a room as good as Keith Moon, Joe
Walsh, or the boys in Led Zeppelin.

When I returned to my hotel room in Kansas City and opened the
door, guess what I saw? My room looked like a bomb went off in it.
First of all, the furniture was gone. At least, I couldn't find any of it at
first sight. There was no art on the walls or lamps anywhere, and all the
curtains and drapes had been torn down (apparently to ensure that if
the victim attempts to ignore the room trashing and simply pass out on
the floor, the early-morning sunlight will make life miserable).

When I say this room was trashed, I mean it was destroyed! As I
entered the blast area, I found pieces of furniture on my balcony, some
tied over the side. The bed was in pieces, the mattresses were hidden in
closets, and the blankets not used for tying together the Christmas
tree–sized mountain of furniture in another area of my room were
nowhere to be found. Even the pillows were gone. I walked through the
room, giggling like a high school kid, feeling like I was now a true part
of rock 'n' roll history. I loved it. I took a few photographs and then sat
on the floor and thought about what to do next . . .

That's when I smelled it: someone had taken a slash in my trashcan
(that's British slang for peeing). It grossed me out a little. I may be a
pig, but I am a cultured pig. I didn't want to give Rod the satisfaction of
me asking him or anyone else in the band for help, so I decided to call
the front desk and ask for a new room. I would tell them I had a

problem closing my curtains, I was worried about the light waking me . . . *fucking genius*!

I dialed the front desk. "Hello, Mr. Salas, can I help you?" the desk clerk asked.

"Hello, ma'am, and yes you c . . . "

"Mr. Salas, are you there?"

"Hello, ma'am, I am here and I . . . "

"Mr. Salas are you there?" Click.

After she hung up, I called back. The same conversation happened again, just like the first time.

Then it hit me like a sausage to the head. I remembered the round piece of metal from inside the phone that fell out of Rod's chest pocket. Motherfucking Rod Stewart, you got me again! He knew I would pick up the phone first thing and call someone for help, so he took the microphone out of the phone so no one could hear me.

I would have to deal with the matter in person. I grabbed one small suitcase from the rubble, along with my bathroom bag, and walked downstairs to the front desk. The girl working the overnight shift was hot and knew I was the lead guitar player for Rod Stewart. (In 1988, people weren't used to seeing celebrities or even semicelebrities like me up close and personal. It's not like that now, with social media giving us front-window views to what a celeb does 24/7, and where talentless nobodies are famous for doing nothing.) We were rock stars playing sold-out sports arenas and appearing on MTV, and she was excited to see me.

I explained to her that I was really tired and, because my curtains wouldn't close properly, the sun would surely wake me. "Oh, I am *so* sorry, Mr. Salas, but the hotel is sold out," she said. "Let me see what I can do." After a moment, she came back. "We do have one of our beautiful two-bedroom suites available, so take that for tonight, and when our maintenance man shows up tomorrow morning, I will have him fix those curtains."

"Thank you, my dear," I said. "Write your name down and let me get you backstage passes for the concert tomorrow night."

Her voice instantly flipped from a thirty-year-old's proper business-like voice to that of an eighteen-year-old squealing girl. She was indeed excited. I know what you're thinking . . . did I invite her up to my room for a little slap and tickle?

No, no, no. I was indeed tired, but I think she would have paid a visit if I'd asked.

My new room was a palace. Not as nice as Rod's suite, of course, but still better than anything I'd had before. I slept like a baby.

I also forgot to get a wake-up call. Later that afternoon, when it was almost time for our lobby call, no one had any idea where to find me. There was no record of my changing rooms, except with the girl who worked the graveyard shift. When my phone finally rang, awakening me from my princely slumber, it was tour manager Henry Newman. He proceeded to chew my ass out. The hotel management also discovered my trashed room and all the damage, and the shit was hitting the fan . . . of course, they thought I did it. All this madness broke out while I slept like a babe in a king-sized manger.

"Why didn't you tell me what room you were in? The hotel says you owe them over five thousand dollars for all that damage!" Henry yelled.

All I could do was smile in my suite, feeling like the cat that ate the mouse.

Rod got the kid good, all right, but the kid stayed in the picture. I may have been young, immature, and inexperienced, but I am not stupid. My street smarts came in handy, and at the end of the day, I think Rod loved that about me. In many ways, we were a lot alike growing up, two blokes with humble beginnings and athletic backgrounds who worked hard for everything they had. I knew Rod woke up thinking Little Stevie must be curled up on that floor with no blankets and the sun beating down on his forehead, when all along, I was sleeping in the most beautiful room I'd occupied in my life.

Later, I mentioned the pee in the trashcan. Rod made a sour face. "I didn't do that! That's disgusting!" he said. I could tell he wasn't lying. Rod may have been a rock 'n' roll cad, but he still had class . . . even in leopard tights.

We drove out to the countryside on the outskirts of Kansas City to play our concert. After sound check, I decided to go for a walk along a nearby creek. I saw frogs the size of Frisbees, which scared the shit out of me! I then walked through the parking area where people were tailgating, saying hello to girls and thinking, *that's right—get a good look, then when you see me tonight onstage you can say, "Hey, that's the guy from the tailgate party!"* I would never do that today. I'd just sit in my dressing room, answering e-mails. When I was young, it was really exciting to sneak amongst the crowd.

When I got to the dressing room, someone was playing The Rolling Stones song "Bitch," off their *Sticky Fingers* LP. "We have a horn section," I said to Rod. "We should cover this song one night!"

Rod's eyes burned into me. "What? That's the competition, mind you!"

Why is he yelling at me? After all, I loved The Faces' version of "Street Fighting Man," which was also the competition's song.

I also got what he was saying. I was a very competitive jock, and so was Rod. That was another reason he liked me. Even to this day, when I get on the stage, I want to take down any other guitar player. It's not personal; it's just my natural competitiveness. I like to win. Rod must have seen it that way with Jagger. Rod was big, but never bigger than Mick.

Rod once told me a story about Mick deceiving him, and I could tell it still hurt. After the Stones lost Mick Taylor on guitar, Rod saw Jagger somewhere. "Mick," Rod asked, "You're not gonna steal Woody from me now, are ya?"

"Oh no, Rod, I would never do that to you."

The next thing Rod knew, Woody was out of The Faces and in The Rolling Stones.

Mind you, it goes both ways. In 2001, I received a call to play with Mick Jagger as his guitarist and musical director. For a couple months, we talked in detail about what he wanted done. We would often meet for dinner during rehearsals. One night at Chan Dara, a very cool Thai restaurant in Hollywood, Mick, his bodyguard, and I were having a bite. "Mick," I asked, "just how did you get my number to call me for this gig?

In his big, tarty British voice, he said, "OHHH I GOT YOUR NUM-BA FROM RRROOOD STEEEUUUWART." Then he chuckled a bit. "Na, I can't do that . . . "

"Do what?"

"You know, by making fun of Rod, I am really making fun of meself, both being British singers and all, aren't I?"

I could tell he had respect for Rod, but he also had a competitive streak in him.

After we played the sold-out Kansas City show, about two hundred people showed up at our hotel, ready to party. Most were girls. I took the band van to the hotel, but Rod wasn't in it. "Where's Rod?" Henry Newman asked me.

I had met a few blondes in Dallas that were from Kansas City, and they were backstage and beautiful. I had a lovely affair with one of them in Dallas, and she was with me now in Kansas City, but the other was still fair game. She was a natural blonde, about five foot eight, with a great lean body and *huge* real boobs. She too was missing.

What followed was one of the craziest things I have ever seen. I was in the front of the hotel, grabbing my guitar, and an ordinary, wine-colored Toyota or Chrysler pulled up. The blonde was driving. I peered into the window. Ducking down in the passenger seat, wearing a Frank Sinatra hat, was Rod. She brought him back not in his standard limo, but in that everyday car! She must have been tripping to get him into the car; as I've said, he was about style. But that was Rod. He liked to take the piss and have a laugh, and that was indeed really funny. We proceeded to party like rock stars.

The next afternoon, we jumped back on our plane and headed for Denver. Rod's friend from Kansas City would become a good friend of mine, staying in touch with me for years after moving to L.A. and living up the street from me. However, I would never see my blonde again.

She worked for AT&T and gave me a free phone card so I could call her long-distance for free (remember long-distance phone bills?). We spoke a few times, but that was that.

It was getting close to showtime at the Fiddler's Green Amphitheater. We had warned Rod about the volume. He didn't like it, but he also didn't want to pay the massive fine we'd receive if we didn't keep the volume down. All the papers had carried on their front pages the story about the noise ordinance and the numerous complaints from local citizens.

The crowd was going nuts as the curtain dropped and we slammed into "Hot Legs." Well, maybe not slammed. It was *so quiet* that it sounded like a transistor radio. Try as we might, we just couldn't feel the music, and Rod was getting frustrated. We kept trying to get into it, but to no avail. We were uninspired.

Then it changed. Rod said something in the mic about INXS holding the record for the loudest-ever show and drawing the most-ever complaints from the neighborhood. "We can beat INXS, boys. Turn it up!"

Rod's competitive nature won out. He wasn't about to have a shit show and be outdone by INXS. The crowd went bananas and we lit it up. We were so unified behind Rod, like an army or a football team in the red zone. We kicked ass! Of course, the city officials were going nuts, but Rod loved it. By cranking it up, he said to them, "I will pay your bullshit fine!" (It was a tidy sum of money.)

Towards the end of the show, we ran into the side dressing room and waited for our first encore. I saw these rocker dudes hanging out. The next night, Denver would host the huge Monsters of Rock Festival at Mile High Stadium, and The Scorpions were on that bill. They were backstage watching us. Whether they would admit it or not, all the rockers loved Rod Stewart. He got all the girls and made all the money. Sure, people would tease him about his shenanigans, or the song, "Do You Think I'm Sexy," but never to his face. After our second encore, Rod said hello to The Scorpions and asked if they wanted to sit in and jam with the band. Of course they said yes!

The Scorps are the nicest guys. I was already chatting backstage with Rudy Schenker, because in 1987, we'd run into each other when I was invited to the opening party of MTV Europe in Amsterdam. What a party that was! I was at the Sonesta Hotel, drunk and depressed about my then-girlfriend Julie Airali, because I'd just found out she was cheating on me and had fallen in love with some guy while I was working in Europe. Granted, I was a douchebag, banging every girl in sight while in Europe. Once "Walk the Dinosaur" became a hit with Was (Not Was), I was really out of control, but when you're an immature kid, somehow that part gets forgotten. Instead, I was like, "How could you do this to me?"

Late that night, Rudy Schenker walked into the Sonesta bar. *Wow, the guy from The Scorpions!* We started drinking and talking, and he was so cool. He really lifted my spirits, so naturally, I was excited to see him backstage at my concert a year later.

As we walked onstage for our third encore, Rod said to The Scorpions, "Guys, next song, get your guitars and let's jam." They went to get their guitars while I kicked into the intro to "Stay with Me," and we just blew the roof off the place. (Well, it was an open-air amphitheater, and there was no roof, but if there was . . .)

After the song, The Scorpions were excited to come onstage. As we ran into our dressing room again, Rod said, "C'mon boys," signaling us to run out the back door and into the waiting limos. We did a runner to the hotel while the crowd cheered for more. Once in the limo, I turned to Rod. "What about The Scorpions? We left them standing on the side of the stage with their guitars on!"

Rod just looked at me with a devilish grin. "Ahhh, maybe next time."

We all felt a little guilty, but we had to admit, Rod pulled a cold-blooded baller move and it was funny.

At the hotel, Jimmy Buffett was hosting a great party in the rooftop ballroom, and everyone but Rod headed up there. He asked me to call him if I saw any talent (his word for beautiful girls). The party was going off, and there were indeed tons of beautiful girls. I was excited to meet the East Memphis horn section from Muscle Shoals, touring with

Jimmy Buffett. The boys told me some cool stories about making the Rod Stewart *Atlantic Crossing* record, one of my favorites. As we were talking, I saw these five *super*hot girls, so I excused myself and went to say hello. They were not the nicest girls, because they knew they were hot shit, but they were friendly enough. Except for the hottest one, who was, quite frankly, a bitch.

I started fetching champagne for the girls. A couple were vibing with me, but I wanted to break down the bitchy one, who was so stuck up and full of ego . . . I had to have her! She brought out my competitive streak. She drank her champagne and we talked about superficial things like cars and wealthy people, which bores me to tears, but I was determined to win this battle. Then I said, "Well, girls, I have some Cristal champagne in Rod's suite. Would you like to try some?"

There were no hip-hop guys walking around and talking about Cristal back then; it was indeed a rare commodity, an indulgence for the rich. Well, my stuck-up girl lit up. "Oh, I have never tasted that, but I would love to," she said.

I explained to her that Cristal was an acquired taste, at least for me, and I found it overrated. "I much prefer Dom Pérignon," I said.

I called Rod's room. "I've got five hot ones," I told him.

"Come to the suite. There is a little party going on here."

I grabbed the gals and headed to Rod's and that awaiting bottle of Cristal. As always, Rod was a super host, dazzling the ladies with his British charm. My girl, the ice queen, was starting to thaw a little, which made me think, *Salas, you bastard, you're gonna do it!* I then explained to Rod about the girls wanting to try Cristal. He looked at me funny. "Stevie boy, meet me in the kitchen."

I told the girls to hang tight, and I met Rod in the kitchen. Then he broke the news. "There was our tour cooler that was holding the bottle of Cristal that I was saving, along with other booze and soft drinks, but to my shock, as I looked into the bottom of the cooler, I saw that the Cristal was empty," he said. "Someone already drank it! Most likely the horn players." (Those guys are their own breed, and would always bag the good booze and drugs while the guitar players always searched for talent.)

We both stood there for a minute. I had to think fast, but then it occurred to me how that chick had been a bitch to me all night and I was eating her shit, taking her rude comments . . .

Fuck it. I reached into the cooler with all the melted ice and bottles in it, grabbed the empty Cristal bottle, and *plup plup plup.* I held it under the melted cooler water and started filling it up. "What are you doing?" Rod asked.

"They want Cristal, and I am gonna give them Cristal!"

Rod thought I was crazy, but he grabbed some champagne glasses and left the kitchen. I took the almost full bottle of dirty melted cooler ice and squeezed some lemons into it, and, for good measure, poured in a little beer and cheap champagne for some fizz and color. I filled the champagne glasses and walked out to present it to my mean, stuck-up debutante and her hot, stuck-up friends. As I handed them the glasses, I reminded my mean girl about my theory that Cristal is indeed an acquired taste and that I thought it was overrated.

She took one sip, then another. In her smug, stuck-up, snooty tone, she said, "Stevie, you're right. I see what you mean . . . it is an acquired taste."

Needless to say, I didn't get laid that night, but I have laughed about this story for twenty-five years. Sure, it was mean, but chalk one up for the little guy, the guy who gets blown off by stuck-up girls like that every day. After all, if I weren't in Rod's band, that girl wouldn't have given me the time of day.

The next day, I was invited backstage by The Scorpions at Monsters of Rock. I was excited, since I was a massive Eddie Van Halen fan and they were the headliners. No one wanted to come to the concert with me except Carmine, so we went together. Hanging with big brother Carmine is always the best, because it seems like he knows everyone everywhere. He remembers every woman's name, every roadie that ever toured in the last twenty years, every agent and manager . . . he is something to behold.

When The Scorpions saw us, no one mentioned how we'd iced them on the side of the stage the night before. Instead, Rudy Schenker shouted in a strong German accent, "Stebie, look! I have *gute* German *bier*! With great pride, he handed me a German beer he'd flown in from the fatherland.

That's some old-school rock star shit. You would fly in items you loved, like a special cheeseburger from a weird restaurant. There was no Internet, so things came by expensive courier after an expensive long-distance phone call. Not just food, either. When Rod wanted to catch a soccer match in England, he would call long distance from his hotel room at about three bucks a minute and have someone back home put the other end of the phone to the TV speaker so he could listen to the match live . . . for two hours!

After we drank our German beers, Carmine and I walked around, greeting people. I met Jason Newsted, who had just joined Metallica, and then I got seated on the side of the stage five feet from my hero, Eddie Van Halen, to watch him do his thing.

Later, I was invited to a VIP room, where I saw my dear pal Dave Weiderman, who always believed in me. He was and still is a big shot at Guitar Center, the huge retailer. Before I landed the gig with Rod, I played a lot of opening slots on bigger concerts, showcasing Colorcode for record companies. Dave would lend me amps and speakers for free from Guitar Center. Now Dave was sitting with the man himself, muthafuckin' Edward Van Halen, whose first and second records changed my life. I didn't care what the critics thought; I *loved* Eddie V.

I walked up and said hello to Dave, who introduced me to Eddie. Eddie stood up, hugged me, and shook my hand. "Have a seat," he said. He ordered me a drink.

That's when I pulled the stupid fan thing I've never pulled, before or since. "Eddie, oh my God, I am your biggest fan and I started playing guitar because of you," I said.

Eddie looked at me. "Shut the fuck up, Stevie. You're making me feel like an old man. Now drink your drink."

We would hang out on and off over the years, and I would become good pals with Sammy Hagar as well, jamming a lot in Mexico with him.

Here is some trivia, and I might be the only guitar player who can say this. Three days after he left Van Halen, Sammy called me and asked me to be his guitar player. I also got a call from David Lee Roth about possibly playing with him. These weren't calls from their managers. Both singers called me personally. I would have loved to play in a band with either, but at the time, I had my own pretty lucrative recording contract, so I stuck to my own thing.

As for Eddie . . . many years later, my then-girlfriend, actress Nikita Ager, had a hot friend who was spending a lot of time with Eddie. We would often double date, which I loved, because I could ask Eddie to tell me stories about the early records. That same year, Nikita and I were hanging in Vegas and joined my pal from the Stone Temple Pilots, Dean DeLeo, and his then-wife at an STP concert (Dean's wife used to date Jeff Golub when I played with Rod). We were chilling backstage when a kid from some new, faceless alt-rock band came up and said, "Dean, I love your records and started playing guitar because of you, etc. etc."

I looked at Dean and smiled, thinking how that was me with Eddie Van Halen that night in Denver.

14

SCARED ONSTAGE

No Bollocks, No Glory

I was where I belonged. I relished the giant stadium and sports arena stages we were playing, but that doesn't mean I never dealt with stage fright. I have always felt a bit of stage fright, a good thing because it reminds you to do your best (not just try your best) and be on your game.

Rod and I shared something in common when it came to stage fright. One time, I asked him, "Why don't we do a surprise show at the Roxy?"

"Why?"

"Because it's a cool thing to do for the fans, don't you think?"

That's when Rod told me he was afraid of playing small crowds.

Funny thing is, so am I. When I walk onto a stadium stage, I feel like a king. I walked onstage at the Toronto Rocks SARS Festival in 2003, and there were nearly five hundred thousand people, but I felt calm enough to circumcise a baby. Likewise, Rod could walk out to a stage in a sold-out sports arena and hold the people in the palm of his hand, making the arena feel like a small, intimate venue, which is a true gift. Oddly enough, in an actual small, intimate venue, he told me he feels awkward.

I'm exactly the same. When you walk into a small venue and see the people in front of you, it's very intimidating. You feel like they can see you for who you really are, just a normal bloke, a regular person. That's not part of the grand illusion that live rock promises, nor part of why most people go to concerts: to become a part of something larger than themselves so they can escape from the reality of their lives for a night. When you walk onto a stadium stage, you feel the power of God. When it's going good, there is no better feeling in the world. Once you taste it, you might spend the rest of your life chasing it. Talk about addictive! I think that's why so many rock stars take drugs, because the high of the big stage is the real bitch. It is very tough to match a high like all of the adrenaline and cheering people.

One thing Rod taught me was that you have to always, *always* keep your cool and never let the crowd know you're nervous. The same goes with women. Sometimes, I would feel so outclassed with a worldly six-foot-plus model fresh off the Concorde with a purse full of lettuce (money). Or, perhaps, having dinner with an actress who, months before, I had watched on TV.

Often, I would push myself to do crazy things when scared, to try to prove to myself I could be bigger than the fear. Take my fear of heights. Once, I was in Baja California with all my high school friends, high as a kite on tequila. I was dancing on a giant pirate ship, really a nightclub mounted into a cliffside above the ocean. To face my fear, I climbed onto the mast over the dance floor (the thought of bouncers trying to kick my ass over this stunt was scary, but exciting, too). I pushed myself further, jumping from the ship onto a big rock cliff. I was teasing death. This was really stupid, because had I fallen, I would have landed on the jagged rocks below and ruined my friends' good time. Still, I felt *so* alive! And I didn't die!

Another time in Cabo San Lucas, I stood on a table above the middle of the dance floor in a club called Squid Row, looking down on hundreds of people as they danced. I was again on fire, thanks to my favorite fiber, tequila. I saw my bro Jimi Dunlop standing on the upper level, about twenty-five feet off the dance floor and a good fifteen feet above me. Jimi screamed my name and leaned over the railing with his hands down like a trapeze catcher. I didn't know he was kidding, so I ran as fast as I could on that platform towards him and took a leap of faith . . .

Once airborne, I saw the shock in his face. Not a good idea, I realized, but it was too late: I was airborne and committed. The crowd roared as I flew through the air towards Jimi and his outstretched hands. He managed to grab me. Barely. My legs kicked in the air, high above the crowded dance floor, while a panicked Jimi desperately tried to pull me over the rail. Had he dropped me, I would have definitely broken some bones. To this day, neither of us knows just how I made that jump.

The bouncers quickly surrounded us, but thank God, I was already a little bit famous there. "Oh, it's the Indio," the head bouncer said. (Mexicans think all Indians are wild and crazy.)

The crowd went wild! The high was untouchable, very much like rocking a stadium. I was scared, but pushed myself to take that leap. I often liked doing crazy things like that when I was young.

Famous women aren't the only ones who can intimidate you. While on tour in Florida, I met a beautiful, very buff woman who turned out to be a professional wrestler. Word was she was the champ, private jets and all, but since I never watched professional wrestling, I had no idea. I knew she was strong, though. Her name was Debby, but she went by the name Medusa. Bernard Fowler, Carmine Rojas, and I nicknamed her Muscles. I thought to myself, *Muscles is very nice and very beautiful, but Stevie, she also has the ability to pick up your little 150-pound ass and throw you through her bedroom wall . . .*

That triggered my "fight the fear" response. As we started becoming intimate, I pushed the envelope and held her tight, spinning her around on the bed and kissing her. She stopped, looked at me with an amazing expression of happiness, and said, "My whole life, guys have always been so afraid of me and never make me feel like a regular girl, but you just are so confident."

I didn't have the heart to tell her I was scared shitless.

As a young man who thought of fear as a weakness, I can't tell you how lucky I was to witness Rod Stewart's nervousness about going onstage or chatting up girls. It let me know that I was okay, and that being nervous wasn't a weakness. Rod and the boys taught me that I needn't worry, because once you get that first kiss out of the way or hit that first power chord that ignites a giant PA system, the nerves will calm, releasing all the energy inside and lighting up everything in your path.

15

DADDY, I'M COMING HOME

It was 1987. I had been in L.A. for a couple of years since leaving my parents' house, trying to make it in the music business. I was working on a few really cool projects, had a buzz in Hollywood with the press, and enjoyed growing relationships with major music managers and record company execs. From where I sat, my future looked pretty promising.

When I say things were clicking, I mean they were *on fire*. The sessions and music I played were oddball things that most people would never think could be huge—but they were. Between the summer of 1987 and spring of 1988, I played guitar and coproduced a track for an oddball group called Was (Not Was). Out of nowhere, we scored a huge number-one record with a weird song, "Walk the Dinosaur." We traveled throughout Europe, where I also lived part of the time, and played *Top of the Pops* in England.

Don and David Was were wacky writer/producers from Detroit that would never get a record deal in today's bullshit music business, but in 1987, when you could get signed for your originality and talent, they actually had a run on several different major labels. I didn't get them at first when former P-Funk bassist Bootsy Collins and I met Don at Jamie Cohen's CBS Records office in Century City, but after hanging with Don, I fell in love with everything about him and the band. Jamie was Bootsy's A&R man, and he thought Don might be a good producer for the record we were recording, *What's Bootsy Doing?* (What's with the question marks after *What's Bootsy Doing?* and *What Up Dog?* Clues that both these artists would become a big part of my life? Hmm, not sure . . . I will have to consult with the Ouija board.)

In that meeting, we played some four-track home demos I'd made for Bootsy to show Jamie the funk-rock hybrid sounds we were putting together (the demos included the original riff groove to my song "Stand Up" from the first Colorcode record that would come out in 1990). Don heard my guitar and must have liked it, because when I got back to my guesthouse in Beverly Hills, he called and asked me to play on his record.

I also served as a staff producer for the legendary David Kershenbaum, who, during the 1970s and 1980s, hung many of the seventy-five gold and platinum albums he produced on the wall—from artists like Duran Duran, Joe Jackson, Supertramp, Laura Branigan, Cat Stevens, and Tracy Chapman. David would give me what a lot of the L.A. music executives thought were the weird records to produce, like . . . rap. What was rap? In 1987, it wasn't so popular or known, but I was into it.

David also worked on music-based soundtracks. While working for him, I had just finished a full guitar score and appeared in a weird film about two kids who travel in time and love rock 'n' roll. I had no idea *Bill & Ted's Excellent Adventure* would make it big and become so iconic . . . but the biggest rush of all was being in the movie. Not that you saw my face. When you watch the movie again, skip towards the end. Look for George Carlin and his very white face while "he" rips the guitar solo. Then see if you notice the very brown hands on the fret board. In true Hollywood fashion, they dressed George and me exactly alike, shot him from the neck up and me from the neck down, and edited the two takes together.

That led to 1988, when I spent some time jamming with keyboard legend Thomas Dolby, which helped create the reason and momentum why I landed the audition with Rod. I also jammed and auditioned for Andy Taylor. Andy had just quit Duran Duran, one of the world's most popular groups in the 1980s, with chart toppers like "Hungry Like the Wolf," "Rio," and "Save a Prayer." Andy eventually ended up at the Record Plant to produce Rod's fifteenth studio album, *Out of Order*. Andy's manager, Randy Phillips, also managed Rod . . . a lot of connections that would soon involve me.

All my parents could see, though, was an ass-broke kid, living hand to mouth while working on a nearly impossible dream that might never come true. Don't get me wrong: my parents, and especially my dad, had always been my biggest supporters. Dad loved and believed in me, and had not only told me but shown me that hard work and dedication pay off. However, I was smart enough to know that while he appeared to be positive and supportive on the outside, he was deeply concerned.

One morning, the phone rang. It was dad. Very gingerly, he said, "Son, I am not saying that this music thing isn't going to work out for you, but I want you to maybe, *just maybe*, think about what you might want to do, *just in case* this music thing actually doesn't work out." He paused, and then quickly added, "I'm not saying it won't work out, but I just want us to talk about potential ideas."

My dad was so awesome. He didn't have a lot of money, but he did give me endless amounts of love. That's all a kid needs, and I really appreciated it.

"Dad, I am getting close, but don't worry, I will think about a backup plan," I said.

I had no backup plan, nor would I think of one. I had seen visions my whole life. I needed to trust them, because for better or worse, they always came true. They still do.

We talked for a while. After we hung up, I suddenly felt insecure. *God, what if I don't make it? What in the hell am I gonna do with my life?*

When I was in This Kids, and later in L.A., I had seen so many broken people well past their prime who still refused to give up their dreams of making it in music. It still hurts me to this day thinking about their pain. I wish I could make everyone's dream come true, but I needed to focus on mine, because I didn't want my dad to worry. I wanted to make him proud.

Back to 1988. After the concert in Denver, I started to feel I was over the hump and within reach of my mini-goal to not get fired before we played San Diego. I had bigger goals, but I also set mini-milestones— make it to San Diego . . . don't get fired before playing the L.A. Forum . . . and *I gotta play* Madison Square Garden.

In Seattle, I noticed Debbie Gibson was playing the smaller venue next to our arena, the Coliseum, so I walked over after my sound check to say hello to Debbie and my friends in her band. I am still pals with her guitar player Tommy Williams, who now plays in The Hooters. (Later in 1988, we would appear together in all the guitar magazines around the world in a Hamer Guitar ad. Ironically, we appeared with Eddie Martinez, who I replaced in Rod's band, and Jeff Thall, a guitar player I would hire fourteen years later to take my place on the Lamya project I was music directing for Arista Records boss Clive Davis in New York . . . small world, right?)

Afterwards, I met up with Steve Pross from Island Records, who was in Seattle hanging out with Susan Silver, who managed a little unknown Seattle band called Soundgarden. I had seen Soundgarden play at Club Lingerie in L.A. with my friend Aaron Jacoves, who did A&R for A&M records while Aaron and I were working on the *Bill & Ted's Excellent Adventure* soundtrack. I would be Steve's first signing at Island Records, which was still a secret. However, it was no secret that he was one of the first major record-company guys who knew the Seattle scene was about to be something substantial, so he spent a lot of time up there.

Before the show, Steve and Susan were hanging out with me in my dressing room. As we walked into the hallway at showtime, a local security guy became aggressive, pushing Steve and Susan and a few others out of the way. "Clear the hall—Rod Stewart's coming through!" he yelled.

"I'm not here to see Rod Stewart; I'm here to see Stevie Salas!" Susan yelled back.

I quickly ducked out, thinking, *oh shit, I hope Arnold Stiefel didn't hear that. I can't get fired before San Diego!*

Luckily, he didn't.

On August 2, we left Seattle on our way to play in Reno. I could smell the Pacific Ocean that I love so much and San Diego closing in . . . I was going to make it!

When we landed in Reno, we jumped into the limo bus, and the driver told us about this crazy chicken-ranch place, The Mustang Ranch. It was an old-school whorehouse in the middle of the Great Basin Desert that was like a saloon. In other words, in the middle of nowhere. I never would have believed such a place could exist in the modern world, but the driver said it did, so Rod thought it would be fun for us to go there and see it, not for sex, but for a good laugh.

We checked into the Harrah's Casino Hotel in Reno. When I got to my room, I freaked out. My round bed was covered in a leopard-print spread, with little round leopard dingle balls hanging from it and a mirror on the roof! Oh man, this must be the motherfucking Englebert Humperdinck suite to the max! I took photos of this to show Big Al and the gang back home.

The limo picked up the band for our "cultural field trip" to the legendary Mustang Ranch, but Rod decided not to go. He wanted to rest his voice, since we had San Diego and then three sold-out nights at the L.A. Forum coming up.

When we arrived at Mustang Ranch, a bell rang. All the ladies walked out, stood in a line, and one by one said their names and hellos. There were chubby ones, old ones, beautiful young ones, beautiful cougars, cross-eyed ones . . .you name it. After they said hello, if you didn't pick one, you sat around the bar drinking with everyone, including the girls.

The ladies were really nice, but I was very intimidated. I never have been into prostitutes. I wanted to do it, but not for the sex. I believe that life should be filled with comedy and adventure, and this place was packed full of both. I wanted to just be able to say I did it, but I was too chicken (perhaps that's why they call it a *chicken* ranch?).

At the bar, a really funny chubby gal pushed up on Carmine as he told Puerto Rican jokes, while a very pretty young girl chatted up Jeff. Meanwhile, I think due to my baby face, plus the fact I looked terrified, these hardcore Darth Vader–type ladies kept trying to convince me to go to the dark side with them. I was mad at myself for being a coward, but I was just that. None of the guys wanted to get laid; after all, we were surrounded by beautiful women who threw themselves at us every day on tour. Still, we all wanted someone to go for it, just so we would have some fun band stories to share.

Everyone balked, except one guy who decided to take one for the team. I'm not going to throw him under the bus and tell you who it was . . . *Oh no, not me.*

The band was ready to leave the ranch and go back to the hotel and gamble. However, we had to sit in the parking lot and wait for Jeff to come out. Once he did, we were on our way.

At the hotel, I met two beautiful showgirls; soon, one was drinking in my suite with the round bed. She had a boyfriend, so she didn't *really* want to fool around, but she understood that I needed "artistic" photos of that bed. We agreed that we needed a beautiful, naked five-foot-ten blonde to make the photo work; coincidentally, she fit the bill. I may not be a Marco Glaviano or a Herb Ritts, but I shot in black and white and faked it pretty good.

The next day, she came over again for lunch, and she spent the afternoon in my wacky room, walking around naked and drinking coffee. Now don't judge me, I know I said I was going to clean up my act, but what I was doing was not for my own enjoyment, nor was it for queen and country . . . this was for *the arts.* I gave her two tickets to the concert that night, but no backstage passes, because she wanted to bring her boyfriend. I am not the kind of slimeball guy who can fool with another man's girl and act like his friend, but when I was playing the show, I saw them both in the front row rocking out and felt bad for the poor guy.

A few days later, on August 7, I woke up in my deluxe room at the Four Seasons in L.A. in the best mood, because I knew I'd made it. Tonight, we would play Devore Stadium in San Diego, and I had over fifty backstage passes to give to my friends and family, including my dad!

My day started with breakfast at Dukes, my normal spot on Sunset Boulevard. Dukes was known as the rock 'n' roll breakfast place, and all the musicians hung out there. The original Dukes on Santa Monica Boulevard was the best, but even though they moved it to Sunset, just off Doheny next to the legendary Whisky a Go Go, it still had the swagger. I spent a couple hours with my girl, Lynn Oddo, at the hotel pool, but before I knew it, the band was on our plane leaving Burbank, bound for San Diego and my big homecoming.

This was really a big deal, and my success was not reserved just for me. My success belonged to all my family, friends, my old band This Kids, and all the fans, agents, promoters, writers, and managers who supported me growing up in San Diego.

North San Diego County used to be thought of as musical hicksville. I remember my girlfriend in 1984, Suzanne Beveridge, telling me about a girl with bad North County hair. When I asked what that meant, she said, "a small-town haircut like a person who has never been to the city or read a fashion magazine." I may have been a small-town kid from North County, but that was okay, because in North County, we don't hate our people after they break onto the national scene. We take pride in their success, always supporting them. My hometown people supported me, just like we supported pro surfing greats like Banzai Pipeline master Joey Buran, and just like we would soon support local pro athletes Tony Hawk and Shaun White. Oh, by the way, Tony Hawk is the greatest skateboarder who ever lived, and Shaun White is the greatest snowboarder who ever lived. Surfing, skateboarding, and snowboarding are considered the coolest sports on the planet. So much for North County being hicksville!

On the flight down, we hugged the coastline, and I pointed out Oceanside and Carlsbad to Rod. He was already glued to the window, because he was checking out the train tracks along the coastline. He is obsessed with trains.

When we landed at San Diego's Lindbergh Field, I was pumped. I jumped into the waiting limo, and to my surprise, the driver knew who I was. We had never met, but he knew I was a San Diego boy making a big homecoming. The local radio stations had been talking a lot about it.

I didn't bother going to the hotel. Instead, I went straight to the stadium, because I knew my old This Kids manager John Cross had arranged a private limo for me, and both Dale and Big Al were waiting for me backstage. Winston, my drummer from Colorcode, and my then bass player Ralph were hanging out in downtown San Diego, waiting for the show. Since Winston really knows planes, he recognized the sound of the Viscount when we flew our approach pattern to Lindbergh Field, so he too headed to the stadium to meet up.

When I got onstage for sound check, the promoter Bill Silva made a point of walking over to congratulate me and shake my hand. We'd known each other since I was really young. I was so happy to be alive!

After sound check, my friends and I jumped into the limo and took a quick forty-mile drive up to my dad's house in Oceanside. I gave my dad and stepmom Helen their tickets and passes, and then we hauled ass back to the stadium, where I got ready to hit the stage. I was more nervous than normal, because almost everyone I'd ever known growing up was in that audience. Another thing: with Rod, I was a different person onstage, not the local guy who played the backyard parties, high school dances, and clubs, so I was a little worried I might look like a show-off in front of my friends, many of whom had known me since grade school. I didn't want them to think I had changed. *Oh well, there is nothing I can do but be myself. I'm just gonna go out there and rock.*

Then my heart started beating a little funny. Some anxiety set in, but I calmed down and reminded myself to be a pro. This wasn't This Kids doing our regular Wednesday-night gig at the Distillery East club in Escondido with DJ Rockin' Stevie W. There were thirty-five thousand people out there waiting to hear the great Rod Stewart, and I had best get it together.

We walked onto the stage just as the sun was starting to go down, and it was very humid. "The Stripper" music was cranking, and the crowd roar sounded like five 747s taking off. I noticed the crew drying off the white canvas stage floor that said OUT OF ORDER in big black letters. One of the crew guys said, "Be careful. It's really wet out there."

I walked over to my guitar tech, fellow San Diego boy Jimmy Cheese (his real name is Jimmy Phillips, but Winston renamed him Jimmy Cheese because he had stinky shoes). Jimmy handed me my black Fender Stratocaster. It was the same Fender Strat I put together from parts right up the freeway at Joe Orndoff's Musician's Exchange music store in Carlsbad, the same Strat my bro Jay Jardine used to fix for me, and the same Strat local legendary guitar builder Scott Lentz refinished for me when I was in high school. Like me, that Strat was North County born and bred. In a matter of seconds, me and that Strat would hit the ignition button . . .

"1-2-123-crack!"

With Tony Brock's crack of the snare drum, Jeff, Carmine, and I moved to the front of the stage like the Guns of Navarone. The lights blew up the stage and the show was on . . . but within seconds, I almost experienced a total disaster. When I reached the front of the stage, there was a big wet spot, and although my boots had rubber on the bottom, I started hydroplaning, almost eating shit in front of thirty-five thousand people, including all my friends and family. *Thank you, sweet angels, for catching me at the last second.* That slide freaked me out, and I needed to shake it off quick.

As soon as I saw Rod twirl the mic stand and sing, "Who's that knockin' on the door?" everything fell into place, and I knew I was going to be okay.

The show was weird for me, because I could see *so* many of my friends in the audience. Right out of the box, high school friends Lauri Randall and Sharon Carpenter walked to the front of the stage, looking full of mischief. *Oh my God, what are you guys doing?* Then they threw some panties onstage at me and started giggling and dancing. Jimmy Cheese grabbed the panties and placed them on my mic stand. At the end of that song, Arnold Stiefel and Annie Chalice from his office were sitting sidestage next to me. He saw the panties and yelled at me in a big queen voice, "This is a Rod Stewart show, not a Stevie Salas show. Take those panties off that mic!" Jimmy Cheese grabbed them, but I knew Rod didn't give a shit about stuff like that. I was just glad the panties Lauri and Sharon threw were clean ones.

I felt a little embarrassed hamming it up onstage, but I shouldn't have worried about it, because what started happening about midway through the show really tripped me out. Suddenly, a lot of my friends who I had known for most of my life started acting crazy, as if I was some strange rock star. They were screaming and going wild, grabbing at me! At one point, Big Al's older brother, Mark Carrasco—the same Mark who grew up down the street—grabbed my leg after the audience rushed the front of the stage. At first, I thought he was goofing around. (It reminded me of a time at the San Diego Sports Arena, when I got to the front of the stage at a Kinks concert. While lead guitarist Dave Davies was singing and playing, I slowly untied both of his shoes and then tied one shoe to the other. Then I thought how uncool it would be if he fell, so I quickly untied them.)

I thought Mark was doing something silly like that, but when I glanced at him, he looked possessed as if in a rock 'n' roll euphoria. While playing, I leaned down and said, "Mark! Mark! It's only me!" He snapped out of it and let go of my boot.

One of the proudest moments of my life came when Rod introduced the band, because when he said, "On guitar, from San Diego, California . . . " Did that stadium light up! My hair stood on end. Twenty-five years later, as I write about it for this book, my hair is standing up again.

My sisters Rachel and Sandy were in the crowd, as well as my mom, stepmom Helen, a ton of cousins, and of course my dad. The crowd was screaming the whole show, but my usually very energetic and talkative dad couldn't move or say a word. Helen later told me he sat there frozen, with an odd, puzzled look on his face. It had only been about a year since he made that call to me in L.A., worried about the son he loved and his future. Perhaps the spectacle of a stadium show was too much to comprehend. He just couldn't believe that the kid on that stage was *his son*. After all, he'd bought my first Marshall amp and listened to me learning how to play guitar in my bedroom for years. That had to be torture, because I sucked! He helped me buy my first big tour van for This Kids, and he once snuck me six hundred dollars so as not to embarrass me when I screwed up my accounting on the gas card that he let me use for my band. He did everything for me, but I don't think he or anyone else could see this coming. After all, what were the odds?

My dad would soon get used to seeing me on the big stage. He made it out to more Out of Order Tour shows, and later traveled around the world with me on my solo tours. One night in Japan, I introduced him to a crowd of two thousand. When the spotlights hit him, he stood up and waved to the crowd as they chanted "CHIEF! CHIEF! CHIEF!" When dad waved to acknowledge them, he cocked his arm and waved his hand in an up and down motion. Later, my A&R man in Japan, Jun Sato, said "Papa-San waved like pope giving blessing to cloud." He meant "crowd."

However, Helen told me that after the San Diego concert, dad didn't say a word all the way to Oceanside. He was still in shock.

16

SHOWTIME
AT THE LOS ANGELES FORUM

We parked for a couple of solid weeks at the Four Seasons in West Hollywood. It was a fantastic place to stay, because there were always rock stars and movie stars hanging out. This leads me to something bizarre I learned: high-profile celebrities like to make friends with others they feel are high-profile celebrities. Before I was in the band, I would meet famous people who would often act a bit guarded toward me. Now that I was in a big band playing the Forum, famous people would come up to me, give me their numbers, and want to hang out. Whether in Hollywood, New York, London, or anywhere else, once you get a touch of fame, you pick up a brand new set of insta-friends.

In Tokyo, most of the non-Japanese celebs would go to a few certain spots. Since you were famous and they were famous, and you spoke the same language, you would find yourself becoming insta-pals. I saw actor Robert Davi a million times in L.A, and we would never say a word to each other. In Tokyo, we were tight! We hung out all night, and he showed me family photos and all the trimmings. Back in L.A., it was business as usual. We never spoke . . . so weird!

My typical day in L.A. began with me kicking Dale off my couch and waking up whatever girls were crashed out. My friend Heidi Richman, who more or less ran Hollywood in the 1980s and early 1990s, would come over with a pack of her hipster, trendy beautiful friends, and we would go to the pool. I did things there that I would never have done before I was in Rod's band, like walk up and casually shoot the shit with people like Paul Shaffer from the David Letterman show or Klaus Meine from The Scorpions. It wasn't just me; they would do the same! (I didn't think about it then, but these rockers and actors most likely would say hello because Dale and I never had less than fifteen girls with us at the pool.)

What an exciting time to be in L.A. One night, I was sitting at my own table in the L.A. China Club with Winston Watson, my drummer, when David Bowie walked up to my table in front of *tons* of other rock and movie stars to shake hands and say hello. Bowie was only my favorite artist in the world! No one knew that the reason he visited was because I knew his girlfriend, who was with him. David was dressed oddly in a kind of baggy clown suit, and Winston didn't know who he was. After David walked off, Winston asked, "Who was that weird-lookin' dude bugging you?"

My eyes blew open like saucers. Under my breath, I practically screamed, "DAVID BOWIE!"

Winston looked at him again and realized he had iced Ziggy Stardust. Man, was he bummed!

To everyone else in the crowd, it looked like David Bowie came to meet me at my table. I knew it wasn't really as it appeared, but I didn't care: it was the coolest bit of PR I had ever gotten.

Superhot soap star Eileen Davidson and I started running around together, going to her house and to concerts. The best thing ever was when I walked into the trendy Hollywood Canteen restaurant. While standing at the front, waiting for my table, Paul Stanley from KISS got up from his table and walked across the room to say hello. That's the same Paul Stanley that I idolized as a kid. Paul is a friend to this day, and I am not sure if he knows that he was a massive inspiration to me. I'll bet he doesn't care, since he was a massive inspiration to a zillion guys like me.

While having lunch on Sunset Plaza one afternoon with my pal Slim Jim Phantom from the Stray Cats, Paul walked up with British actor and singer Michael Des Barres (you might remember him from the 1980s and early 1990s TV show *MacGyver*; he played Murdoc). I had been touring Europe nonstop because my *Back from the Living* CD was a big seller there. In a fairly pissed tone, Paul said, "Man, Stevie, I was in Europe and I couldn't open a magazine without seeing your face."

That was a proud moment for me, but I learned to never let those moments go to my head. My big brother, Bootsy Collins, told me to always remember that these people aren't my real friends, but my business friends, which is cool.

A couple years after the Rod and Colorcode tours, I had some emotional problems related to this exact subject. When my first record didn't sell like everyone predicted it would, people stopped treating me the same, and it was bumming me out. I called Bootsy, who told me, "You're all right, Stevie; you just tricked yourself into getting your feelings hurt. See, since those people really weren't your friends, then your feelings weren't really hurt . . . you tricked yourself."

God, I love Bootsy. He is always right.

The Four Seasons was fun, but it was really hard to sleep at night because my phone kept ringing off the hook. Between girls who wanted to hang out and party, friends who wanted to party or wanted tickets to one of our three sold-out Los Angeles Forum concerts, record-company friends and execs, publishing-company friends and execs, and my managers at Bill Graham's office who wanted to talk about my new recording contract, plus the people closest to me—Allen Carrasco, Dale Lawrence, Vinnie Chavez, and Lynn Oddo—I was lucky to get four hours of sleep a night. The Four Seasons used to charge a dollar just to make a phone call, and you had to pay some sort of toll on top of that. My phone bill was running hundreds of dollars a day.

I had three shows at the Forum, but a million people who wanted to go. This became a problem, because I was only allowed six tickets total for the three shows. On the first night, I invited my girlfriend Lynn and her actress girlfriend, and it was an amazing night for us all. I think Lynn was blown away; I know I was. The band was now rocking with monster truck force, and we were all coming together, looking after each other. I was the kind of kid that if anyone tried being a badass, talking shit or messing with Rod or any of the boys in the band, I would not hesitate to start throwing blows. By the time we were playing in L.A., the whole band felt that way about each other. We were bonding, becoming brothers.

After the show, we would all hang at the backstage L.A. Forum Club. This was extra cool for me, because it was one of my hangouts before I was in Rod's band. Now, it was over the top. All the people working there were really proud of me, too.

Meanwhile, Jeff Golub taught me so much about guitar playing. I developed my vibrato from watching him, and he taught me why maple necks sounded different than mahogany necks. Most importantly, after the concert, Jeff taught me how to swing from a chandelier at the Four Seasons. He looked like one of the three musketeers, but instead of a black cape, he wore his standard-issue white Four Seasons robe. He would later also teach me how to wear a lampshade on my head, which isn't as easy as it looks.

The next day, I hit the pool, and about a dozen girls joined me. I powered down iced tea to help relieve my hangover, and I enjoyed talking on the phone that the Four Seasons set up for me poolside. All twelve gals with me were either old or new friends. No, I didn't sleep with them all; don't be ridiculous! I probably slept with about half of them, but who's counting? It was the late 1980s, and that's what you did. Don't gasp or think *mal* of me. After all, it's really not my fault. I was not a plumber, orthopedic surgeon, accountant, or stockbroker (a stockbroker would have slept with all twelve. Those dudes are insane). I was a rock star playing three sold-out nights at the L.A. Forum, and my situation comes with the job. If you read the rock star handbook, written by our elder rock lords Led Zeppelin, Van Halen, and The Rolling Stones, you already know that.

We were the kings of L.A., so you can imagine the buzz. Our shows dominated talk on the radio and local news; everywhere we went, we were greeted as heroes. One of the local rock radio stations, KLOS, kept talking about our set list. They were hoping we would play the Rod Stewart classic "Every Picture Tells a Story." In the dressing room we talked about it, but Rod wasn't sure. He said he had never really played that song in concert, which surprised me.

For the second show, I invited Big Al and Dale, who went bonkers with all the girls. They learned the value of an all-access pass, that's for sure. Dale would often push it with his passes and girls, using his wild Rod Stewart–like blonde hair and all-access pass as a way of breaking the ice. Deep down, Rod really liked Dale, but Dale was always nervous around him. Dale *always* wore a hat around Rod, so as not to have a spiky hair competition with him. Meantime, Rod would fuck with Dale to no end. While in our dressing room, Dale would walk in and Rod would stand up out of the blue and chase him out of the dressing room, barking, "No ponces in my dressing room—now get out!"

One night in Sacramento, we did a runner to our limos, and Dale wasn't where he was supposed to be. He was working this girl and didn't hear us stop playing. What happened next blew my mind. We ran up to the cars, and Rod's was the first limo in line. When he reached it, Dale was leaning into the open door, making out with the chick! I was like, *oh shit!* Dale looked at Rod and quickly reached for his hat. While staring straight into Dale's eyes, Rod grabbed the hat and dropped it to the ground, then stomped on it. Then he sped off. I was in tears laughing. I had invited Dale and Lynn Oddo onto the private plane for that show. Being the good sport that he is, Rod had a good laugh about it afterwards with Dale.

During the second L.A. concert, several beautiful girls in the front row were going crazy, screaming and grabbing at me. They were so beautiful that I did something that I had only read about in rock magazines. I grabbed backstage passes and after the last song, while touching fans' hands from the stage, I placed those passes in the girls' hands. The four girls met me in the Forum Club, and I found out a couple were not only beautiful, but also supersweet and kind. We all hung for a while, then exchanged numbers. I made plans to see them at the Four Seasons pool.

As they were leaving, the blonde girl, Dina, and I started kissing (Dina happened to be the reigning Miss California). I noticed her friend watching us, and it made me a little uncomfortable, for good reason. That other girl was not her gal pal from the O.C. It was her *mother*. I was so embarrassed. I had turned into a bit of a rock 'n' roll cad, to be sure, but I did respect my elders.

After the girls and their mother left, Dale, Big Al, and I went to Pennyfeathers, a late-night dinner hang on La Cienega Boulevard. When we were there, I couldn't believe who was sitting next to me . . . the singer Sheena Easton. I'd always had a mad crush on her, so I instantly chatted her up, inviting her to come to my third L.A. show. To my surprise, she dumped her restaurant date and accompanied me back to the Four Seasons for a wild night of love making . . .

I wish! Here is what really happened. She sat next to me, but all I could do was say hello. For some reason, I got all geeked up and couldn't talk to her. What a loser, right?

The next day, I received a phone call from my ex-girlfriend, Julie Airali. Julie was a very serious girlfriend in my life. I had met her a few months after I moved to L.A. in 1985. Like me, Julie wanted to be a rock star. Like me, she also loved partying and dancing in the clubs, and like me, she was wild. We loved each other so much, but we drove each other crazy. Neither one of us was faithful to the other. Who could be at that age in Hollywood, where everything was a go, for better or worse?

As I mentioned earlier, I was working in Europe in 1987 when I started hearing that Julie was cheating on me with a new guy, and they were serious. I was stuck in Europe going nuts, and I couldn't get home to find out what was going on. That made me crazy. Why should I be crazy really, right? I was dating so many girls in Europe, but when you're young and stupid . . . I managed to get her on the phone, and she said it wasn't true.

She lied. After I got home, we saw each other. All seemed okay until I flew to Detroit to record with Bootsy Collins. When I was there, she took up again with her new boyfriend. I flew back to LAX, and she wasn't there to pick me up as planned, so I called her house and her sister told me everything.

Man, was I crushed. I suffered from the worst broken heart of my life. To make matters worse, Julie had joined a band to which I introduced her, and they won some contest and were off to Japan to play. Soon, I would see photos of her with her new boyfriend everywhere.

I am not saying that I deserved payback, because I was quite possibly the worst boyfriend in history, but Julie and her new boyfriend didn't know I was in The Rod Stewart Band when they presented their tickets at the second Forum show . . . their tickets to nosebleed section seats. Julie was with me when I was homeless and starving in L.A. Here I was, three years later, onstage at the Fabulous Forum. I must admit, it felt great to know that her guy had to watch me dominate in front of eighteen thousand people. Later, she told me that when I walked onto that stage, she couldn't believe her eyes. All she could do was cry.

Julie and I are still great friends, just like I am with all my ex-girlfriends. They all forgave me and understood that it was just the way it was at that crazy time. Ohhh, to be young and stupid. Recently, while talking with my old bandmate Rick Braun, he said it best: "There will never be another time like the late eighties and early nineties."

The night for our last Forum show arrived. We still hadn't played "Every Picture Tells a Story," so KLOS decided to turn up the heat by playing the song once every hour throughout the day, with a broadcast plea for Rod to perform the song.

I brought a model gal pal to the concert. I'd met Ashley at one of Big Al's photo sessions. (Al was a pro who had shot quite a few surf magazine covers, starting with our hometown surf magazine, *Breakout*, but he sometimes would shoot fashion. Did he have a way with the ladies!)

Ashley had never been this deep backstage, where only the all-access passes work, so she didn't know the rules. About halfway through the show, I went behind our stage to change guitars, and Ashley thought it would be okay to walk onto the stage to talk. All I heard was "Hey, %^*+^#, let me go! +^%*" When I looked up, I saw two guys carting her away as her arms and legs flailed in the air. Not good.

I asked my tech, Jimmy Cheese, to make sure she was okay. Then I walked back out to rock. We were near the end of the show, and what a great show it was. I was tripping out a little, thinking about Ashley, but also the fact that Billy Duffy, the guitar player from The Cult, was staring at me all night from the second row. I was a little intimidated, but I got over it.

Then Rod walked over to Carmine, Jeff, and me. "Let's do it," he said. "Let's do 'Every Picture Tells a Story.'"

I didn't know the intro yet, so Rod kind of sang it to me. *Well*, I thought, *what the hell. Here goes nothing.* I proceeded to screw that intro up *so* bad. The cool thing, though, was that no one really caught my mistake. They knew I was trying to play the intro, but all would be well as soon as Tony Brock counted us off into the drop D chord.

After that, Rod's voice and body language was cocked and loaded like a superhero on full wail, singing, "I spent some time feeling inferior." Did the Forum ever explode!

The L.A. shows were a massive success. Sure, Rod's mate and old guitar player Jim Cregan hated my playing, as well as the band in general, but who could blame him? He was the man in charge for years, and we were doing it our way, not his. For him, it must have been like seeing another man sleeping with your woman. I know I was screwing up a lot of his guitar parts, but that's his fault: he made his parts too hard! Just kidding, Jim.

It angered us when the *Rolling Stone* review came out and said we weren't great. The reviewer sounded like a person married to the past. Jeff, Carmine, and I were rocking out with an up-to-date vibe, not trying to recapture the old sound at all, yet making sure to respect it while bringing Rod's music into the future.

Rod knew we were mad, and that's when our leader shined in our eyes. He stood up and said, "Did everyone in that crowd go crazy? Was every show sold out, and did the radio talk about how great we were? Don't worry about this review, it doesn't mean anything . . . we were great!"

We were his band, he was our singer, and no one could come between us. We were the boys.

17

AMBULANCES AND HELICOPTERS

Rod started having issues with his voice early in the tour, which resulted in the cancellation of some shows. While I didn't know for sure, it occurred to me that all the partying and drinking until sunup didn't help. I now know it affected Rod's voice, but in 1988 I only knew two things—nothing and sweet fuck all.

When I sang lead vocals in my own band, I learned this lesson the hard way.

On my first solo world tour in 1990, and for many tours that followed, I tried my best to keep the party-in-every-city tradition that I learned from Rod and the boys intact. Consequently, come showtime, my voice would often be shot. When I toured with Rod or Terence Trent D'Arby as their guitar players, it wasn't a big deal if my voice was shot, since I only sang background vocals. However, when I had to handle both the guitar and lead vocals on my own tours, I ran into problems.

During my 1996–1997 tours of Europe and Asia, I played a string of sold-out shows in Japan. Every night, like a good rock star, I would chase the fun. Since I was really famous in the Land of the Rising Sun, plenty of it awaited me. One night, I pushed it too far and stayed out all night with a wild model from Brazil who was in Tokyo for a shoot. At around 9:00 a.m. the following morning, while still going strong, we called it quits. She needed to get to the airport, and I had a big concert that night, along with a ton of press and promotion beforehand.

I left her hotel. Since it was such a beautiful day and I still had a super buzz, I decided to walk back to my hotel. Yes, that meant taking the walk of shame (still wearing my clothes from the night before). As I strolled through the streets of Tokyo, the Bee Gees' "Staying Alive" playing in my head, I wore an appropriately 1970s-style shirt with a big collar, which made me want to strut walk. So I did. I felt like a mix of a very tall and together Bernard Fowler (I'd seen him get his strut on many times) and a very tall John Travolta. However, I would bet that, to the people on Tokyo's streets that morning, I looked like the very unto-gether short Native American Stevie Salas. I'm sure I looked like an idiot, but it wasn't the first or last time. Plus, who cares? When you're famous, you can do stupid shit like that.

When night arrived, I played the last of my three-night stand of packed Tokyo concerts at the Blitz to promote my new *Alter Native* CD. Big stuff. While 2,500 people in the hall anticipated me giving them a great show, I arrived tired and hungover. Before performing, I was on hand for a massive meet-and-greet filled with Tokyo press, mo-vie stars, rock stars, and music execs. I was running late, trying like mad to warm up what little voice still remained. I also was flashing back to 1988 and Rod. This happened to Rod a lot during the Out of Order Tour.

Now, I knew how he felt. It was hitting home in the worst possible way.

I had no choice; I couldn't cancel the show. I sucked it up and prepared to make an ass out of myself. I walked into the meet-and-greet room and tried to talk, but only squeaks and whispers came out. I was embarrassed and in a shit mood, but I shook all the hands and posed for all the photos while feeling like a loser. Yes, that woman was beyond beautiful, incredibly wild and fun, and it indeed was a fantastic night . . . but was it worth it? At the time, after a bottle of Don Julio tequila, I thought so, but at this moment of truth, I knew I'd definitely blown it. Music was my life and the reason for so much of my good fortune.

Weren't these the moments I dreamed of, playing sold-out concerts for thousands of people who wanted to hear songs I wrote? I was ashamed that I had put the party first.

The Tokyo experience took me back to 1987, when I played guitar on an Elektra Records album for a UK artist at Wisseloord Studios, near Amsterdam. Def Leppard was recording the *Hysteria* album at the same time, so I became friends with Joe Elliott, the singer. His band's record was about to explode on the charts. In 1988, Def Leppard toured the world, playing a lot of the same cities and venues back to back with the Out of Order Tour. Our planes were parked next to each other at airports, and we'd often run into each other at the hotels.

One night in San Francisco, I joined Joe and his wife, Carla, for sushi. Carla and I were drinking and carrying on, but Joe wasn't. "Have you quit drinking, Joe?" I asked.

"Stevie, in order to give the audience their money's worth, I have to live as clean as I can if I want to hit those high notes every night. That means no drinking."

Man, that's dedication, I thought. Then I ordered another saké.

Back in Tokyo, I wished I had listened to Joe.

I squeaked hello to the band, along with the promoters, Masa and Toshi from Smash. Then, like a big boy, I walked onstage to pay the price for my night of wilding. I joined Brian Tichy, Rei Atsumi, and Melvin Brannon Jr., and we hit it pretty good. I still felt like a dirtbag, because I knew people in the audience paid a lot of money to see me, and I was doing them wrong.

Before that night, I never really understood how bad it must have made Rod feel when he struggled onstage to find his voice. Trust me: when you can't deliver the goods, you can stand in a room with twenty thousand people screaming your name and still feel like you're alone.

In a way, I was lucky. At least I could burn some notes on the guitar and play extended jams to save my ass—as well as my non-voice. Plus, I was never that good of a singer, so perhaps some people didn't notice my voice was shot. However, when you're Rod Stewart, a.k.a. The Voice that sang the soundtrack of many people's lives, sold two hundred million records, and inspired legendary singers from Robert Plant to Terence Trent D'Arby, people wanted and expected to hear the goods. When you can't deliver, it leaves you with an empty, shameful feeling.

Unfortunately, we were dropping shows due to Rod's throat problems. Around the time of the three big L.A. Forum shows, we flew to Las Vegas and Santa Barbara to set up, sound check, fill the concert hall with sold-out crowds . . . and then announce we were canceling. We were ready to play, but Rod's voice didn't quite make the flight.

When we canceled a show, a moment of near-silence would follow . . . at first. Confused fans talked amongst themselves, trying to confirm that what they had heard was indeed fact. After they digested that information for about two minutes, we started to hear rumblings that sounded like tidal waves building far out on a reef. The realization was setting in: the night they'd planned with the expensive dinner, hot new outfit, and, in some cases, rented limousine was all for nothing. The tsunami built as it moved closer to shore, slowly at first, and then with much haste. Just like that, the crowd would erupt, yelling and booing like pissed-off maniacs. I even saw girls cry hysterically, as if someone had died . . . it was nuts plus!

At the Santa Barbara County Bowl, we faced a big problem. A *big* problem. To get off the grounds from the backstage dressing-room area, we had to exit through the sold-out crowd of five thousand at the small venue—the same crowd now approaching full riot mode. Our managers, along with the promoters, had to think fast. We needed to escape to our plane or we would remain locked backstage for hours as they cleared the crowd and surrounding roads. I'm not sure whose idea it was, but it involved a small, van-shaped ambulance sitting backstage. We lay down in the back, squeezed in like tinned sardines. We piled on top of each other and then covered up with blankets and sheets so no one could see us through the ambulance window.

Slowly, the ambulance and its nervous cargo left the backstage area into the screaming madness, inching through the maniacal crowd. I kept thinking *Santa Barbara . . . wine and cheese . . . isn't this the good life crowd?*

To Rod, I'll bet it sounded like the Brixton riots. Inside the ambulance, we were really squished and uncomfortable. Had anyone farted, Rod would have fired them.

We cancelled a show in Las Vegas on August 6, knowingly ruining that Saturday night for thousands of people. We knew we would face the music (pun intended) and head back to Vegas to make it up to the fans. Twelve days later, we boarded the plane and headed to the Nevada desert to try again. This time, the promoter wanted to make sure everything was beyond perfect for Rod.

When we landed in Las Vegas, I took part in a series of events that, to this day, remains some of the craziest shit I have ever seen. To my surprise, a bunch of helicopters landed next to the plane, where our limos usually awaited us. We ran along the tarmac like commandos into the awaiting helicopters. The choppers took off in a military-style sequence like a scene from *Apocalypse Now*. Before I knew it, we were hauling ass at a low level in single file down the Vegas Strip! I shared my chopper with Rod's manager, Arnold Stiefel, who appeared a little freaked out about flying in a helicopter. To fuck with him a little, I started rocking back and forth, trying to get the chopper to shake while howling like a madman. As we boogied down the strip on our rock 'n' roll special ops mission, Arnold started to melt down. "STOP IT, STEVIE! STOP IT!" he yelled at the top of his lungs.

Eventually, we landed in the parking lot of the Aladdin. Black limos pulled up next to the choppers. This confused me, since we were only twenty yards from the private backstage entrance. How long does that take to walk, fifteen seconds? Then again, why walk when you can ride in style? We jumped into our personal limos, which took us into the backstage area and dropped us off for the show.

I used to read about shit like this in *Creem* magazine in my dad's mobile home. Now, it was actually happening to me! The decadence of the moment was as old school as it gets, truly one of the greatest rock 'n' roll memories of my life.

What created this memory, more than anything, was that our singer had his voice back together and we could fly down the Strip and give the Vegas fans a great show.

18

THE MTV AWARDS ... WHEN MTV STOOD FOR MUSIC TELEVISION

I woke up at the Ritz Carlton in Chicago at the crack of noon, pretty beat after a long run of Canadian concerts as Labor Day weekend began. I was amazed how much the Canadians could drink, and not just the fellas, but the gals, too. My size twenty-eight pants were getting snug, which wasn't good, since we were getting ready to play on the MTV Music Awards in a few days and I needed to look lean and mean on TV. Millions would be watching.

Rod booked the band into a Chicago recording studio. His recording engineer, George Tutko, flew in from L.A. Bands never played live on the big TV shows in 1988, because they just didn't know how to make live music sound good on TV. Instead, they would lip-synch, which was *really* embarrassing. In Europe and England, lip-synching was the norm; I even did it many times on the big UK music show *Top of the Pops* while thinking nothing of it.

If you think that's weird, then check this out: lip-synching at live gigs was normal, too. I'll explain that better. In 1987, with Was (Not Was), we would spend promotion days performing "Walk the Dinosaur" on tons of TV shows in England and continental Europe. We lip-synched on all of them. At night, we would go to a big club where people were dancing to a DJ, set up gear, and lip-synch "Dinosaur" to the crowd. It felt really weird to do that, but only once did we get shit for it. In

Norway, after a lip-synch club promotion, I was sitting in the dressing room with Don, Gemma, and some of the band members when a guy barged in, really upset about us lip-synching. In broken English, he said, "Why did you doing that pretend play?"

One of the Was (Not Was) singers, Sweet Pea Atkinson, was a straight-up Detroit pimp. I was worried he was about to bury his entire Florsheim shoe up that guy's ass. I understood the dude's frustration, and I felt like an idiot faking the song.

Twenty years later, I had to lip-synch in front of a million people in Times Square for New Year's Eve 2007 with *American Idol* winner Jordin Sparks. Even worse, there were megamillions watching on TV around the world, so this was really silly. We played two songs, but only the second song, "Tattoo," was broadcast. One of my best friends, TV writer and host Spike Feresten, was cohosting the event for Fox. He also hosted his own late-night talk show on Fox, and I used to write music gags for the show. We thought it would be funny if, during the first song, Spike grabbed one of my guitars from my tech, Alex Alvarez, and crashed the stage, pretending to be playing with us. Normally, you could never do something like this, especially with an *American Idol* winner, but it pays to have huge connections in the music business— and I do. Jordin's manager, Stirling McIlwaine, was also a close friend, and he loved Spike (who wrote for *Seinfeld* and won an Emmy for the famous "Soup Nazi" episode). After I laid out the plan, Stirling said, "OK, but be careful with Jordin."

Then Spike arranged for the Fox camera crew to capture the footage so we could use it on his talk show later that year.

We started lip-synching our song. Jordin was dancing and the sea of kids were screaming . . . then Spike flew onto the stage like a kamikaze, bouncing off me and then over to Jordin, who looked at me with a puzzled glance. I was her music director, and I forgot to tell her what was going to happen! I acted pissed off, yelling at my tech and security guys, telling them to grab this stage crasher. Security grabbed him and chucked him off the stage, and it was all captured on film. Jordin is such

17. Too Rolling Stoned. (Courtesy of Stevie Salas Archives)

18. The Singer. (Photo: Bruce Kessler)

19. King Size Children. (L to R: Jeff Golub, Tony Brock, Randy Phillips; courtesy of Stevie Salas Archives)

20. Arnold, Get to the Chopper! (Courtesy of the Stevie Salas Archives)

21. The Boys Bringin' It. (L to R: Tony Brock, Jeff Golub, Carmine Rojas, Me, Rod; photo: Allen Carrasco)

22. Soul Mate. (Courtesy of the Stevie Salas Archives)

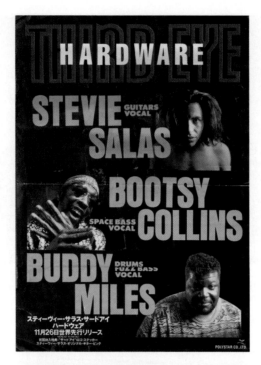

23. You're Kidding, Right? (Courtesy of the Stevie Salas Archives)

24. You Gotta Love Your Friends. (L to R: Matt Sorum, Tom Peterson, me, Sass Jordan, Brian Tichy, Rick Nielsen; courtesy of the Stevie Salas Archives)

25. It's a Big World. (Photo: Invisible Hands Music UK)

26. Anything Is Possible! (L to R: Jimmy Page, Me, Zakk Wylde; courtesy of the Stevie Salas Archives)

27. Papa-San. (Courtesy of the Stevie Salas Archives)

28. A Little Less Shattered. (Courtesy of the Stevie Salas Archives)

29. 25 Years Later, and It Still Feels Like a Dream. (Photo: Greg Hackett)

30. How Did a Native American Guitar Player with a High School Education Get a Job at the Smithsonian? (L to R: Me, Robbie Robertson [formerly of The Band], Tim Johnson. Photo: Jefferson Miller)

31. There Is No Place Like Home. (Courtesy of the Stevie Salas Archives)

32. I Am Too Young for This! (Photo: Kimberlie Acosta)

a pro that she never flinched, nor did she ever ask about what had happened. She just kept dancing and lip-synching.

The reason Rod and the band booked time in the Chicago recording studio was to record a live version of "Forever Young," Rod's new hit single. Rod didn't want to lip-synch the album version on TV, so he thought we should record a high-quality live version for the band to synch. Rod could then lay live vocals over it on TV. This was a much cooler approach. I was pretty confident, since I had spent a lot of time in the studio as a staff producer for David Kershenbaum, and I felt my studio skills were evenly matched with the other guys in the band. We spent all day recording. It was a great experience.

In 1988, nothing in pop or rock music was bigger than the MTV Awards. In my view, they were more important than the Grammys and American Music Awards, because they were so cool. All the biggest and brightest came to the MTV Awards, which only artists and their guests could attend. Today, they pack in tons of punters and make them all act like they're having the wildest night of their lives. The real players don't go to these events any more. Or, if they have to attend, they leave as fast as they can. When I was working with Mick Jagger in 2001, he showed up at the MTV Awards and walked the red carpet for all the TV and press, then cruised into the venue and directly backstage into a waiting limo to take him somewhere else. It gave viewers at home the idea that all the big stars were there, but in fact, it was bullshit.

Not in 1988. The MTV Awards had true music credibility, and it was a great honor to be there.

On Tuesday, September 6, we met on set at the Universal Amphitheater at 10:00 a.m. to rehearse for the MTV Awards. That really sucked, because to me, a rock 'n' roll night owl, 10:00 a.m. was like 6:00 a.m.! We were opening the awards, a very big deal, so we needed to block for the cameras. I brought a special guitar from the Hamer factory, an early-production Californian model that owner Jol Dantzig gave me. It was a hot-looking bright yellow, a shape almost no one in the world had ever seen, since it was one of the first Californians made. I put that guitar on the cover of my first Colorcode record; eventually, the Hard Rock Café bought it from me for their La Jolla wall. That fulfilled another dream of mine: to have my guitar on a Hard Rock Café wall. Now, there are nine Stevie Salas guitars in Hard Rocks around the world, but get this: in Honolulu, where surfing is the sport of kings, they mounted my Carlsbad-made Scott Chandler surfboard on the wall, next to my guitar. To me, that was the ultimate tribute.

In my dressing room at Universal, something crazy happened. Superstars walked in and hung out, talking to me. I was and still am a *huge* music fan, so when Steven Tyler and the other Aerosmith boys walked into my room, I freaked out! It was weird to be viewed as an equal by guys like the great Aerosmith guitarist Brad Whitford, but to him, I was one of the boys, not some stupid kid fan. Aerosmith was soaring on the charts, in the midst of one of the greatest comebacks from drug hell in music history with their platinum record, *Permanent Vacation*, which churned out five big singles. They were huge when I was a kid, and they were huge again.

Brad and I talked about amps and guitars, and he seemed to really care about what I said about tone and playing . . . fucking weird! Then bass player Tom Hamilton joined in, saying he couldn't use the Spector bass because it was sonically too big for his band. I sat there and thought, *this is a conversation me and This Kids bass player Paul Martinez could have.* You always think that when you're in a little local band, if you make it big, things will be different. Other than the money and comforts, band members still talk and fight about the same things.

We were staying at the Universal Sheraton hotel. So were a ton of the other artists. Legendary actor Telly Savalas, the bald-headed star of *Kojak*, was hanging out in the hotel lobby (someone told me he lived in the hotel when he was on the West Coast). I saw MC Hammer with something like fifty dancers, which I guess he wasn't paying, because many of them walked around stealing food from old room-service trays in the hallways. I felt bad for the girls. I didn't dig that shit. These dancers were about to appear on the MTV Awards, and Hammer should have treated them better. INXS was hanging out, too, and, like us, they were surrounded by lots of girls and party favors. Like us, they were touring a massive hit record, in their case *Kick*. Also like us, their shows sold out wherever they played. It was yet another time our paths crossed.

We spent most of show day backstage, dealing with rehearsals and wardrobe. It was an amazing day, because I met so many of my heroes. I saw Dick Clark from *American Bandstand*, whom I had watched since before I could remember. When he walked towards me, I smiled, and he stopped and shook my hand. "Hello, Stevie," he said. "I hope you have a great show tonight with Rod."

I was in shock. As the producer of the show, he was on the case.

As we neared showtime, someone yelled, "Stevie, you're late! They're waiting for you in hair and makeup!"

I ran towards the makeup room. As I started scaling the stairs, I noticed Steven Tyler walking down towards me. I am not normally shy, but I was freaking out inside, so I looked straight ahead as I ran past him. When I reached the top of the stairs, I heard this scratchy voice say, "Hey."

I stopped dead in my tracks. Steven gave me a dead-on look. "Who, me?" I asked.

"Yeah, you. What's your hurry? You look like you're running from the schoolteacher or something!"

I told him I was late for makeup, but he made me walk down and formally shake his hand and say hello. As I walked back up the stairs I was on stun . . . I couldn't believe what had just happened to me.

Twenty-five years later, while filming Steven Tyler for a documentary film I am producing about Native American musicians, I told him that story. Funny, he didn't remember it at all, but it sticks with me as one of the most amazing moments of my life.

We'd rehearsed our show appearance with the live version we recorded in Chicago, but as showtime drew close, I could hear mumblings backstage.

Something was wrong. Rod's voice was bothering him again. The last thing you ever want as a famous singer is to appear on national TV and sing like shit. At the last minute, we made the switch from our live, band-recorded version of "Forever Young" to the studio version, with the band and Rod lip-synching. I was so bummed, but I completely understood. The last thing I wanted to see was our hero embarrassed . . . but boy, did we get the piss taken out of us by the bands seated in the front row when we lip-synched live!

I walked onstage and said hello to the host, Arsenio Hall. To my surprise, my old pal, Thomas Dolby, walked to the front of the stage to say hello and shake my hand. That made me look pretty cool to a lot of people, including our keyboard player, Chuck Kentis, a big Thomas Dolby fan. I then said hello to Matias, the guitar player from The Scorpions. Matias was sitting with a gal I knew years before, Ami, now a backup singer for Mötley Crüe. She was half of the awesome Motley Crüe *Nasty Habits* duo. The other half, Donna McDaniel, was as talented and sweet as they get. She and I would spend some time together. (She sang on my *Electric Pow Wow* CD in 1993.)

Since we were opening the awards, we took our place on the stage. That's when I noticed many of the front-row seats were empty. As they started counting down to thirty seconds, in walked INXS and Aerosmith to take those seats. Right away, the great INXS front man Michael Hutchence started making silly faces at me. I tried hard not to laugh, because it was showtime. It was no use.

We started lip-synching, and the boys in Aerosmith and INXS fucked with me and Carmine. When Jeff Golub and I stepped up to fake our big guitar solo, all the guys stood up in front, doing the two-finger V over their lips while their tongues darted in and out, the universal sign for you know what. If you ever watch a recording of that performance, you will see me cringing and laughing. That's why.

On that night, there was no way I could have known that nine years later, Michael Hutchence would make his last appearance on a live stage, sitting in with my band Nicklebag at the Viper Room in Hollywood. I also played guitar on his solo record. He was indeed a fantastic rock star. I still miss him.

After we played, we took our second-row center seats. I brought my girl, Lynn Oddo, and Dale Lawrence, but Dale had to sit up in the nosebleeds. Lynn had an all-natural body reminiscent of a classic bombshell actress. She borrowed a crazy green dress that my singer friend Laura Hunter wore in the *Disorderlies* movie. It looked great on Laura, but on Lynn and her curves it was beyond . . . so beyond that Arsenio Hall called her out on TV and made her stand up for the world to see.

While this happened, Jeff was going crazy alongside me, because young porn star turned legit actress Traci Lords was sitting in front of him. I had hardly ever watched porn growing up, so I had no idea who she was.

Later, while I was in New York, a friend who would become a major part of my life, Tonjua Twist, happened to watch a rerun of the show. "Who was that girl with you at the awards in that cheesy dress with all the holes in it?" she asked.

Tonjua was winding me up. She was one of the youngest fashion editors at *Vogue* magazine, but what she said was true. Lynn's dress was an L.A. dress, not a New York City dress. High fashion or not, Lynn still looked insane in it.

The MTV after-show parties were amazing. It felt so great to fit in on my own star power and credits. In the past, I relied on one of my record-company pals, like a Jamie Cohen or Frank Chackler, to get me into these events. I felt so alive.

After the awards, the band had a few days off, so I drove south to stay at my parents' house in Oceanside. In the morning, when I went for a jog in my neighborhood, people walked out of their houses, cheering and clapping for me. I'd lived in that house since the end of tenth grade, which meant my poor neighbors suffered through many horrible-sounding band rehearsals in my parents' garage. I guess my appearance on the MTV Awards made it okay.

19

GARDEN PARTY

One night in 1985, Rick Perrotta ran into Studio A in Los Angeles, wearing a necktie around his head like a hippie's headband. He danced like a 1950s teen idol while strumming Ricky Nelson's famous acoustic guitar—the one that said "Ricky" in leather. Ricky had been recording at Baby O studio, which Rick owned, but Ricky was not there. However, his gear was, so Rick thought it would be funny to prance around with his guitar while we laughed and screamed "Ricky!" like star-crazed girls.

It remained funny until the following week, when Ricky Nelson returned and freaked out. Word was, he packed his acoustic guitar a certain way and could tell when someone messed with it. (Sadly, a few months after this scene, he would die in a tragic plane crash in Texas.)

Flash forward to September 16, 1988. I boarded a late flight at LAX, bound for New York City. Ricky's megahit, "Garden Party," was stuck in my head on nonstop playback, even though I don't really like the song. I was en route to making another dream come true—playing Madison Square Garden. The first show sold out so quickly that promoters had to add a second show, which also sold out. It surprised us, since we were already playing two sold-out nights at Jones Beach Amphitheater, just a half hour away on Long Island.

Rod's *Out of Order* album was selling great, and the tour was hot! Our band now ran with Rolex precision, as tight as nine guys could get, both musically and personally. We trusted and believed in each other. Sure, I still got my balls broken from time to time—after all, I was still the overconfident little brother who needed to be kept in check—but I was doing my share of ball breaking, too.

I once made the mistake of losing my cool a bit when Rod teased me about the intro of "You're in My Heart" (which I now played perfectly). "Fuck that shit!" I yelled.

Rod, being ever the secure badass that he was, said, "Ahhh ha ha ha! No one ever tells me that! Ahhh ha ha!" He laughed in my face, which made me laugh, too.

During the flight to New York, the beautiful British actress Finola Hughes sat next to me. She had starred in some soap operas, but I really knew her from the John Travolta movie *Staying Alive*, in which she played the hot diva with a bad attitude. On the plane, she was anything but a diva, but me? That's a different story. For reasons I still can't figure out, I pretended to have no idea who she was. As we chatted away, she mentioned acting, so I said something like, "Ohhh, you want to be an actor?"

"Well, I am an actor."

"Have you ever gotten a speaking role? Do you have a SAG card? If you need help getting an agent, perhaps I could help out." I even asked if she had to waitress on the side while hitting various auditions. What a shit!

Finally, Finola broke it to me that she was a big movie star. I was like . . . *oh my!*

She was such a great person. We talked throughout the red-eye flight, and I invited her to see one of our Madison Square Garden shows. After we landed, we collected our bags and walked out with our drivers, who were waiting at baggage claim. She walked to her tiny limo, while I stepped into a crazy superstretch. I don't remember why I had a limo this size, but no matter.

Ten years later, I was attending a Hollywood party with Slim Jim Phantom when we ran into Finola and her husband, the photographer Russell Young. I said hello and reminded her about our flight and my practical joking. We all shared a good laugh. A small-world story: in 1989, Russell Young (who Finola would marry in 1992) shot some amazing photos of me in London that appeared in many magazines when my album *Colorcode* was released there.

I checked into the Ritz Carlton on Central Park South and slept most of the day. Late that afternoon, the band left for Long Island to play our first sold-out show at Jones Beach. It rained on us, but it was still fun. We were planning a late night out on the town, so I walked into the Ritz Carlton bar early and ordered myself a drink. "Garden Party" was still playing in my head . . . the mind is a funny thing. While I was having my drink, pop star Julian Lennon walked in. "Hey, are you waiting for Carmine?" I asked.

He flashed his classic boyish grin and sat down with me. I tripped out a little, because there is a lyric in Ricky Nelson's song about John and Yoko being at the show—"Yoko brought a walrus / there was magic in the air." Now, I would play the Garden, and Julian Lennon would be at *my* garden party.

Two years before, Carmine and Chuck Kentis played in Julian's band when he toured to support *The Secret Value of Daydreaming*, and Carmine was his music director. Julian is an incredible artist and songwriter. We are the same age, so Carmine served as his big brother, too. During the next twenty years, we would run into each other all over the planet.

One night much later, I heard noise in the front yard of my Hollywood Hills house. To my surprise, Julian was in the front yard barfing in my bushes, and my neighbor, Heather from Texas (remember her?), was helping him out. In Hollywood during the early 1990s, you never knew what surprises lurked in the bushes. Or anywhere else.

Jeff wanted to pop by a club and see the rockabilly killer Robert Gordon play, so I left with him, with a later plan to meet Carmine and the gang at the China Club. Jeff and I rode in a giant white limo, which looked funny parked on McDougall Street, deep in the heart of bohemian Greenwich Village.

Earlier at the Robert Gordon gig, I got super stoned on some chronic, and it made me really paranoid. After the show, Jeff wanted to hang at the Scrap Bar, but I was so freaked out from the weed I told him I would meet him inside. I sent the driver into the pizza place on the corner to get me a slice and proceeded to trip out people who peered into the back of the limo and saw me. I kept the doors locked. Everyone around the Scrap Bar looked like a drug addict, Hell's Angel, or some type of rocker. I even saw Billy Idol's lead guitarist, Steve Stevens, walk past. Steve was an idol of mine, too. Since I was so stoned, I could hear my voice echoing in my head. I thought it best to stay locked in the back of that limo. I was so high, I might have even been wearing my seatbelt.

I finally went to sleep around 4:00 a.m. Three hours later, the phone rang. I was a little discombobulated. "Hello?"

To my surprise, it was my friend Pippa, with whom I'd been partying recently in Montreal. "I'm in the lobby," she said.

"What lobby?"

"Yours!"

Apparently, she and her little friend Courtney started drinking and decided to take the all-night bus to New York City to surprise me. In Montreal, Pippa and I were growing very fond of each other, but we had never been intimate. That changed in New York after she walked into my hotel room. She socked it to me in English *and* French.

Later that morning, we were hungry, but I had only been to New York one other time, so I had no idea where to take Pippa for breakfast. I wanted to order room service, but when I saw the cheapest thing on the menu was an eighteen-dollar peanut butter and jelly sandwich, I thought, *we'd better go out and find a spot*.

That afternoon, we said our good-byes when I left for our second concert at Jones Beach. While at sound check, I got a message that someone from Island Records was on the phone for me at the Jones Beach ticket office. Three weeks earlier, Island Records had signed me to my first recording contract, and no one knew about my record deal in the Rod camp.

I freaked out. I didn't want Rod or Randy Phillips to hear anything about my Island deal, because they didn't need to worry about my loyalty to the tour. After finally gaining their total trust, I didn't want to upset the apple cart. I picked up the phone. "Hello?"

It was Pippa. Since she'd been with me when I received my Island contract, she knew all about it. She was also smart enough to know that someone would actually find me and bring me to the phone if it was a legit call from a record company. She decided to stay in New York long enough to see our show, so I sorted out tickets and passes for her. We would enjoy an on-again, off-again love affair for years. Eventually, we stopped all that madness, and we remain the best of friends.

The next day, the band took a quick flight to Portland, Maine, and played another sold-out show, but I was a little sluggish onstage due to the fact I'd lost my mind stuffing myself with Maine lobster beforehand. When we returned to New York, we headed straight to the China Club, where Carmine had set up a bash. The China Club was practically our home base in NYC.

Once inside, I met Fatima Bergstrom, a supertall Swedish model. I have never been insecure about being with women taller than me. When I saw her, I didn't care if dating her meant I would have to carry around a stepladder! She brought along two other skyscraper Swedish friends, whom Rod dubbed The Swedes. The next night, Fatima and The Swedes met us at the hotel. We threw ourselves into a big New York night out, dropping into the D Bar, China Club, MKs, and finally Nell's. I arrived as happy as a pig in mud, with a tall beautiful model on my arm who had legs up to her neck (Rod was onto something when he wrote that lyric in "Hot Legs").

However, something happened earlier in the evening that knocked me off balance. Carmine knew four really fun girls that worked at *Vogue* magazine—Kate, Inga, Elizabeth, and Tonjua. I couldn't get Tonjua out of my head . . . *what was wrong with me?* The Swedes were in the limo with us, but so were the The Voglets, as we called them. Tonjua hated me right away, giving me a hard time the whole night . . . not that I didn't have it coming. Since she was dishing me so much shit, I decided to leave her a little something to think about. When we dropped off The Voglets in front of their destination, another club, Tonjua stood up to leave the limo. I reached over and grabbed her cool, stretchy ruffled pants and yanked them to make her jump. I don't know how it happened, but she moved as I yanked, and her pants crumbled to her ankles! She turned bright red and socked me in the arm. I headed home with Fatima, who I was mad about, but with Tonjua still on my mind.

The next night, Carmine, Rod, and I took off for a private bigwig fashion event. When I arrived, the first person I saw was Tonjua. I almost didn't recognize her. The previous night, her hair was slicked back, but now, this green-eyed Cherokee Indian's long, beautiful hair was free. I knew right then something was terribly wrong with me. She said, with a big smile, "If you mess with my ruffles again, I will cut your heart out."

When I was in fifth grade, I rode my bike to a Cub Scout meeting behind my elementary school. A little girl in one of the front yards sometimes stopped me. "Hello. What's your name?" I asked.

"Tanya."

I don't know why, but when that little girl said that, it triggered something in my mind, like it was supposed to mean something to me. I always remembered that moment, for reasons far beyond me. That is, until I saw Tonjua. That long-ago memory came back, leaving me short of breath. I knew this was a sign, something I needed to take very seriously. Eventually, I did.

We left our New York hub for a few days to play The Centrum in Worcester, Massachusetts, along with the Civic Center in Providence, and the world-famous Boston Garden, home of the Boston Celtics. The Boston Garden opened on my birthday, November 17, but in 1928—

making it just a tad older than me. I'm not kidding when I tell you it was the oldest, crustiest place we played on the Out of Order Tour.

The sports fan in me didn't care. I walked around the arena looking at (and, sorry to say, *smelling*) the history while taking photos of the sixteen NBA championship banners hanging from the rafters. Larry Bird, Kevin McHale, Robert Parrish, Danny Ainge, and their Celtic teammates spent the 1980s battling it out with my Showtime Lakers. This was the Celtics' greatest run of success since they dominated the 1960s, and this old arena with the parquet floor had absorbed it all.

When we went onstage that night, George Thorogood was hanging out on one side of the stage. I smiled as I thought back to my best pal, Big Al, singing George's big hit, "Who Do You Love?" while I strummed the guitar in eleventh grade. Earlier that afternoon at the Four Seasons, while in the lobby, I saw a guy who looked like George, but I paid him no mind. The dude was talking to a lot of our people, so I asked Carmine, "Who the fuck is that George Thorogood looking muthafucker hanging out over there?"

Carmine gave me a funny look. "That's George Thorogood."

Oh.

After the show, we flew back to New York, and Carmine and I met The Swedes at the China Club, but I still had Tonjua on my mind. The next day, I met Tonjua and The Voglets at the Patricia Field party. I had never seen so many beautiful models on a catwalk. These women were stunning . . . was I not in Oceanside anymore! Remember in *Star Wars*, when Obi-Wan Kenobi said, "Be careful, Luke, your eyes will trick you"? He was right. All the girl models turned out to be dudes.

That night, we played the first of our two shows at Madison Square Garden, and I was in a pickle . . . over girls. *Okaaaay, let's see, I will invite Fatima the first night and Tonjua the second.* That's what I did.

While in the dressing room, Carmine's grandma showed up in our dressing room. What a firecracker! She was barking orders at everyone . . . even Rod. She was an exceptional woman, the heart of Carmine's world, and he glowed in her presence. It was beautiful to see him like that. Later, before we went onstage, some big shots from the

Garden, as well as the New York Rangers NHL hockey team, walked into the dressing room and presented Rod with a Rangers jersey that had "Stewart" laminated on the back. They shot a few photos, and then Rod said his good-byes. After they left the room, Rod rolled up the jersey and chucked it into the trash. "C'mon boys, let's give it to 'em," he said.

The house lights dropped, the crowd roared, and the band left the dressing room. Except for me. I reached into the trash can and grabbed that jersey as a souvenir. I still have it today.

When I walked onto the Madison Square Garden stage, I had a feeling that was beyond my control. I almost started crying. My subconscious took a moment to let the enormity of the journey soak in, to realize exactly where I was and what it took to get there. I took a moment and kissed the stage, giving thanks.

We lit up the Garden. The band, as always, showed no mercy. When the smoke cleared and the first show was over, we knew we'd kicked ass.

It's really weird. You can be the most seasoned band in the world, but whenever you play L.A., New York, or London, your nerves are always on edge. Something about those places makes every concert feel like the first. When the shows go well, you feel a tad higher than the top of the world.

Remember my new friends at Island Records? This time, they actually did show up in person—causing me to worry all over again. I tried to keep them away from management and Rod, because I was so afraid they would find out I had a record contract. The band was working together, really trusting each other, and I didn't want them to think I wasn't committed to the tour and in with both feet. Rod, Randy, and Arnold never caught on. For the moment, my secret was safe.

The second show also was off the hook. Fatima really wanted to go, but I had already asked Tonjua, so I danced a little wiggle-wiggle to keep Fatima from getting too angry. Afterwards, Rod was ready to party in a big way. Tonjua and my buddy Ray took his town car to meet Rod and Kelly Emberg at MK.

That's when I walked straight into a hornet's nest. The Voglets were there. So were Fatima and The Swedes. So was I . . . with Tonjua on my arm.

Oh shit. "Why didn't you call me after the show?" Fatima asked.

"Uh uh hmm well, ummmm . . . "

Ever the streetwise hipster, Tonjua peeled off to the bar, leaving me to catch hell on my own. I didn't know what to do, so I ran to the closest person I had to an on-site father figure to seek advice. I told Rod what happened. "Okay, you'd better sit here next to me until this blows over," he said.

That's what I did.

I know, I know . . . what a coward. I bailed on both girls and I felt like shit.

Then Rod and Kelly started getting into it, and she was crying. Our great, triumphant night in which we conquered Madison Square Garden was going south in a hurry.

MTV VJ Downtown Julie Brown sat next to me at our table. She and I drank and talked until Julian Russell, the owner of the London club Stringfellows, took us out for a late bite to eat.

I needed to make it up to Tonjua. The next day, I called Bill Graham Management to book a couple of tickets for us to see Sandra Bernhard. To my surprise, Spider Middleman was playing sax with Sandra. He was an old L.A. friend who worked with me on the *Meatballs and Spaghetti* cartoon soundtrack. At Sandra's show, I also signed a bunch of autographs, which I wasn't used to doing. A lot of people in the crowd recognized me from the Out of Order Tour.

During the night, I realized Tonjua was more than just another girl. Even though neither of us wanted to move any further forward, it felt like we were falling in love. Perhaps it was just me. After all, I would soon find out she still had a boyfriend in L.A.

The band spent many nights in New York City during the tour, with more concerts added at the Meadowlands Arena, across the Hudson River in New Jersey. The Voglets and The Swedes kept us company constantly. When we would leave a restaurant or club with a load of girls, my job would be to walk all the girls outside and out of harm's way, so the paparazzi couldn't shoot photos of them with Rod.

Our partying and madness reached an all-time high. It led to a night when Rod, Carmine, and I were stuck in traffic on Madison Avenue, our limo packed with a ton of girls, including The Voglets. The girls decided they were going to strip us, and they proceeded to go nuts, attacking us and ripping our clothes off. We were stopped dead in Madison Avenue gridlock when, at about 2:00 a.m., Rod threw open the limo door and fell into the street with at least four girls tearing at his clothes. I fell out next, my shirt torn off and my pants around my ankles. I clutched my private parts as I tried to roll off the street. The girls screamed and laughed as people in the surrounding cars tried to figure out what the heck was going on.

From flat on my back on Madison Avenue, I looked towards the front of the limo. I saw Rod running down the street, weaving through the traffic in bright, tight leopard-print underwear, his pants around his ankles and girls chasing him. I heard someone in another car yell, "Oh my God! That's Rod Stewart!"

During our final night in New York, Rod, The Voglets, a couple of other gals, and I were inside the China Club, playing truth or dare. At first, we rolled out harmless stuff: "Truth: what year did you lose your virginity?" or "Dare: stand up and scream, 'I'm a nympho!'" Soon enough, it grew crazy. To meet one dare, one of the girls had to get up and order drinks with her tits hanging out. On another, Rod walked across the room from our table to the bar and ordered drinks—with his pants around his ankles. He was so awesome that he could pull it off with the regal look of an aristocrat.

What was my dare? To stand on top of the table and drop my pants. No problem. Even though I wasn't wearing underwear, I knew my long

T-shirt would hang over the old wedding tackle. I stood up and dropped my pants. Then one of the girls reached over and pulled my T-shirt up.

I jumped back down. It was too late. It was freezing cold in New York, and you know what happens to a fella when it's cold. "It's so small!" Inga exclaimed.

"It's not that small; it's just freezing in here!"

Rod leaned over. "You're just like me, mate. Next time it's cold, before you pull your trousers down, reach down there and warm it up a bit."

My garden party turned out to be a lot better than Ricky Nelson's. I played Madison Square Garden three more times in my career, but Cat Stevens and Rod were right . . . the first cut is the deepest.

20

HAWAII NINE-0

It's not like I needed a vacation, since every day on tour felt like one, but it excited me that we were playing two shows at the Blaisdell Arena in Honolulu. I have always loved the beach and sun, not to mention surfing, so you could say Hawaii is my kind of place.

The plan was to play our two shows in Honolulu, then take five days afterward to recover. That's my idea of a dream week: playing my guitar and rocking fifteen thousand people in a sports arena, surfing in the day, and meeting sun-tanned women at night—while drawing a chubby salary . . . Thank you, God!

Since the flight from Atlanta to Hawaii is about the same distance as flying from Los Angeles to London, we didn't take our own plane. The nine of us flew commercial on American Airlines, along with Don Archell and Tracy, Rod's hair and makeup girl. Just a few months earlier, I took my first-ever first-class flight, which blew my mind. Now, after flying everywhere in our private plane with our own flight attendants, crossing the country first class on a commercial plane almost felt ghetto. I thought about that for a minute and realized I needed an attitude adjustment. I reminded myself to be thankful, because this good country living could vanish just as quickly as it had appeared.

We had to make a stop in Los Angeles. When we arrived, Dale was waiting to join me on the flight to Honolulu. This would be our second

trip to Hawaii together. His decision to pay for my first trip in 1985
when I was broke would now reap big dividends for him.

That night, we checked into the New Otanni Hotel on Waikiki
Beach. I should have been tired after eleven hours of flying, but
couldn't be bothered. Once I smelled that Hawaiian air, I was ready to
rock. The band was having a dinner party at a swanky steakhouse later
that night, but I couldn't wait that long to get out, so Dale and I jumped
in a taxi and hit the beach. We stopped at a new club that Dale heard
about, and as always, we showed up at the back door with my Rod
Stewart all-access pass. A security guy stood there, talking to two young
surfers, and I could see they were trying to do the same thing—skip the
front-door line, get in for free, and be treated to VIP status. We were
standing behind the surfers, waiting for our turn to name drop, when
one of the big Hawaiian security guys lifted up a surfer by his collar,
saying, "You want in free, bruddah?" He bitch-slapped him a couple
times really hard. "You still want in free, VIP?"

Dale and I looked at each other in horror and then I quickly slipped
my backstage pass into my pocket. We turned around and sheepishly
walked away with our asses tucked in like a couple of scared dogs.

We showed up to the band dinner party. As always, tour manager
Henry had the place decked out in beautiful girls and froufrou drinks.
The whole band showed up, but the boys weren't their usual peppy
selves. After dinner, most of them grabbed girls and headed back to the
hotel to chill.

Not me and Dale. We decided to go to the Pink Cadillac, a livelier
hangout filled with young people our own age. The last time we were in
Hawaii, we'd met the Camacho brothers, who owned the place. We
were hoping to say hello again. My pass worked like a charm at the front
door, getting us access to the owners' private table in the VIP area,
which was loaded with beautiful people. We partied late into the night,
dancing and drinking with all the tourist girls. Some of the ladies were
really wild and sexy, but I was attracted to this beautiful, conservative
brunette from Calabasas, in the Los Angeles area. She was sweet and
kind and had these soft eyes that really got to me. There were a lot of

other wild girls that, I could tell, wanted to go back to the hotel and get all *Lord of the Flies* naked and wild, jumping around on the bed, but I was stuck on my sweet girl. Plus, I only wanted to hang out with her, even if it meant holding hands and talking all night. My new lady's tall blonde friend was dancing with Dale.

When the club closed, we headed back to my room for drinks. My girl was only drinking water, but this was her idea, which made me happy. The girls had been in Waikiki for a week and were leaving in the morning. After we reached the hotel, Dale split with his blonde, leaving us alone.

We laid on my bed with all the windows and doors open, talking while enjoying the sweet Hawaiian air. She then asked me if I would please make love to her. "Excuse me?" I asked. She said it was her last night in paradise, and she wanted to have an affair to remember. I sure didn't see that coming!

Before we could move forward with her great idea, she shared a few concerns. She was a bit of a germophobe, and her insistence that I use condoms, no matter what, seemed over the top. Fine by me.

The moonlight blasted through my open windows and doors as we made love until sunrise. The whole experience seemed surrealistic. It wasn't like twenty-two-year-old college-girl sex, but much deeper. She held me intensely and seemed to be filled with sadness as well as joy. I really felt a bond with her, which hardly ever happened with me.

When she left, she refused to give me her contact info. Strange, since we both lived in L.A. "I can't tell you why, but I won't be able to see you ever again. I will never be able to thank you for how you made me feel tonight," she said.

I was confused. "What is it, are you married?" She swore she wasn't. She hugged me tightly and left.

I never saw her again. I was really bummed out, because we shared something really intense.

Meanwhile, Dale's blonde friend got his number. A few months later, she called Dale to tell him that her best friend had just died from leukemia. The girl who was with me in Hawaii.

These best friends knew the end was near, so they decided to take a final trip to Hawaii. She told Dale how wonderful her girlfriend felt after our night together, and that it was everything she'd hoped for.

The news cut my heart like a knife. I broke down and cried.

The next day, Dale and I rented mopeds and took a ride around Waiki-ki, looking for banana pancakes and coconut syrup. After we ate, I decided to show up for our sound check at the Blaisdell Arena extra early. We had to rent a lot of gear for the two Hawaii concerts, which can be risky business, since you never know if the gear will be in great shape or not.

My gear was fine. Man, was it *fine*!

A man walked in. "Stevie Salas?"

"Yeah, that's me."

"I brought you these Marshall amps that Jimi Hendrix used for the *Rainbow Bridge* concert and movie."

"*Really?*" I plugged those bad boys in and blew one up right away. No big deal, since our techs fixed the tubes. I then hit the "on" switch. Within five seconds, I had "Foxy Lady" on blast!

I was also excited to be playing the same arena where I saw Elvis play on TV as a kid. I always remembered him walking around with a ton of leis around his neck . . .What a great day! I was in paradise, playing with Jimi's amps, and now all I needed to do was find a shitload of leis to make this experience complete . . . no problem!

Other than the stadium festivals, we had not played with an opening act, but for the two Hawaii shows, our old pals Hall and Oates were opening. Or, I should say, our old pal and his partner. Only my man John Oates ever bothered to say hello. The skinny cat, Hall, always showed up with a bucket of ice.

We played the first show, and I had a different vibe than normal. The Hawaiian people were so friendly and sweet. I would look out into the packed arena and see and feel love. The *aloha* spirit. Perhaps it was my inner aborigine picking up on the deep soul in the room, I'm not sure, but those smiles were infectious.

After the show, Henry informed us that we had another high-end dinner party to attend. He pulled me aside and said that a very wealthy, older six-foot blonde fan wanted to meet me. *Really, Henry?*

You might think this is strange, but I didn't fall for girls who assumed that, just because they were so fine, they could arrange to be with me. Guys with money do this to girls all the time, and I think it's lame. I want a girl who has some personality, can make me laugh, and can laugh with me. If she happens to have a few bucks, that's gravy, but it's not important.

I told Henry to keep the gal on ice. "If I'm feeling it, I will decide then to meet her," I added. He agreed.

When I got to the dinner, I played it cool, working the room and having fun with the boys and some of the friends and family members. I noticed the six-foot power blonde sitting at the bar, smartly dressed and very beautiful. I finally went over to say hello, but I made my vibe clear, that I was not some bimbo guitar player chomping at the bit to be with a woman. After about three minutes, she said great things about the concert that made sense musically, cracked a joke that got us both laughing, and bought me a drink. Five minutes later, we left for the hotel.

What can I say? She met the criteria.

Our private Out of Order Tour plane featured two incredible fun and beautiful flight attendants, who took care of us like family. As it turned out, one of the band members was receiving more care than the rest, elevating him from family to big daddy status.

For several months, our fun-loving trumpet player Rick Braun had been getting jiggy with one of the flight attendants. Not that anyone in the band or management knew it; we didn't. I'm sure the flight attendant didn't want anyone to know, out of concern for her job security, and Rick didn't want anyone to know . . . because he was married. I have a feeling that Nick, our trombone player, knew, because he and Rick were like peas and carrots. Me? I had no idea, nor did I care. That stuff was none of my business . . . but it became everyone's business in Hawaii.

From what I gathered through various mumblings, our flight attendant knew Rick was a married man and was okay with that. I know people who mess with married men and women always say that they are cool with it, but I don't know if that's ever really true. Before the second show, Jeff and I caught wind of some crazy shit happening around our hotel beach. Our flight attendant was freaking out. Why was she even in Hawaii? I wondered.

I started putting things together. I saw Rick and his wife together, then I saw the flight attendant acting weirdly.

That's when I found out. Let me tell you, I was surprised. None of us knew how the crafty Rick pulled this one off; it wasn't like he had animal magnetism. Jeff and Carmine figured he had to be hung like a donkey. Nothing else made sense. I do know that the tall, handsome, creative, lanky sweet-hearted party animal was not a wolf like Jeff, Jimmy, Carmine, or Rod. Or me, for that matter.

On the other hand, our flight attendant was a strong, ballsy kind of a gal, not to mention incredibly sexy. I figured she was the predator in that relationship, having sized up Rick as an easy kill. I'm sure Rick was just happy to be tiptoeing in those tulips.

When we boarded the bus to go to the Blaisdell for our second show, I saw Rick sweating bullets, and not from the Hawaiian humidity. Well, every fella knows that chicks have ESP for shit like that. A simple odd look or wisecrack from another woman, complemented by a barely noticeable, uncomfortable reaction from a fella, can spell out a whole crime novel to a woman. That's what it did. By the way Rick was stressing out, I figured his wife was bringing the heat.

Sammy Hagar once told me that, even if his first wife were to walk in on him with another woman, under no circumstances would he break from the story of I DIDN'T DO IT. She could catch him butt-ass naked with a girl, buns up and kneeling, wheeling and dealing, and he would still say, "I DIDN'T DO IT."

Rick was not Sammy Hagar. Rick was a sweet guy . . . a sweet guy who was fucking up, but still a sweet guy.

It was just a matter of time before Rick, his wife, and the flight attendant carried on with bursts of tears, mixed with yelling and drama. Poor old Rick looked like he was in hell. None of the boys teased him on this one. We were unified brothers looking after each other, but we all knew there was nothing we could do to help. Rick would have to ride out this shit on his own. We were all there for him if he needed to talk, but we figured this was going to play out. Badly. Which it did.

After the two gigs and heavy family drama, everyone decided to take the rest of their vacation in Maui. *Fuck that!* Carmine and I wanted to stay in Waikiki, where the action was. C'mon, we just played two sold-out nights at the Blaisdell. There was no way I was going to Maui.

Rod and the band, including Rick and all the static, left Waikiki for Maui, while Carmine, Dale, and I stayed behind. That's when I pulled off another massive move, thanks to Henry. Rod had an insane all-glass suite that took up the entire top floor of the hotel, with a wraparound balcony to boot. It was truly my dream house. The tour booked and paid for the suite for the entire week, so Henry told me I could have it. When Dale saw the place, he practically shit his pants!

Now that we had the sickest party pad in Hawaii, it was time for the party to start. Carmine introduced me to his local friends, Peter and Leslie, who knew everyone on the island; soon, we were hitting all the spots. We would start at some great restaurant, then move to a club and dance for a while. Let me tell you: Carmine can shake his round ass on that dance floor! We would then visit the Pink Cadillac to cuss and lie, or to a rock club called The Wave to jam with the band. I love Carmine so much, and I really love the bass line he played on Bowie's song "Let's Dance," so every time we would jam, I'd get him to play that bass line for me. I was always hammered by this point, and so was Carmine, but he would still kill it.

Finally, our Hawaiian holiday ended. It was the greatest vacation I'd ever had. Several years before, I almost went to Hawaii with my friends for my high school graduation present, but I asked my dad to use the money to buy me a Marshall guitar amp instead. At the time, it was a tough choice, but in the end, it was the right choice. I ended up making it to Hawaii playing my guitar.

We spent our final day in the ocean and on the beach, with a stereo on the penthouse-floor balcony blasting East Memphis soul music we could hear all the way to the sand. Yes, Dale, Carmine, and yours truly lived and loved wildly and often that week. The food was great, the drinks were zesty, and we always left the girls smiling.

21

CANADA LOVES ROD, BUT . . .

By August 29, we had already been in Canada for ten days on our first swing through the country, playing multiple sold-out shows and constantly turning up in the news and papers. We were popular throughout the U.S., but in Canada, they treated Rod almost like the second coming of The Beatles.

Except in Montreal. We left from Toronto one day to play a quick concert in Saratoga, New York. When we flew back to Montreal, you would've thought they'd never heard of us.

Canadian customs, that is. As soon as we landed and walked to customs, the Canadian love was gone. Let me write this in a French accent: In Toronto, we were big shots. In Montreal, we were shit.

First off, they made us empty our plane. That meant every piece of gear, luggage, bottle of wine . . . *everything*. We'd been living on that big plane for two months, so there was a lot of stuff to unload. We knew then we were in for a long night. We started out acting cool, but the customs guys were total assholes to us. After a while, we started turning into obnoxious assholes, too. We had all been drinking, but Rod was really living *la vida loca* that night. Kelly Emberg and baby Ruby were with us, too, and I could tell Kelly was tired. Any mother knows how busy a baby keeps you, but when you add a giant global touring act and its nine grown-up babies into the mix, you can imagine how tired one might be at midnight. Needless to say, she was kind of crabby. Rod didn't help. Or, I should say, he couldn't help himself; he was winding her up like mad.

While the plane was being unloaded on the tarmac, the customs officials lined us up in a room single-file to show our passports, one by one. When Kelly reached the front of the line, the biggest customs prick of them all exploded. His eyes bugged out like Marty Feldman, and his face turned from pasty white to a lovely shade of bright red (the color actually agreed with him). He then yelled out in broken French English, "Whot eez dis! Dis eez a federal document!" What the heck was he carrying on about?

All of a sudden Kelly screamed, "What's that?"

I saw Rod hide behind a potted tree, with a classic Rod Stewart tight-lipped, open-eyed look and a wide, ornery smile. I looked over the counter and saw Kelly's passport opened to the photo page. Someone had taken her passport when she was asleep and drawn a squirting penis next to her photo. To make matters worse, the penis looked like it was shooting sperm in the direction of her head. That drawing was a familiar sight on the Rod Stewart tour . . . it was called a knob (British slang for penis).

There were a couple of unwritten rules in The Rod Stewart Band:

1. If you get drunk and fall asleep on the plane, during any travel, or in a bar during a good night of drinking, you may wake up with eggs in your boots, shaving cream in your hair filled with cigarette butts, peanut butter behind your ears, a Magic Marker mustache, or a knob drawn anywhere on your person; and
2. Always keep your important documents hidden well. Otherwise a knob would certainly find its way onto them.

When I first joined the band and was fucked with nonstop, I found knobs on all my things. At first, I would get mad, but after a while, I just pretended I didn't know about it. Before a show one time, someone in the band drew two huge sperm-squirting black knobs on my white stage speaker cabinets. I said *fuck it* and went onstage and played, not saying a word. Soon, the knobs were cleaned off. Another time, I had just received a new white vest from Lipp Service. I walked into the dressing room only to find a big squirting knob on the back of it, rendered in black marker. I took the stage and rocked the show. Every time I stood next to Rod or sang into the mic with him, I spun around so everyone could see that knob on my back. By acting like I didn't care, we all had more fun.

I learned to play it cool from Rod himself. At one show at the Saddledome in Calgary, we were in the dressing room while Rod was outside with a group of corny church ladies that had won a meet and greet with him. They were called The Canadian Lady's Debutante Society or something like that. While Rod was talking to them, the band built a little platform and stuck a wooden chair with wooden slats on top of it. We then took a big silver fire hydrant off the wall and, in heavy black marker, drew some squirting knobs on it. We wrote, in big letters, "Stomach Pump 5 Gallons of Sperm." Then we shoved the hydrant hose up the bottom of the chair slats so it looked like an enema hose. We added some other signs on the wall to make the place look like a hospital. We wanted to wind up Rod about the old famous myth that he had given a bunch of guys head and had to get his stomach pumped (a total bullshit rumor, I might add).

Little did we know that Rod planned to walk into the dressing room with all the Cornball Square Ladies Society. When they arrived, he saw our massive build-out—and so did all the ladies. Without so much as a blink of his eye, he said, "C'mon ladies, let's take these photos." He slyly slid himself in a perfect position so our chair setup was directly in the photo behind him and the ladies. He didn't cringe once, but I sure was cringing! When I saw him play the situation like that, I knew Rod Stewart was the king of them all.

I was in a good mood, because that late August afternoon in Calgary, I received a phone call from Morty Wiggins at Bill Graham Management, telling me I had just been given the biggest recording contract in Island Records history for a new artist. I was busting at the gut wanting to tell someone, but I had to keep it a complete secret from Rod and the band.

Canada brought us good luck. After I left The Rod Stewart Band, Canada brought me good fortune; it still does. Here are just a few things that happened for me over the years. First, I made big records with Sass Jordan and The Jeff Healey Band. (Jeff was the great blind guitarist featured as the house band in the Patrick Swayze movie *Road House*.) Then, I played two sold-out nights at Massy Hall in Toronto with my band Colorcode, the SARS Festival with The Rolling Stones, AC/DC, Rush, and many others in front of nearly five hundred thousand people, and landed my first executive producer credit and hosting role in a TV series with my music comedy show *Arbor Live!* Now in its fourth season, it is like a combination of *The Larry Sanders Show* and *The Office*. I also spoke at the governor general's mansion in Ottawa about the importance of funding the arts, and I even landed my two-year stint at the Smithsonian's National Museum of the American Indian in Washington, D.C., and New York City because of a speech I gave at Jukasa Studios on the Six Nations Indian Reservation.

The Canada connection definitely started with Rod. We were playing sold-out show after sold-out show, and as soon as we would leave the country, they would book more shows for us.

The one and only time I felt bad luck in Canada happened a few months later, when we were in Toronto for Thanksgiving. *American* Thanksgiving, that is. It might have been my first Thanksgiving not spent with my family back home in Oceanside. We were staying at the Four Seasons, but since our Thanksgiving was not a Canadian holiday, there was nothing planned for the band.

The day started out pretty cool, because my Minneapolis musician friend St. Paul Peterson, the lead singer in The Family, Prince's band, was at my hotel with his badass musician brothers Ricky and Billy. They were in town to play Massy Hall with The Steve Miller Band and wanted to keep their Thanksgiving football tradition alive. We were in semiuptight Yorkville, without a football field in sight, so we started a game right there in the street. For a minute, it made me feel like a normal kid back home, playing in front of Allen Carrasco's house with Joey Buran, Tom Kerr, and all the neighborhood dudes.

We were playing Maple Leaf Garden that night, so after our sound check, my Ovation guitar rep, Rick Wheldon, and I drove over to Massy Hall to watch St. Paul and his brothers sound check with Steve Miller (I endorsed Ovation acoustic guitars from 1988 until 1991). I invited them to meet Rod and the boys at a special Thanksgiving dinner we were having upstairs at the Four Seasons.

After our shows, we made it to the hotel. It looked like it was going to be a great hang. We hosted a ton of beautiful Canadian gals there, as well as plenty of good Canadian whiskey, but when the dinner came, we were missing something very important . . . good food! They served little round red potatoes with slices of turkey breast. That's it. We were a little depressed, but what the fuck, we were rock stars in a country full of people who loved us, so we got over it and hit the town.

It seemed like we were constantly staying at the Toronto Four Seasons. Soon, we had a regular group of girls that would come and party all night. My room was always packed, and in the morning, it would often look like the scene of a massacre with half-naked women passed out all over my bed, couches, chairs, and floor.

Remember the girl I'd met in Miami who said that Tony Brock called me immature? Well, she showed up one night. I had now been on the tour for months, rather than three days, and I was seasoned enough to know she was cuckoo. She was like the girl in the movie *Nurse Betty*, who really thought she had something going on with this actor on TV. ("Nurse Betty" is the nickname of my son's mother, too, but not because of craziness.)

The Miami girl was now in my room, telling me things about "Roderick." *Who the hell was Roderick?* She was worried about "Roderick" because of this, and "Roderick" needed that, because . . . *blah blah blah*. Then I realized she was talking about Roderick *Stewart*. "Roderick" . . . I've never heard Rod called by his given first name before or since. We could tell she was nuts, but she didn't have a place to crash that night, and all the girls thought she looked beautiful walking around naked in her high heels, so we let her crash.

One of my friends looking after me was Leslie, a flight attendant. She took me to my first-ever after-hours booze camp (that's what Canadians call a secret late-night drinking bar), and she also took me for my first-ever slice of pizza. *Slice of pizza?* In 1988 California, you would only buy a whole pizza; we didn't yet have places that sold single slices. Since Leslie was a flight attendant, she could fly out and hang with me in cities like Winnipeg. Winnipeg was the first city where I appeared in the newspaper because of the place I ate dinner. It was news, I guess. *The band had reservations here, but ended up there, and Rod had veal, and Stevie fell in the snow, etc., etc.* It was weird.

When I walked into the Winnipeg Arena for the first show, I was freezing. I looked around and discovered the whole floor was covered in ice beneath the wooden deck. It was a hockey rink, the home of the NHL Winnipeg Jets! I never knew they left the ice under there; I thought they froze it before each game. We weren't watching too much hockey back in San Diego, so what did I know?

While in Winnipeg, I ran into my old San Diego gal pal, Tanya Glickman, whose boyfriend, Marty, was our singer in This Kids after Pat Pinamonti left. She was living in Winnipeg, going to school.

After the last show, Leslie, Tanya, and I ended up at a cool late-night jam spot called The Blue Note, along with Rod, the band, and a bunch of other gals. We joined in and rocked. I sang a James Brown song, and Rod loved it. He thought about having me sing it during my funk-guitar solo in the middle of "Do You Think I'm Sexy." I never ended up doing it, but we came close.

The following week, as November ended, we came back to the Four Seasons. We ran into Bob Dylan, who had stayed at the Four Seasons in Vancouver when we were there in August. Among those in Dylan's band was the now-famous bass player Kenny Aaronson, who I had seen in the Rick Derringer Band opening for Foghat when I was eleven, thanks to my sister Sandy and brother-in-law Steve. Kenny was a close friend of Jeff Golub's, because they played together in Billy Squier's band for years. It was Kenny's birthday, and he was not feeling well. Jeff pulled me aside and said, "Let's get a few of our Toronto girls, and get them to do something special for Kenny, since it's his birthday."

I would never say no to my big brother Jeff, so we grabbed a couple of the more adventurous ladies and asked a favor. We took the elevator to Kenny's floor and got the girls to strip naked (except for their high heels). They walked down the hallway and knocked on Kenny's door, while Jeff and I hid with a camera. Kenny opened the door, and the biggest grin stretched across his face when they serenaded him with "Happy Birthday." Jeff and I couldn't stop laughing, and then Kenny saw us.

Jeff Golub is a good friend to look after his boy that way. I got some great photos, too!

The next night, while having dinner with Rod and Randy Phillips, Randy looked me dead in the eye. "So you signed a big recording contract as a solo artist with Island Records?"

I sat there and swallowed the lump in my throat as they both stared at me. "Uhhh, well, ummm . . . yeah, I did, but I don't want to leave the band." Then I asked, "How did you know?"

"I know everything," Randy said. Which he did. He has always been one of the most connected people in the music business. That hasn't changed, since he now runs AEG, the massive music company.

"Guys, I was gonna . . . "

Rod interrupted, laughing. At me. "What's so funny?" I asked.

He shook his head and mumbled something beneath his breath, while continuing to laugh. "What?"

"For years," Rod said, "the guys in my old band were always trying to get a major-label recording contract, never doing it. Just like that, you go and get one."

I could tell Rod was proud of me and not angry. Nor was he worried, because Rod was not insecure at all. I say this because you would be surprised how many egotistical superstars wish their band members ill will when they try to strike out on their own. Not Rod.

I then told Rod and Randy the truth. "I've been signed since August, but I didn't want you to know, and then worry that I wouldn't give my all for the band."

Rod knew that we were all in a great place as a band, not only blowing the crowds away, but also having fun doing it. We weren't just saying we were great. We *were* great. There is a big difference.

22

WHAT? NO LOVE FOR ROD IN D.C.?

After a great night that included another lights-out concert, this time at the Civic Arena in Pittsburgh, I had to say good-bye to my beautiful new friend Natalie. She dressed like a Native American girl, and the combination of her long blonde hair, soulful smile, gorgeous curves, and moccasins proved to be too strong for me to fight.

We jumped on our plane and flew to Cleveland to play the Richfield Coliseum. During this stop, someone in the promoter's office gave me a message from my boys Don and David Was. They were in town playing a concert and wanted to visit me at sound check, but the promoter didn't think they would make it due to their promo schedule. I was happy to hear from Don, but bummed that I wouldn't be able to see them.

Only a year earlier, Don, David, and I, along with singers Sweet Pea and Sir Harry, clocked a lot of studio recording, TV taping, and passport stamping time when the *What Up Dog?* LP came out in Europe. It spawned several hits, including "Walk the Dinosaur," "Spy in the House of Love," and the song I coproduced, "Out Come the Freaks." Hearing from them brought back those memories.

After our concert, Jeff Golub and I thought we would stay in Cleveland for the Was (Not Was) show, since Jeff was close to his hometown of Akron. Instead, we heeded Henry Newman's advice and stayed with the band.

Hearing from the Was (Not Was) boys led to a funny side note: Rod's daughter, Kimberly, used to like to run up behind me, giggle while pulling my shirt, and call me "Mr. Dinosaur Man." She was maybe ten years old, but because I was in the video for that song, she saw me all the time on MTV.

About eight years later, I ran into Kimberly backstage at a Rolling Stones concert. She had grown into a young woman, but I teased her a bit and asked, "Do you remember what you used to call me?"

She blushed and smiled. "Yes . . . Mr. Dinosaur Man."

By this time, my aging process had begun. For all I know, she could have just been calling me Mr. Dinosaur Man because of that!

When we hit the stage in Cleveland, it was *game on*. After our regular set, we played a few encores and then jumped into limos for the ride to Rod's plane. Our tour book said we were headed for Indianapolis, since we were playing there the next night, but Rod wanted us to fly to Chicago instead. The plane changed direction and headed to the Windy City. We checked into our hotel, and Rod told everyone to meet in thirty minutes at the hotel bar so we could hit the town and do our thing.

During this time, Rod started changing our travel schedule a lot. He based it on which cities he felt had the best wine, women, and song. After all, we really liked to have fun! Atlanta, L.A., New York, Toronto, and Chicago became our main hangouts. Since we had already spent a lot of time in Chicago, people treated us like locals. We knew exactly where to go, and on which nights, to find whatever we fancied. If we weren't sure, our great brown leader, Carmine Rojas, sorted it for us. He brought in his team of gal pals, Brooke, Patty, and Ginna, who were our Chicago tour guides.

The next afternoon, we flew to Indianapolis to play Market Square Arena. After the show, we flew back to Chicago. Once on the flight, we engaged in our band ritual, with Nick Lane and Rick Braun mixing the mudslides. After five months on tour, Rick and Nick had the drink mixing down to a precise science. Rick mixed the booze and ice into a blue, barrel-shaped container, and then Nick performed his customary Ricky Ricardo Latin rumba shake on one knee, tossing the container of mudslides over his head and not stopping until he achieved the perfect blend and temperature. Some of us would even chant "Babalu" to fire him up. I have no idea what was in those drinks, other than Bailey's, but Nick and Rick were indeed chemists. I assumed it was because they were horn players, and aren't horn players better at math than drummers and guitar players?

When they felt the mix was just right, they poured drinks into our glasses. We gathered around each other, thinking of ourselves as proper gentlemen, but most likely looking like a sweaty pack of gay caballeros. Then someone would set the pitch, and we would sing our customary "Mudslide" song in perfect harmony. The song stuck to the notes of "Amazing Grace," but we substituted the word "mudslide" for "amazing grace." We sang it like college frat boys, reminiscent of the movie *Trading Places*, when the old college goons at the tennis club sang their alma mater's fight song to the girls. That's what it was like, except for one thing: we'd sing "Mudslide" like the old spiritual, with Rod's scratchy, soulful tone holding down the middle. I'll bet we could get the grande dame of Deep South cinema, Scarlett O'Hara herself, to peel her panties off and throw them at us.

Back in Chicago, our full days off gave us the freedom to partake in guilt-free madness. However, my days were filled with meetings. The first was with Elektra Records exec Mitchell Krasnow, who a year earlier had given me a development deal that enabled me to work on my own music for my solo career. I had turned him onto my close friend, Amp Fiddler, the keyboard genius who took Bernie Worrell's place in George Clinton's band. Mitch played Amp's demos, telling me he planned on offering Amp a recording contract. Amazing news! Since I was signed to Island, I couldn't go further with Mitch, but I owed him a lot, since the demos that I made for him at Elektra helped me with my Island deal. Furthermore, Mitch introduced me to then-Elektra A&R exec Steve Pross, who made me his first signing when he moved over to Island.

I also met with Jol Dantzig and Frank Untermyer, the owners of Hamer Guitars, the guitar company I endorsed. Jol educated me about old late-sixties Marshall amplifiers, selling me a 1969 hundred-watt super lead head and a 1968 mini-Plexi fifty-watt that I still use to this day.

Then it was back to the boys. After the sun set in the early December midwestern sky, the boys piled into the limos. We started with a proper dinner somewhere, which I loved, because with Rod, it was like getting an education in fine dining. He was a perfect blend of pub-drinker bloke and classy Englishman, so I never felt intimidated, but empowered, like I belonged, too.

Rod was in rare form. He told our limo driver to take us to Alexander's, one of our drinking spots. When we pulled up, a line of people crowded the front. As always, we sent our limo driver up to the security guy to ask him to tell the owner The Rod Stewart Band was inside and we needed a secure table. I saw a couple girls I knew in line, so I jumped out of the limo to say hello. Rod had a look on his face that meant some shit was about to go down. Out of the corner of my eye, I noticed his blonde rooster head poking into the driver's section of the limo through the boot. "Watch," I whispered to the girls.

He worked his body through the boot like a drunk, slithering snake until he sat in the driver's cabin. He slid behind the wheel of the limo. The people outside turned their heads towards the limo as the engine roared. He dropped the gas pedal to the floor, which lifted up the car as he dropped the tranny into drive. I won't say he lit the tires up, but it was pretty damned close. He blasted off while all the people out front watched the limo driver freak out, running like a madman after the car while yelling, "Hey, come back!"

We had stolen our share of limos on this tour. Each time was as good as the first, and this was really funny, since our driver was running down the street in hot pursuit. The poor, sweaty driver returned to the parking lot, pacing back and forth, not quite sure what to do. Since I was standing there watching this spectacle, I could have been cool by telling him not to worry and that we do this all the time, but I thought fuck it— let the poor bastard sweat. In the end, I knew he would get a fat tip, plus he would always have a great story to share with friends and family about the great Rod Stewart stealing his limo.

After fifteen or twenty minutes, the big black limo pulled into the lot with Rod behind the wheel. Try to picture that spiky big blond hair and signature snout as a proper limo driver, rolling the stretch into the parking lot. Rod, the band, and the girls calmly walked up to the Alexander's entrance as if nothing had happened. With his proper British accent, Rod thanked the limo driver while handing him the keys. Into the club we went.

Following two nights of 24/7 partying, it was time to get back to work. We jumped on the Rod Stewart plane and flew to Cincinnati to play the Riverfront Coliseum. The boys were half hungover and half chomping at the bit to get back onstage to resume what we really did for a living. If you were to bear witness to any of our parties, you might think that partying was indeed our main gig.

I was excited about Cincinnati because my big brother, Bootsy Collins, lived there, and I hoped to coax him out to the concert. Not to be. When I called him, he told me in that classic Bootsy voice, "Ahh Stevie Bubba . . . Uhhh, I don't need to be out there when I ain't on the charts. But Big Brotha Bootsy loves you indubitably, Baby Bubba." I really wanted him to see me on the big stage, since he'd first worked with me during the days when I starved. However, I understood where he was coming from.

Like every other show, we opened with "The Stripper" theme; before I knew it, we were halfway done with the show. We went offstage to rest up for our second set when I heard someone talking about Poison lead singer Bret Michaels. He was a big star, and normally guys like him would receive super VIP status, but Rod and the boys could give two shits about a glam metal band, so he wasn't in our backstage area. I wasn't a Poison fan, but I was still excited to meet him. Little did I know that in 1991, one of my best friends, lead guitarist Richie Kotzen, would join Poison as a baby-faced twenty-one-year-old, causing a bit of madness (but Richie can tell that story in his book). I would also spend years working at the Rocket Plant studio of Poison's drummer, Rikki Rockett, where I would record and produce my records *The Electric Pow Wow* and *Back from the Living*, as well as Sass Jordan's *Rats* record. I always found the guys in Poison to be supernice.

I decided to walk around backstage and look for Bret, but I couldn't find him anywhere. When I asked our security guys where he was, they told me they punked him, putting him in the after-show room for contest winners . . . all the way on the other side of the arena. *SHIT!*

I only had fifteen minutes or so before taking the stage. *Fuck it.* I grabbed a few drinks and ran through the backstage hallway until I got to the room. I opened the door, and there was Bret with his then-girlfriend Suzie Hatton, an up-and-coming singer. They were sitting in there all alone! I introduced myself, gave them a drink, and we had a great little hang. Bret was very nice, and I felt guilty that we had disrespected him, but he didn't seem to care, or perhaps not even know—so no harm, no foul. As we talked, I heard the arena crowd start screaming, signaling the start of the second half of our show.

I jumped up, said good-bye, and ran as fast I could in my cowboy boots to the stage on the opposite side of the arena. I heard Jeff's guitar making noise, which meant the band was already onstage. It freaked me out, because Jeff and I start the second set together. I ran up the stairs, and my tech Jimmy Cheese handed me my pink Hamer right as Tony Brock counted off the tempo, signaling the dual-guitar opening for "Dynamite." *Phew!* Just made it!

Our schedule changed yet again after the show. Our tour book said we would stay in Cincinnati, but instead we flew to Washington, D.C.

On the flight, I told the guys about Bret Michaels, but they were like, "Why do you give a shit about that guy?" They meant nothing personal, but they were considered some of the best musicians in the world, and their old-school sentiments about bands that can't play and singers who can't sing ruled their way of thinking. I can't blame them. I came from a different generation, and I didn't give a shit either way, as long as they were cool (that would change for me as I got more seasoned). On this tour, if I was your friend, that meant I was a friend of your music, too, whether I liked it or not. Why? Because I feel a person's music is part of who they are.

In 1994, another guitar player friend from my generation said something about this subject that made a lot of sense to me. Zakk Wylde and I were in Milan, Italy, playing at a big summer rock festival that Aerosmith headlined. The night before the show, we met some members of the band Jackal, which was opening the festival. (Remember the song with a chainsaw solo? That's Jackal.) These southern boys were very nice, just like Bret Michaels, and we liked hanging out with them.

The next afternoon, when Jackal took the stage, Zakk and Brian Tichy grabbed me from my dressing room, and we walked up to the side of the stage to watch our new friends play. Well, Zakk being Zakk, he started clowning the guys and saying shit like "Yeah, smell the glove!" When the drummer did a drumroll, Zakk said, "I hope the drummer doesn't explode!" He has a really loud trucker voice, and although I thought it funny as shit, I felt a little bad for the guys. After all, who wants to be associated with Spinal Tap jokes?

"Easy, Zakk. Those boys are nice guys," I said.

Zakk looked at me with a *what the fuck* face. "Stevie, just because you like a guy doesn't mean you gotta like his music."

His comment made a lot of sense. I always hated seeing a friend's shitty show, then feeling obligated to lie by telling him how great it was. On the other hand, if I was getting paid to produce or musically direct your band, then I was straight up and often ruthless. For a friend's gig, I would rather lie than hurt anyone's feelings.

On one of my Colorcode tours in Europe, bass player Melvin Brannon Jr. and I came up with some good things to say to our friends who were in bands we hated. For instance, if a band member saw us and asked, "Did you see the show? What did you think?" I would say with an energetic, positive voice, "Man, you guys were up there *doing it*!" This way, I would no longer have to lie, and I also wouldn't hurt anyone's feelings.

When our plane landed, Rod was in the mood for a drink. After we checked in at the hotel, he and I went straight to the bar. We started casing the room, feeling out Washington, D.C. After a long minute, we noticed that no one gave a shit about us. *Weird.* We always caused a commotion when we walked into a bar, but in D.C., not one girl looked at us a second time.

What followed was a slap in the face. Some old lawyer-looking dude walked into the bar, and all these young, hot but conservatively dressed girls went nuts, saying under their breath, "That's Congressman Blah Blah Blah, and that's the lawyer for Senator Chabba Chabba . . . "

That grossed me out. Sure, politicians are allowed to have groupies, too. What I don't like are political douchebag hypocrites that do the same shit we rockers do, including buying girls drinks with our tax dollars, but in public look down on us like we're degenerates.

After about thirty minutes, Rod had had enough. "I'm going to my room," he said, so we walked into the elevator and called it a night . . .

Almost. Alongside us were two superhot conservative girls. I figured that Rod, ever the competitor, wanted one last penalty shot. He grew focused, and I knew something good was about to happen. When you're Rod Stewart, you can do something as simple as drop a napkin and ten people will dive to the floor to pick it up. In this spirit, he had developed a maneuver I'd seen him pull a million times, and it worked every time. Naturally, he figured he possessed the Da Vinci code to crack these D.C. ice queens.

He looked straight into the girls' eyes. They looked back into his. He slowly stretched his arm out, holding his room key. He paused . . . then dropped the key.

In any other elevator, in any other city, the girls would dive to the floor, try to help him pick up his key, and take it from there. These two girls looked at the key, peered back into Rod's eyes . . . and looked away. *Oh my God . . . I didn't just see that!* I thought I'd seen everything, but *brrrrr*, their shit was icy cold-blooded to the tenth power!

Rod couldn't believe it. We looked at each other, half laughing and half stunned. That doesn't happen to *Rod Stewart.* He picked up his key (probably for the first time since "Maggie May" came out almost twenty years before this night), and called Henry Newman. "Call the band and the pilots, then get the plane started," he said. "We are leaving."

It was just after 11:00 p.m., so we could make Atlanta in a couple hours and find friendlier allies. We drank on the plane, so by the time we landed, we were half bagged and on fire. We walked into the waiting limos and set off to our favorite family hangout, full of wholesome hometown love: The Gold Club, our favorite Atlanta strip club. It was indeed packed full of southern goodness. Many of the girls were becoming actual friends, hanging out with us for more reasons than sex, though that was always an option.

Rod, Don Archell, and the band walked into a private room filled with about twenty naked girls. Most knew us pretty well, so we knew they wouldn't sell stories to the tabloids. Rod and Carmine's friend Jeanie was the queen bee of The Gold Club. Jeanie was a superfun, beautiful, six-foot blonde with a body like an Olympic athlete and a great attitude. She was fit plus, not quite an American Gladiator or female wrestler, and not at all manly. However, if you angered her, she could choke you out pretty good. She always talked to Rod, and again stood facing Rod, with her naked backside to Don, Jimmy Roberts, and me. She bent over to say something into Rod's ear, causing her muscular legs and ass to almost touch Don's face. He grimaced a bit, pulling his head back, but without breaking stride, the old silver fox cupped his hand and held it up just under her bodybuilder butt. "Couldn't ya just see a big pair of bollocks hanging right there?" he said to Jimmy and me. He meant no offense to Jeanie, who was quite beautiful and a good friend, but his tart British humor would not be denied.

The next day, we flew to Louisville to play Freedom Hall. Louisville was the hometown of Tonjua Twist, my New York obsession. She asked me to get tickets and passes for some members of her family, including her stepmother, so I did.

She failed to tell me one small detail. While I sat in my dressing room, the guys were talking about this hot, older, provocatively dressed blonde at the backstage entrance. That blonde was asking for me. Carmine was puzzled, since he seemed to know all the sexy, hot, provocatively dressed older women in America (he knew the young ones, too). I knew Tonjua's sisters and stepmother were waiting to come backstage, but I'd hoped to sleep off my hangover before the show.

Now I was curious. Time to find out who this mystery older woman was. When I got to the entrance, the hot, older, provocatively dressed blonde said, "Hey Stevie, Tonjua said to meet you here."

"And you are?"

"Tonjua's stepmom."

These days, cougars fly across all these shit reality shows, like *Housewives of Dayton* or *Sexy Gold Diggers of Newport Beach*. But we're talking 1988. I didn't know anyone with a mom who looked like that. Tonjua's real mother and father were Kentucky Cherokees, but Tonjua's stepmom was not a southern gal at all. She was Swedish. Plus, she was a nice enough person . . . but indeed caused a commotion backstage. My instincts told me she'd known some wild days, especially when she recalled her days modeling in London and hanging out with Josephine Wood, the wife of Rolling Stones guitarist Ronnie Wood.

Years later, through Bernard Fowler, I would get to know Jo Wood pretty well. One night, while hanging out in her and Ronnie's hotel suite, I asked her about Tonjua's stepmom. "I heard you and she used to have a lot of fun together partying with Fleetwood Mac," I said.

Jo's mouth dropped open and she made a funny face. "Shhh! Don't talk about that, Stevie!" she muttered under her breath.

Hmm . . . wild days indeed.

From the dressing room, I called Tonjua. She said she was a little worried about the boys and her sexy stepmom backstage, but I told her she was just fine and the guys knew to behave themselves. "After all," I said, "she is your stepmom, and they all love and respect you."

After the show, we did a fast runner back to the plane. When we landed again in Atlanta, we went straight to The Gold Club, but this time to load up the limo with girls for an after-hours party at Club 112. We had the next night off, and since we occupied most of the top floor of the Ritz Carlton, including a huge party suite, we decided to ask some girls to come by our hotel the next night for a proper dinner party. We invited a blend of straight, beautiful, conservative, college-type girls mixed with wild strippers. At this point, after months on a tour where one has seen and done everything, one must find new ways to be entertained. People watching always provided good entertainment.

All of us knew that the upcoming night would be the last big party of the tour. We only had two shows remaining before our Christmas break, so we wanted to make this a night to remember. Our crew arranged to have all the party favors on hand, and Rod made sure to set up a formal dinner. There were about a dozen of us between the band and our crew, along with twenty-five invited girls. A good omen, I thought, since Jan and Dean's "Surf City" was one of my favorite songs. (Remember the refrain lyric and do your math, people!)

At 8:00 p.m., the ladies started showing up. Naturally, the conservative models and college girls were on time, even a bit early, while most of the strippers arrived late . . . or later than that. The drinks started flowing. The smart, conservative models were so animated and excited to be there, telling clever stories about the Hamptons, mama and daddy, and fine wine. Ever the charismatic host, Rod kept the conversation and drinks flowing splendidly.

Soon, we sat at a long, classic wood table, and dinner was served. I was too stupid to notice if anyone was doing any cocaine, but I did see a lot of uneaten steak and lobster. I'm not going to spill the beans on whose plates were untouched . . . though after I finished eating, I wondered if I should put Carmine and Nick's plates in the fridge in case they got hungry later.

Meanwhile, I felt something brush my leg beneath the table. I didn't want to alarm anyone, so I slowly peeked and noticed Tony Brock crawling on his hands and knees, snooping through all the conservative girls' purses. I knew right away what he was up to, so I looked up and tried to make sure none of the girls noticed that he wasn't sitting in his chair. Tony was grabbing the girls' cameras, a little trick we pulled a lot. (When you shot photos back then, you visited the local drug or camera store and dropped off your film to be developed before knowing what the photos looked like. When people hung out with rock bands, they always brought cameras; Tony knew that.)

Tony grabbed a few cameras from the straightest, most uptight girls and snuck back into his seat. He then passed the cameras to various band members underneath the table. One by one, we would excuse ourselves to use the facilities. While in the bathroom, we shot photos of our private parts in funny or unflattering ways, always making sure to keep our faces off camera. Once most of us had a run or three, we snuck the cameras back to Tony, who slid under the table and dutifully returned them to the girls' purses. While Tony was on his mission, Rod would usually tell an extra charming story to hold the girls' undivided attention.

By midnight, it was pretty easy to tell which girls were gamers and which were not. A lot of times, girls will show up, thinking about a potentially serious relationship and not acting too wildly on the first night. They wanted to make a good impression, normally a cool thing, but *not* on our last party night of the tour. We wanted a party to remember—or, if it was *really* good, perhaps forget.

The fastest way to get chatty, conservative girls to leave is to secretly ask some of the wild ladies to prance around naked while we act like nothing unusual is going on. For some reason, that makes conservative girls a little uncomfortable, although, if it's your lucky night, one or more can become competitive. After all, they are used to walking naked backstage at modeling shows. Either way, we achieve our desired result: the squares leave.

After watching some of the naked girls walk around and then sit at the dinner table, many of our guests smiled uncomfortably, thanked us, then said good night. As we exchanged good-byes, they asked, "Can we please take a photo?" Depending on his mood, Rod sometimes posed.

Or not. Either way, most of us would pose for some good night shots, then the girls would be on their way. We all knew that first thing in the morning, each girl would run to the store to get her film developed so she could show her friends and family the pictures of her great night out with a famous rock band. I cringed, thinking about these poor girls rushing to pick up their photos, only to realize that everyone at the developing shop thought they must be animals. I almost couldn't bear to imagine the looks on their faces when they opened the envelope, expecting to see nice, classy shots of themselves dolled up with Rod and the band, carrying on like old chums, and then seeing a close-up of Carmine Rojas's hairy ass or Jeff Golub's nutsack.

Now that I am a father, I feel kind of bad about some of the stuff we did. At the time, though, I was learning all the rock 'n' roll tricks from the boys. It seemed like harmless fun; for the most part, it was.

The music grew louder, and the party favors were in full effect. Soon, the room was filled with naked girls. One by one, we started losing band members. I was dancing and having some fun with four or five girls (who's counting?) when I started wondering where some of my big brothers were. I took a look around and saw, to quote my diary, "pure chaos." Rod and the boys were carrying on throughout our huge party suite, but I couldn't find Jeff. Earlier, he was on fire as I saw him walking through the party with a lampshade on his head, but now he was nowhere to be found. Since he was so hammered, I was a little worried.

I looked for clues. I noticed all the chandeliers were still connected to the ceiling, so he hadn't been swinging from them. Then I saw water running from underneath a bathroom door. I grabbed a couple of girls for a search-and-destroy mission into the bathroom. The master bedroom featured a huge, mini-Caligula bathtub, and when I walked in, it was overflowing with bubbles. They were more than a foot above tub level, but no one was inside, so the girls and I started out the door . . .

I heard a sound. The girls kept walking, but I stopped and turned around. Three big, round, bubbly balloon shapes surfaced . . . it was Jeff and two girls, laughing their heads off. I could only see their eyes and teeth. Jeff's head looked like a big lion mane made of pure bubbles. "There you are!" I said. I laughed and returned to the party.

Before I knew it, an old friend of the band, sunrise, decided to make an appearance. She peeked through all the cracked curtains, bright as ever. Soon, we closed down the party and headed to our rooms. Before we did, someone had the great idea to get a band photo (note to all party people: *never* take photos at the end of a wild party). We lined up by the piano like an old sports team, with some of the guys standing shoulder to shoulder in back, while some were down on one knee in front. As we lined up, we realized Jeff wasn't there. A few seconds after we shouted for him, he walked out of the master bedroom wearing a dress. We had no idea whose dress it was, and neither did Jeff, but it was a very nice dress. He was the best-dressed person in the photo.

The band members were hammered. Normally, one or two of us might be like this at a given party, but this time, all of us were beyond ripped, so it took a minute to get lined up for our proper end-of-tour party photo. Finally, we faced the camera. Jeff was standing just behind Rick Braun, who was on one knee. Right before we shot the photo, Jeff reached under his dress and pulled out his knob, then gently placed it on Rick's shoulder without him knowing.

We snapped the photo. Jeff's wiener quickly retreated beneath his miniskirt, and Rick never had a clue. I still don't know who shot the photo, or who has it, but I hope I never see it!

My wake-up call felt as gentle as a dull knife to the forehead. My diary says, and I quote, "I woke up in my bed with two naked girls in my room and I don't know who they are . . . I must have blacked out." I don't remember the after-party in my room, but I do recall walking like a zombie from the hotel toward the limo, feeling like 140 pounds of hell and thinking I might barf for the first time on the tour. The rest of the band wasn't looking much better, including the singer. We resembled Bruce Willis at the end of the first *Die Hard* movie.

During our flight to Charleston, West Virginia, we operated on ghost protocol. After a short nap, I walked through the plane to have a look around, and all seemed normal. Jeff was unconscious in his white robe with green hospital pants and sporting black Reeboks, looking as if someone had shoveled him into his two seats. Carmine was passed out like a peaceful Puerto Rican baby while gripping his banana. The only thing that seemed odd was the usually dapper Don Archell asleep with his mouth wide open, catching flies. It was so quiet that the plane engines could lull you to sleep.

I stared out of the window, pondering my actions the night before and my life in general. I had dreamt of nights like that since I first strapped on a guitar, but had I gone too far? Some might say what happened was disgusting, while others might call it glorious. Don't lie . . . If you were being truly honest with yourself, you'd want to be there. You may not want anyone to *know* that, but it's true. I have learned over the years that a lot of the rock 'n' roll fantasies of my youth, once fulfilled, were almost never as great as they were in my mind. I also know that the mystery of the great unknown can drive a man crazy, so I am thankful to have experienced these opportunities firsthand. Most people can only dream about many of these things. I never want to wake up one day and say, "I wish I would have done that," because every time I have done it, I have learned something.

Yes, having five naked girls in your bed is awesome—but is it as awesome as being in love with one person? Yes, traveling the world to exotic locations with rich and famous people is really incredible and sometimes a blessing, but does it match staying at home with my son? No way. You've gotta have balance.

I know nights like our final tour party can feel like a shot of pure, uncut Colombian cocaine. Once you feel that high, if you're not careful, you can waste a lot of your life trying to relive that feeling. When that happens, you become a cliché. They don't call it "partying like a rock star" for nothing! Partying is cool, as long as it doesn't stop you from taking care of business and family. Really, when you think about it, was it any different for modern rock stars like Rod, Keith Richards, and

Steven Tyler than it was for eighteenth-century rock stars Mozart, Bach, and Beethoven? You know those fuckers were wild as hell, too.

When the show started at the Charleston Civic Center, we were still hungover. Perhaps this party wasn't the best for us when it came to taking care of business, because I believe we played our worst show of the tour. Still, the crowd loved it. Even while hungover, we were as tight as Jedi warriors, and the force was guiding our way. We were mind-locked, making moves with each other without even being aware of it, just like Joe Montana knowing that Jerry Rice will cut left and not right and committing to the throw before Rice even begins his cut. Our subconscious minds trusted each other fully. We had finally become a great band, fitting perfectly like pieces in a puzzle.

Still, it was a shit show.

On the plane ride back to Washington, D.C., Rod and I finally talked about my contract with Island Records, along with my new album. I told him I wanted to possibly record the song "Stone Cold Sober" from his *Atlantic Crossing* record. He thought that was a great idea, and then told me to get home and start recording right away. He wanted me to finish the record before we started our South American stadium tour so I would be fully focused.

At that moment, I experienced another all-time high. I realized I was in a private plane with a band vibrating at a maximum level, playing massive sold-out shows with the respect of musicians everywhere, and I was becoming a real musician. I had so much love, gratitude, and respect for the guys who looked after me and taught me so much and were now my family. I know this sounds corny, but in the song "To Sir with Love," Lulu sings the lyric, "How do you thank someone who has taken you / from crayons to perfume?"

That lyric kept playing in my head, and I couldn't escape it. I knew that, just as Lulu's character had to leave high school and her teacher, Sidney Poitier, I too would have to leave Rod and the boys.

23

THE END AS WE DIDN'T KNOW IT

At sound check that afternoon, I plugged into my rack of hundred-watt Marshall amps and I noticed how relaxed I was on the big stage. No longer were my guitar amps loud and out of control with the volume on six. Now, the volume sat at a comfortable three. The static and panic that had filled my ears during the early days of the tour were gone, and everything was very calm and clear.

The thought of it overwhelmed me, and I almost cried. I looked out at the empty eighteen-thousand-seat arena and thought about the boy who, only six months earlier, walked into Audible Studios in Burbank nervous but confident, scared to death but cocky. Now, he was a rock star. I put my head down and thanked God and all the angels who had helped my dreams and visions come true, and I thought about where I was at that moment—playing in a huge band with my big brothers, who happened to be some of the best musicians in the world. I loved them very much.

It was December 10, the last show of the 1988 leg of the Out of Order Tour. We were ready to break for Christmas, but nobody felt emotional about the tour ending, since we would be back together for the 1989 South American stadium tour that was already booked.

However, I knew in my heart this would be my last show. I knew I would be saying good-bye to the brothers who had protected me, tortured me, taught me how to be a man and party like a rock star, taught me how to be a pro . . . the brothers who loved me. It wasn't going to be easy.

We played to our usual packed, standing-room-only arena of scream-ing fans at the Capital Centre in Landover, Maryland, across the Poto-mac River from Washington, D.C., and we slayed them. I thought it was the best show of the tour. Afterwards, we headed back to the Ritz Carlton. As always, a pack of beautiful girls waited in the hotel bar. Unlike the stuck-up politician groupies earlier in the week, these were wild rock groupies. In D.C., even the rock groupies dress like conserva-tive girls that would gain your mother's approval. Trust me, it matters not if they are wearing leather or silk, if their hair is teased like Barba-rella or cut nice like Rebecca from Sunnybrook Farm. After a couple of Grey Goose and sodas, they all like to swing from the chandelier.

While walking through the bar, I ran into Linda Brill, an old sweet-heart from back home in Carlsbad. What a surprise! During and right after high school, my pals Allen Carrasco, Eddie Binder, and Paul Mar-tinez would join me to go to ice cream stores and talk the girls into giving us free ice cream. Linda worked at a Carlsbad frozen yogurt shop and was not only beautiful but whip smart, and I liked that. Over a period of weeks, I ended up getting several free frozen yogurts . . . as well as her phone number. We dated a lot, mostly going to my This Kids gigs (the ones she could get into, since she wasn't old enough to get into bars, and neither was I, but I had a fake ID).

Linda and I also spent a lot of time at her mom's apartment, where we watched MTV. MTV played videos for about forty-five minutes, followed by fifteen minutes of static . . . full-on, white-noise static. We would eat or make out until we heard the static stop, and the MTV theme, a distorted odd-time guitar-chord riff, would start. Then a guy walking on the moon planted an MTV flag, and a VJ would talk, or a video would start. There were five VJs—Martha Quinn, J. J. Jackson, Mark Goodman, Alan Hunter, and Nina Blackwood. Together, they made MTV the coolest TV show on the planet, the show on which every rocker wanted to see their videos.

While sitting all those nights smooching with Linda, I had no idea that in a few years I would be shooting an episode of the TV show *Fame* and having fun hanging out with Martha Quinn. Little did I know I would soon be watching J. J. Jackson rocking out to me in the front row at the L.A. Forum (his daughter, Tracy, is a great friend to this day). If you would've told me that the beautiful Nina Blackwood, about the sexiest rock chick there was, would spend Christmas at my house with my dad and family in Oceanside, I would have laughed in your face.

There was also Rod Stewart.

It seemed like all MTV ran was Rod Stewart videos. Every time I heard and saw Rod Stewart singing "Infatuation" on Linda's TV, I was unknowingly preparing a bit more for the audition four short years later. "Infatuation" was the song on which I ripped during my audition, sealing my chair in the band.

When I saw Linda standing in the Ritz Carlton bar, I couldn't believe it. I had not heard from her since we stopped seeing each other. While we enjoyed cocktails, she told me about her life and that she was living in D.C. I wanted to see all the sights, and D.C. had plenty, so Linda took me for a late-night drive. We saw the Capitol building, the White House, and many other historic places. It was a very cold December evening, but we wanted to walk around the Washington Monument, so we jumped out of the car. It seemed like it took forever with the ice-cold wind howling in our faces, but we laughed and got through it, feeling for a moment like young kids again. After that, we jumped back in the car and headed to the hotel. When Linda and I dated, it was very innocent . . . just kissing. (Not that I didn't try, mind you. Linda was a very beautiful young lady.)

When we got back to my suite, we started where we left off, kissing like mad. It was weird, because at that moment, it hit me that I must have been a lot closer emotionally to Linda than I realized. She felt the same way, too. We looked into each other's eyes intensely. Linda wanted to show me she was all grown up—and yes, she did show me. It was amazing. (Okay, I know what you're thinking . . . now get your mind out of the gutter. We didn't do it.) Linda was not that kind of girl, but she socked it to me in her own way, which was beautiful.

It felt so great to be together, perhaps the taste of home we both needed. Even though we sat in a superexpensive hotel suite in the most powerful city in the world as adults, that night we were kids again in Carlsbad, where life was safe and simple. Now here she was, three thousand miles from home.

Oddly enough, I would see Linda again the next year at a Rolling Stones concert in L.A. There were almost one hundred thousand people at the L.A. Coliseum, and of all people, I run into Linda Brill walking around the stadium . . .

As it turned out, that Stones concert was a big night for me, because my newfound rock star status enabled me to go backstage and bring my pals with me. While watching the Stones and their awesome background singer Bernard Fowler, little did I know that soon he would become a huge part of my future, not to mention Mick Jagger. That's another book. Perhaps.

It was really late, and Linda had to go home. As we said good-bye, we could close the book on our past relationship and end it well. I shut the door behind her and started packing my bags.

The band met in the lobby, then we all piled into limos to Washington National Airport, hungover and laughing like always as we shared stories of the night before. Naturally, the superhot blonde at the American Airlines counter had been at the concert and knew who we were. Carmine was already chatting her up. Jeff Golub was looking very disheveled as always, but very *rock* in dark sunglasses. He had her blushing about something.

I wasn't my normal wild, annoying self. I was superhappy, and knew my pal Dale was waiting at the airport to take me home to see my friends and family for Christmas. However, I was also a little sad and a little freaked out. My subconscious mind knew what my conscious mind didn't want to know . . . that my life would never be the same. I would have to leave the safety of Rod and the boys and face new challenges, successes, and failures.

In the middle of the madness running through my mind, I heard the beautiful blonde behind the American Airlines counter. "Excuse me, Mr. Salas . . . Mr. Salas?"

Startled, I looked up at her, then deeply into her blue eyes. She handed me a first-class ticket to the rest of my life.

24

IT'S MY TIME TO BURN, BUT IT'S STILL HOT WHERE I'M AT

When I returned home from Washington, D.C., I did as Rod instructed. I headed straight into the studio to start working on tracks for my new record. I so desperately wanted to pull off a hat trick. I needed to please my record and management companies so that I could please Rod and play those 1989 stadium shows in South America.

Once I started the process, I ran into some big problems. I'd changed as a musician and artist in more ways than one. I was a much better guitar player and songwriter than before the tour, and I had matured perhaps a little too much as an artist. Island signed me on the strength of my wild, reckless style that was both rock and alternative, but I seemed to have lost a bit of that angst. Was it too much pop-music discipline? Or money in the bank? I wasn't sure, but everyone was concerned that I had lost my edge. Besides the money from Rod's tour, I also now held all my record-company advance money and publishing money. It definitely took away my desperation, so in a panic move, I bought two houses in order to feel broke again.

My other problem was my band. I had handpicked Winston A. Watson Jr. and C.J. DeVillar for their cool power and style, but now I was used to Carmine and Tony Brock. I needed the youthful madness that C.J. and Winston brought, but I heard all the mistakes, and they were driving me crazy. In return, I drove them crazy. I was a mess! Kevin

Patrick, the head of A&R at Island, asked my other A&R guy, Steve Pross, "Remind me . . . why did we sign him?"

I knew I would not be able to make the record in time to stay with Rod. Perhaps I could go with him to South America, keep writing, quit the band after that, and then cut my record. Then Morty Wiggins, my manager, flat-out asked me, "Do you want to be an artist? Or someone's guitar player?"

Morty was right, but man, did my heart hurt! I didn't want to leave Rod and the boys. It wasn't about Rod's music, the private jets, or the money. My heartache was over losing a band of brothers whom I had grown to love and also to depend on.

On January 10, 1989, I called Rod at his house in England to wish him happy birthday. He started whispering to me under his breath about having to go through all the local papers to tear out photos of him hanging out with other women before Kelly saw them. We shared a couple of laughs. As I started to hang up, he said, "Get that record done, and I will see you soon for the South American tour."

I hung up, depressed. I knew I couldn't go.

I called Rod's managers, Randy Phillips and Arnold Stiefel, and told them I was leaving the band. Randy really seemed bummed. Randy had fought for me to be in Andy Taylor's band, and Randy had fought for me to be in Rod's band. During the tour, Randy once told me that he could look his mother straight in the eye while sneaking money from her purse. Yes, that's dirty indeed, but I appreciated his honesty, and I always knew where I stood with him. Because of that, we remain friends to this day.

During my last year with 19 Entertainment and *American Idol*, I ran into Randy at the American Music Awards. When he found out that I was the music director for *American Idol* runner-up Adam Lambert's big end-of-the-show production number, he was really excited and made a point of watching it. (It turned into a disaster. Adam fell on the stage, and then jumped up and kissed the bass player, causing quite a stir with the TV network.)

I know 1988 was just a small blip on the radar for Rod and the boys, but for me, it was almost as important as being born. In a way, it was my rebirth, sending me into the second part of my life, from a boy to a man. Like that stubborn unborn child fighting his due date and refusing to enter the new harsh world outside the comfort of his mother's womb, I too would fight my rebirth, not wanting to leave the safe cocoon of The Rod Stewart Band, a place where life was light, the concerts sold out, every check cleared, and everybody had a great time.

With the boys, I enjoyed stability, with nothing to worry about. I was only responsible for my guitar parts. Rod carried the heavy weight, and we focused only on our share of the load. So what if snooty critics thought Rod had no credibility? *Who cares when you're playing sold-out arenas all over the world?* In many ways, I was like the spoiled kid brother in a wealthy family, born into private jets and lobster dinners. Rod and the boys spent years building the world in which they lived, whereas I just stepped into it and benefited from their decades of hard work. Rod worked from the bottom up, paying mad dues to get to the top, as did Carmine, Jeff, Tony, Chuck, Nick, Rick, and Jimmy. I came into this family already living in a mansion, so to speak, from nobody to somebody virtually overnight.

I'm not saying it was easy to stay in that place; it wasn't. Rod and the boys were the best and expected you to keep up. The trust they gave me came with a great amount of pressure, as well as the opportunity to deliver and rise beyond my potential.

I believe, as did my father, that a big man lies within every small man. I could have died when I was born with that umbilical cord around my neck, but I didn't. I could have quit Rod's band and told the boys to fuck off every time they belittled me, or every time the pressure to deliver beyond my skill set became unbearable. Instead, I chose to fight for my right to be in that band, even though I wasn't talented or experienced enough. By fighting and succeeding, I not only gained the respect of Rod and the boys, but I also gained respect for myself.

Yes, I had a big ego, but if not for Rod and the boys, it would have been *really* big. Those guys really saved me by keeping me in check, which they did with love and respect. They could always back it up, which made me respect them in kind. They taught me that yes, in our world, we are *the shit*, but when standing around each other, we ain't shit.

Back home, I never had a big brother until my sister married Steve Cottrell. Steve was a winner, and he believed that I was, too. Rod and the boys were the same. They were my big brothers who beat me down when I had it coming, built me up when I felt insecure, fought for me, and taught me what it took to be a great musician . . .

Then I had to leave them. I knew it was my time to burn bright on my own, but it was still hot where I was. Hot and safe.

One of the hardest things is to land a major-label recording contract, which I did, but I couldn't help thinking, *why now?* Yes, I wanted to write and play my own music, and I definitely didn't want to perform songs like "Baby Jane" anymore, but I also didn't want to leave my family.

It didn't get any easier, that's for sure. When my first record with Colorcode came out, I had many problems. Polygram bought Island Records just as my record was released. Warner Brothers, my distributor, lost the rights to distribute the record, so they stopped working it. Problem was, Polygram didn't yet have the rights to start working it, either. So there I was on a sold-out world tour, playing in front of three thousand to five thousand people per night, with no records in the stores. The press and critics loved my record, because it was so far from mainstream; I was in every magazine you could find. However, without records in the stores, I felt doomed.

During that time, I ran into Rod at The Cat 'n' Fiddle in Hollywood. He said, "Everyone says your record is amazing, but that it's not selling, sorry to hear that." He didn't look happy or unhappy. It was just business.

I had an incredible run between 1987 and 1991, leading people to think I was some sort of golden boy, since I was involved in a lot of successful, hip projects. If you were someone on the outside looking in, it might appear that way, but things are not always as they seem. Yes, the Rod tour was the gig of gigs, but no one was lining up for the other projects I took. In fact, I probably got some of them by default.

When I joined The Rod Stewart Band, Rod was a superstar, a legend, but a star and legend some said was losing his shine. He sure proved them wrong! The Out of Order Tour was only intended to be three months long; it stretched into almost two years.

As for my other big projects? I did the unknown movie *Bill & Ted's Excellent Adventure*, directed by the unknown Stephen Herek and starring the equally unknown Keanu Reeves. *Plus*, the film's distributor had just gone bankrupt. I produced the unknown, very left-of-center pop group Was (Not Was), which was crafting songs featuring people like Mel Torme while people were listening to hits on the radio by Poison and Lionel Ritchie. I produced the underground garage band The Pandoras for a tiny label, Restless Records (the band had just been dropped by Elektra, and no one wanted to touch them), I was recording with 1970s funk icon Bootsy Collins, I played guitar on an Eddie Money record, and I produced some tracks for The Tubes. Oh yeah . . . I also was playing funk rock, trying to get a recording contract while companies were selling metal bands left and right. Everyone wanted the next Bon Jovi or Whitesnake, and I didn't fit into that mold at all.

Call it luck or fate, but other than Rod Stewart, my projects were far from most people's radar.

That would change. By the time 1990 rolled around, I looked like a genius. Was (Not Was) had a global hit, *Bill & Ted's Excellent Adventure* was a massive hit movie, The Pandoras' record was getting play on the very hip L.A. radio station KROQ, DJs were spinning Bootsy Collins in the clubs again, the Eddie Money track became a single . . . and Rod Stewart was bigger than ever. The *Out of Order* record sold nine million copies, and his new *Anthology* release sold like mad as well, with the help of a huge single called "Downtown Train."

A lot of the projects I worked on were long shots, but I also knew they came from great artists, and the music was worth playing and producing. (I also needed to make money, and in 1987, it wasn't like I had many other options.) I never thought all this success was due to me, but I also knew that the resulting light shining on me in the music business was a great thing, because people take chances with people who are connected to success.

I can now look back twenty-five years and clearly see how much I learned from Rod and the boys. Would I have won number one in the Best New Guitarist readers' poll in Japan, or number four in *Guitar World*'s Best New Guitar Players readers' poll award in 1990 if it wasn't for Jeff Golub and the things he taught me? Could I have been a successful music director for the American Idols I worked with, as well as Mick Jagger, Lamya, Sass Jordan, Terence Trent D'Arby, and others, if not for the things I learned from Rod and Carmine on how to really rock a stadium? I learned so much from them, and I will never be able to thank them enough for what they did for me.

Before I joined Rod's band, I saw him driving down Sunset Boulevard in Hollywood in an incredible brown custom Mercedes Benz 500 SEL. I never saw a car customized like that, before or since. Around the time I quit the band, I overheard Rod saying he was going to sell that car, so I told him, "That's my dream car! I want it!"

Rod told me I could have it at a great price, so I went to his South American rehearsals in L.A. to say hello to the boys and talk to him about delivery of the Mercedes Benz. When Rod pulled me aside, he said, "I'm not gonna sell you my car."

"Why not?" I asked.

He then told me a story that I have subsequently shared with every young musician with whom I work: "Stevie, when I was young, I was a gravedigger, and I never knew if I would make it as a singer. When 'Maggie May' came out, I got a little bit of money, so I bought myself a little flat. That way, if it didn't work out, I would at least have a roof over my head.

"As it turned out, 'Maggie' was a hit by accident. 'Maggie May' was the B side of my single, which was 'A Reason to Believe.' If not for the one DJ who decided to turn the record over and play 'Maggie May,' who knows if I ever would have had a hit?"

He paused for a moment. "Stevie, a career is full of mountains and valleys. When you're up, you can't stay up forever, but when you're down, you can't stay down forever, either. The key is to keep on moving." He then looked at me very seriously. "Take that money you were gonna use for my car, and go buy a house."

That's exactly what I did.

In 1993, I joined Terence Trent D'Arby for a small get-together at the home of Ronnie Wood's manager. Rod was there, as well as a few others. That night was so much fun, with Terence, Woody, Rod, and myself sharing great stories over cocktails. I was Terence's music director, and Rod had great respect for him. I felt like Rod knew I was no longer a kid, and it stoked me to make him proud. He asked me that night if I would like to come back to the band sometime. At that time, I not only had a big record contract and publishing contract, but I was also producing and writing for a lot of well-known artists, not to mention touring with Terence and Duran Duran. It just wasn't the right time—but I would have joined him in a minute if I could.

I have experienced many successes and failures, mountains and valleys. Over the years, I realized that the guys didn't just teach me how to be a better musician, but also how to be a better man. They also helped me pick up some bad habits, like drinking too much from time to time, but no one said we were saints. In many ways, the things I learned on the Out of Order Tour became the cornerstone of everything I do. I listen to the smallest details, I know that anything is possible even when all seems lost, I know that teamwork is everything, and I also know that when it's showtime, the big players make the big plays. Failure is never an option. Not if you wanna roll with the big boys.

The boys and I still check in with each other and work together on projects from time to time, and it never fails to produce heartfelt laughs. Even though I am as old as dirt, I still get treated like their kid brother. Perhaps this will never change. I hope it never does.

I moved on from the band and onto the rest of my life, but I will never forget when we were the boys.

EPILOGUE

Twistin' the Night Away

Six months into the 1989 leg of the Out of Order Tour, I drove to the San Diego Sports Arena to see Rod and the boys play my hometown. I stood on the side of the stage with Dale and Big Al, watching the show. I must admit that watching new guitar player Todd Sharp onstage was almost like seeing a guy sleeping with my wife. It felt surreal, and not all that good.

During the final encore, "Twistin' the Night Away," Jeff Golub walked over and looked at me with a big smile. He unstrapped his guitar and waved for me to take it. I jumped onto the stage, and as he slipped his Strat over my chest, the sold-out arena filled with cheers.

I started playing and worked my way over to Rod. He was belting out the song, but as he heard the crowd screaming, he looked over—and saw me again by his side. He kept rocking without breaking his flow, like my presence was the most natural thing in the world. As we finished, Carmine and the band gathered around me. Then Rod yelled into the mic, "Stevie Salas, from San Diego, California!" The crowd erupted again.

That was the last time we played together.

When I left the Out of Order Tour, my friends thought the party was over. In some ways, it was, because I was no longer the same person. In the ensuing twenty-five years, I have been on the covers of countless magazines around the world as an artist as well as a guitar player. I have won awards and played on some great tours. However, I was never really that famous. I think my quest was a little different than most; rather than purely huge gigs, I sought collaborations that built my music credibility and stayed true to my roots. I wanted projects that carried depth and meaning, projects that would not only give people great music for their listening enjoyment, but also mean something. So many people in the rock 'n' roll business equate their legacies to records sold, number of arenas sold out, or number of wild stories that they started, or starred in. For me, I want to know that someone liked my songs, maybe learned something from me, and that I was able to collaborate with or help them in some way.

I was able to pass along a lot of the life lessons I learned from Rod and the boys. Just as Rod and the boys were big brother figures to me, I became the same to guitarist Richie Kotzen (who debuted with Poison before developing a very successful career) and Foo Fighters drummer Taylor Hawkins, both of whom also became my good friends. Watching their continued success brings me great pride.

In the 1990s, when my solo career took off, I made more than a million dollars selling records in Europe and Asia. However, like many, I lost a great deal of my wealth in the stock market crash of 2000. I was hitting those mountains and valleys, just like Rod told me when I was so young. However, I have managed to stay in the game for twenty-five years and counting. I would produce just enough solo records to keep my record contract, and when that slowed down, I would be fortunate enough to get a call to work on something big like Mick Jagger's solo tour, a Justin Timberlake release, or *American Idol*.

Could my career have been bigger? Absolutely. But I have done all right. I've seen the world, rocked most of the legendary venues like Madison Square Garden (five times, but who's counting?), have had companies put out Stevie Salas signature guitars and pedals that sold all over the world, and played with many of the most legendary artists in history. I have the lifelong respect of my peers in the music and entertainment industry. Almost every day, I get letters, e-mails, texts, or calls from people who say I have inspired their lives and careers.

People always say in memoirs like this, "Sure, I made some mistakes, but if I had to do it all over again, I wouldn't change a thing." Well, I would. If I could press "rewind," I would have learned how to invest my money properly when I was younger. Most importantly, I would have figured out a way to save the love of my life, Tonjua Twist, who I met in New York during the Out of Order Tour. She would tragically leave this world in 2000.

As for the rest? I wouldn't change a thing.

When I drove past the San Diego Sports Arena that long-ago night in 1984, I visualized myself playing with Rod, Mick, and David Bowie. I'm not giving up on the third part of my vision: I still expect to play with Bowie. I am living proof that anything is possible, if you truly believe.

ACKNOWLEDGMENTS

All love and respect to the Salas Boys, my late father Hilario, who I would lose while writing this book, and my son Shane Silva Salas. Also love and thanks to both of my mothers, Lollie and Helen, sisters Sandy and Rachel, Karen Silva, Allen Carrasco, Dale Lawrence, Steve Pross, This Kids, brother-in-law Steve Cottrell, Jimi and Jim Dunlop, Morty Wiggins and all at Bill Graham Management, Roger Stein, John Cross, Terry and Nikka Costa, George Clinton, Bootsy Collins, Don and David Was, the late great Jamie Cohen, David Kershenbaum, Winston A. Watson Jr., C.J. DeVillar, Brian Tichy, Brian Wright McLeod, Sass Jordan, Stirling McIlwaine, John Marx, Amos Newman, Bernard Fowler, Vince Chavez, Pando, Richie Kotzen, Iain Pirie, Tim Johnson and all at the Smithsonian National Museum of The American Indian, Kenny Hill and Jukasa Studios on 6 Nations, Jerry Montour, Bryan Porter, Julie Farmer and all at GRE, Freddy Kushner, Riki Malwani, Pj Thrasher, Christopher Osceola, Sean Welsh, Bill Laswell, Jun Sato, Kaz Miyayama, Adam Beach, Eric Schweig, Jesse Green, APTN, Robert Mann, Deirdre Richardson, Dana Stewart, Randy Phillips, Arnold Stiefel, and the 1988 Rod Stewart Band.

A very special thank you to my cowriter, Robert Yehling, for the constant push, to Carmine Rojas for sneaking me in, and to Rod Stewart for changing my life.

Cowriter Robert Yehling wishes to thank our agent, Dana Newman, plus Bill Missett, Scott Threlfall, Robert Munger, and most of all, Martha Halda, for your love and support during one crazy but fun deadline.

ABOUT THE AUTHOR

After a difficult, trying childhood, **Stevie Salas** created fun and exciting teenage years in his North San Diego beach town, surfing, fishing, racing motocross, and playing team sports. He taught himself how to play guitar at age fifteen, beginning a career that made him one of the most versatile studio and touring musicians, songwriters, recording artists, and music, television, and motion picture producers of the past twenty-five years. His many credits include: work on number-one box office hit *Bill & Ted's Excellent Adventure*; touring lead guitarist on Rod Stewart's 1988 Out of Order Tour; music director and lead guitarist on Terence Trent D'Arby's 1993 world tour and Mick Jagger's 2001 solo project; collaborations with George Clinton, Justin Timberlake, Bill Laswell, the late Jeff Healey, Was (Not Was), Michael Hutchence from INXS, Bootsy Collins, Sass Jordan, and many other recording artists; music director and consultant for 19 Entertainment/*American Idol* working directly with Daughtry, Jordin Sparks, David Cook, Kris Allen, and Adam Lambert, and Advisor to Contemporary Music at the Smithsonian Institution. In addition, he has sold more than two million albums as a solo artist. He has received many honors and awards, including a Native American Lifetime Achievement Award at the 2009 Native American Music Awards. He is the executive producer of *Rumble*, a Native American music documentary airing on PBS and the Super

Channel. He is also the executive producer and star of *Arbor Live*, the Canadian comedy-music TV series.

A California native of Apache descent, Salas now lives in Austin, Texas, while continuing to produce and collaborate on music, television, and Native American projects worldwide.